Building Neo4j-Powered Applications with LLMs

Create LLM-driven search and recommendations applications with Haystack, LangChain4j, and Spring AI

Ravindranatha Anthapu

Siddhant Agarwal

‹packt›

Building Neo4j-Powered Applications with LLMs

Portfolio Director: Gebin George

Relationship Lead: Sonia Chauhan

Project Manager: Prajakta Naik

Content Engineer: Vandita Grover

Technical Editor: Rahul Limbachiya

Copy Editor: Safis Editing

Indexer: Tejal Soni

Proofreader: Vandita Grover

Production Designer: Alishon Falcon

Growth Lead: Nimisha Dua

First published: June 2025

Production reference: 1230525

Published by Packt Publishing Ltd.
Grosvenor House
11 St Paul's Square
Birmingham
B3 1RB, UK.

ISBN 978-1-83620-623-1

www.packtpub.com

I would like to dedicate this book to my lovely wife, Sreevani Rajuru, for all her encouragement and patience during this journey.

– Ravi Anthapu

I would like to first and foremost thank my loving and patient wife, Rashi, for her unwavering support, encouragement, and endless patience throughout the long journey of writing this book. To my wonderful parents—thank you for your constant belief in me and for being my lifelong pillars of strength. I'm also deeply grateful to my incredible colleagues whose camaraderie, insights, and inspiration pushed me to keep going. A heartfelt thank you to the Neo4j team and community for fostering an environment of innovation and collaboration—your support made this book possible.

– Sid Agarwal

Forewords

For much of my career, AI has been in a kind of nuclear winter, a stasis from which we were told amazing things would emerge in the next 10 years. That winter began to ever-so-slightly thaw with practical applications of machine learning over the last decade but with truly amazing things still a perpetual 10 years away.

And then ChatGPT changed everything.

Today, AI is no longer the preserve of academic journals and ambitious conference talks. It has taken center stage in the IT world and is reshaping entire industries and economies. For technology professionals, it has redefined what it means to build software in the modern era.

The shift has been swift and dizzying. We have all marveled at GenAI-powered chatbots, but amid the excitement and innovation, a serious question has lingered: how can we use AI dependably? Dependability is an important characteristic of systems. It encompasses aspects such as availability and reliability but of particular importance in a world built on AI, it also covers safety, security, and trustworthiness.

It is in the ability to help systems developers make AI trustworthy that Sid and Ravi as authors, make their mark.

This book is a thoughtful, well-written guide from authors with real experience in contemporary graph and AI systems. The authors know the terrain, including theory and architecture as well as code and the deployment pipeline. They have accumulated wisdom that is very worthy of sharing.

The book builds on a classic RAG approach, where retrieval from external data sources meets generation to produce grounded, useful responses. From there, the reader is gently guided into the more sophisticated and powerful world of GraphRAG, where Neo4j and knowledge graphs play a central role in helping foundational models to produce trustworthy results. Along the way, readers are acquainted with examples using modern AI middleware, such as Neo4j's GenAI framework, with a focus on Haystack, LangChain4j, and Spring AI. This middleware helps us to rapidly build and deploy (including on the cloud) coherent, dependable systems supported by knowledge graphs.

The authors write with clarity and authority that reflects their experience. They understand both how to make knowledge graphs and GenAI systems work and how to explain them in a way that's accessible and engaging. But what makes this book particularly outstanding is its developer-first sensibility. There's no hand-waving or marketing speak—just clear, pragmatic advice, and a collection of crisply written technical examples. It is the sort of material that's empowering for developers who are tasked with putting dependable AI systems into production.

Dr. Jim Webber

Chief Scientist, Neo4j

My journey with Neo4j began in 2016 during my master's thesis, where I used it to traverse citation graphs between scientific papers and patents to recommend cross-collection references. Coming from a background of natural language processing, and having worked mostly with unstructured data, I was struck by the clarity of graph traversal and the elegance of the Cypher query language.

Two years later, in 2018, deepset was founded, and the foundations of the open source AI framework Haystack were soon built. Designed for building modern, compound AI systems with a focus on production readiness, the framework quickly gained a vibrant community and with it a growing variety of use cases and deployed solutions. Fast forward to today, and the integration of Haystack and Neo4j feels not just natural but like the next logical step in building smarter, context-aware AI applications.

As one of the maintainers of Haystack, I am particularly excited about this book. It doesn't just present a theoretical case for using knowledge graphs with LLMs. It is a hands-on, pragmatic guide to building RAG-based applications with Neo4j's powerful graph model and Haystack's flexible pipeline architecture with its highly customizable components. As Sergey Bondarenco, who worked on the integration, put it well: "Haystack pipelines are also graphs." Each component is a node, each connection an edge, you can have branches and loops, and when you run a pipeline, information flows from one component to the next. With Neo4j's integration, you can now filter metadata through Cypher, combine vector and structured search in a single query, and enhance context windows of LLMs with structured information.

In a field moving as fast as GenAI, it is refreshing to see a book that is grounded in well-established, robust technology. Ravi and Sid have written a guide that embraces the best of both worlds: the structure and interpretability of graphs, and the flexibility and reasoning capabilities of LLMs. Whether you are just starting with RAG or looking to level up your graph-driven GenAI applications, this book will meet you where you are and take you further.

Dr. Julian Risch

Team Lead (Open Source Engineering), deepset

Contributors

About the authors

Ravindranatha Anthapu has more than 25 years of experience in working with W3C standards and building cutting-edge technologies, including integrating speech into mobile applications in the 2000s. He is a technology enthusiast who has worked on many projects, from operating system device drivers to writing compilers for C language and modern web technologies, transitioning seamlessly and bringing experience from each of these domains and technologies to deliver successful solutions today. As a principal consultant at Neo4j today, Ravindranatha works with large enterprise customers to make sure they are able to leverage graph technologies effectively across various domains.

Siddhant Agarwal is a seasoned DevRel professional with over a decade of experience in cultivating innovation and scaling developer ecosystems globally. Currently leading developer relations across APAC at Neo4j and recognized as a Google Developer Expert in GenAI, Sid transforms local developer initiatives into global success stories with his signature "Local to Global" approach. Previously working at Google managing flagship developer programs, he has shared his technical expertise at diverse forums worldwide, fueling inspiration and innovation. Learn more about him and his work, visit, meetsid.dev (https://meetsid.dev/).

About the reviewers

Fernando Aguilar Islas is a senior solutions consultant at Enterprise Knowledge, leading the design and implementation of AI and graph-based solutions for global organizations. He specializes in semantic solutions, LLMs, graph data science, knowledge graphs, and machine learning. His work spans diverse use cases, including identity resolution with graphs, AI-augmented human-in-the-loop frameworks, and graph-based recommenders. Fernando holds an MS in applied statistics from Penn State and is a certified Neo4j Professional and AWS Solutions Architect Associate. He is passionate about building intelligent systems that drive measurable business impact through advanced analytics, semantics, and graph technologies.

Manisha Mittal is a machine learning engineer with nearly a decade of experience in delivering enterprise-grade solutions at leading technology companies such as SAP and Visa. She specializes in GenAI-based RAG (embeddings and GraphRAG) applications, agentic workflows, and evaluation frameworks, along with in-depth knowledge of LLMs. She has deep expertise across a wide tech stack, including Java, Python, SQL, Hive, Neo4j, React, Node.js, Airflow, and Hadoop. Manisha holds a B.Tech. degree in information technology from the Indian Institute of Information Technology, Allahabad, India, with a strong foundation in scalable application development and AI-driven systems.

Mihir Arya is a UCLA mathematics graduate currently working at Visa as a senior software engineer. His team works heavily in the GenAI space, in the domains of building agentic user applications and GenAI evaluation frameworks, in addition to building and promoting knowledge graphs as a revolutionary alternative to traditional vector RAG among internal developers.

Acknowledgement

The authors are grateful to the **grouplens** team and the **Kaggle** team for making available the Movies dataset, a derivative of the Movie Lens Datasets.

(F. Maxwell Harper and Joseph A. Konstan. 2015. The MovieLens Datasets: History and Context. ACM Transactions on Interactive Intelligent Systems (TiiS) 5, 4:19:1–19:19. https://doi.org/10.1145/2827872).

The authors are grateful to **H&M** Group and the **Kaggle** team for making available the H&M Personalized Fashion Recommendations dataset.

(Carlos García Ling, ElizabethHMGroup, FridaRim, inversion, Jaime Ferrando, Maggie, neuraloverflow, and xlsrln. H&M Personalized Fashion Recommendations. 2022. Kaggle. https://kaggle.com/competitions/h-and-m-personalized-fashion-recommendations)

Join our communities on Discord and Reddit

Have questions about the book or want to contribute to discussions on Generative AI and LLMs?

Join our Discord server at https://packt.link/4Bbd9 and our Reddit channel at https://packt.link/wcYOQ to connect, share, and collaborate with like-minded enthusiasts.

Table of Contents

Part III: Building an Intelligent Recommendation System with Neo4j, Spring AI, and LangChain4j   135

Chapter 7: Introducing the Neo4j Spring AI and LangChain4j Frameworks for Building Recommendation Systems   137

Preface

We're living through a GenAI revolution—where AI is no longer just a backend component but a copilot, content creator, and decision-maker. And yet, many GenAI applications still struggle with hallucinations, lack of contextual understanding, and opaque reasoning. That's where this book comes in.

This book was born out of a core belief: knowledge graphs are the missing link between GenAI power and real-world intelligence. By combining the strengths of **Large Language Models (LLMs)** with the structured, connected data of Neo4j, and enhancing them with **Retrieval-Augmented Generation (RAG)** workflows, we can build systems that are not only smart but also grounded, contextual, and transparent.

We wrote this book because we've spent the last few years building and showcasing intelligent applications that go far beyond basic chatbot use cases. From developing AI-powered recommendation engines to integrating frameworks such as Haystack, LangChain4j, and Spring AI with Neo4j, we saw a growing need for a practical, hands-on guide that bridges GenAI concepts with production-ready knowledge graph architectures.

The vision for this book is to equip developers, architects, and AI enthusiasts with the tools, concepts, and real-world examples they need to design search and recommendation systems that are explainable, accurate, and scalable. You won't just learn about LLMs or graphs in isolation—you'll build end-to-end applications that bring these technologies together across cloud platforms, vector search, graph reasoning, and more.

As you journey through the chapters, you'll go from understanding foundational concepts to implementing advanced techniques such as embedding-powered retrieval, graph reasoning, and cloud-native GenAI deployments using Google Cloud, AuraDB, and open source tools.

Whether you're a data engineer, AI developer, or just someone curious about the future of intelligent systems, this book will help you build applications that are not only smarter but also produce better answers.

Who this book is for

This book is for database developers and data scientists who want to learn and use knowledge graphs using Neo4j and its vector search capabilities to build intelligent search and recommendation systems. To get started, working knowledge of Python and Java is essential. Familiarity with Neo4j, the Cypher query language, and fundamental concepts of databases will come in handy.

What this book covers

Chapter 1, Introducing LLMs, RAGs, and Neo4j Knowledge Graphs, introduces the core concepts of LLMs, RAG, and how Neo4j knowledge graphs enhance LLM performance by adding structure and context.

Chapter 2, Demystifying RAG, breaks down the RAG architecture, explaining how it augments LLMs with external knowledge. It covers key components such as retrievers, indexes, and generators with real-world examples.

Chapter 3, Building a Foundational Understanding of Knowledge Graph for Intelligent Applications, explains the basics of knowledge graphs and how they model real-world relationships. It highlights Neo4j's property graph model and its role in powering intelligent, context-aware applications.

Chapter 4, Building Your Neo4j Graph with the Movies Dataset, walks through constructing a Neo4j knowledge graph using a real-world movies dataset. It covers data modeling, Cypher queries, and importing structured data for graph-based search and reasoning.

Chapter 5, Implementing Powerful Search Functionalities with Neo4j and Haystack, shows how to integrate Neo4j with Haystack to enable semantic and keyword-based search. It covers embedding generation, indexing, and retrieving relevant results using vector search.

Chapter 6, Exploring Advanced Knowledge Graph Capabilities, dives into multi-hop reasoning, context-aware search, and leveraging graph structure for deeper insights. It showcases how Neo4j enhances intelligent retrieval beyond basic keyword or vector search.

Chapter 7, Introducing the Neo4j Spring AI and LangChain4j Frameworks for Building Recommendation Systems, introduces the Spring AI and LangChain4j frameworks to build LLM applications with Neo4j.

Chapter 8, Constructing a Recommendation Graph with the H&M Personalization Dataset, follows from the data modeling approaches discussed in *Chapter 3*, to load the H&M personalization dataset into a graph to build a better recommendation system.

Chapter 9, Integrating LangChain4j and Spring AI with Neo4j, provides a step-by-step guide to building Spring AI and LangChain4j applications to augment the graph by leveraging LLM chat APIs and the GraphRAG approach. It also covers embedding generation and adding these embeddings to a graph for machine learning purposes.

Chapter 10, Creating an Intelligent Recommendation System, explains how we can leverage Graph Data Science algorithms to further enhance the knowledge graph to provide better recommendations. It also discusses vector search and why it is not enough to provide good recommendations, as well as how leveraging KNN similarity and community detection gives us better results.

Chapter 11, Choosing the Right Cloud Platform for GenAI Application, compares major cloud platforms for deploying GenAI applications, focusing on scalability, cost, and AI/ML capabilities. It guides you in selecting the best-fit environment for your use case.

Chapter 12, Deploying Your Application on Google Cloud, provides a step-by-step guide to deploying your GenAI application on Google Cloud. It covers services such as Vertex AI, Cloud Functions, and Firebase for scalable and efficient deployment.

Chapter 13, Epilogue, reflects on the journey of building intelligent applications with GenAI and Neo4j. It summarizes key takeaways and highlights future opportunities in the evolving AI ecosystem.

To get the most out of this book

To fully benefit from this book, you should have a basic understanding of databases, familiarity with Neo4j and its Cypher query language, and a working knowledge of LLMs and GenAI concepts. Prior experience with Python and Java will also be helpful for implementing the code examples and working with frameworks such as Haystack, as well as LangChain4j and Spring AI for Java-based applications.

You'll be guided through building and deploying intelligent applications, so you may need to create free accounts on platforms such as Neo4j AuraDB, **Google Cloud Platform (GCP)**, and OpenAI (or equivalent embedding providers). While no special hardware is required, a machine with at least 8 GB RAM and internet access is recommended for smooth development and testing.

Download the example code files and database dump

The code bundle for the book is hosted on GitHub at `https://github.com/PacktPublishing/Building-Neo4j-Powered-Applications-with-LLMs`. We also have other code bundles from our rich catalog of books and videos available at `https://github.com/PacktPublishing`. Check them out!

You can download the database dump from this link `https://packt-neo4j-powered-applications.s3.us-east-1.amazonaws.com/Building+Neo4j-Powered+Applications+with+LLMs+Database+Dump+files.zip`.

Download the color images

We also provide a PDF file that has color images of the screenshots/diagrams used in this book. You can download it here: `https://packt.link/gbp/9781836206231`.

Conventions used

There are a number of text conventions used throughout this book.

`CodeInText`: Indicates code words in text, database table names, folder names, filenames, file extensions, pathnames, dummy URLs, user input, and X (Twitter) handles. For example: "Install the Hugging Face Transformers library for handling model-related functionalities: `pip install transformers`."

A block of code is set as follows:

```
documents = [
    "The IPL 2024 was a thrilling season with unexpected results.",
.....
    "Dense Passage Retrieval (') is a state-of-the-art technique for
information retrieval."
]
```

When we wish to draw your attention to a particular part of a code block, the relevant lines or items are set in bold:

```
tokenizer = T5Tokenizer.from_pretrained('t5-small', legacy=False)
model = T5ForConditionalGeneration.from_pretrained('t5-small')
```

Any command-line input or output is written as follows:

```
pip install numpy==1.26.4 neo4j transformers torch faiss-cpu datasets
```

Bold: Indicates a new term, an important word, or words that you see on the screen. For instance, words in menus or dialog boxes appear in the text like this. For example: "**Artificial Intelligence (AI)** is evolving beyond niche and specialized fields to become more accessible and able to assist with day-to-day tasks."

> Warnings or important notes appear like this.

> Tips and tricks appear like this.

Declaration

The authors acknowledge the use of cutting-edge AI, such as ChatGPT, with the sole aim of enhancing the language and clarity within the book, thereby ensuring a smooth reading experience for readers. It's important to note that the content itself has been crafted by the authors and edited by a professional publishing team.

Get in touch

To keep up with the latest developments in the fields of Generative AI and LLMs, subscribe to our weekly newsletter, **AI_Distilled**, at `https://packt.link/Q5UyU`.

Feedback from our readers is always welcome.

General feedback: Email `feedback@packtpub.com` and mention the book's title in the subject of your message. If you have questions about any aspect of this book, please email us at `questions@packtpub.com`.

Errata: Although we have taken every care to ensure the accuracy of our content, mistakes do happen. If you have found a mistake in this book, we would be grateful if you reported this to us. Please visit http://www.packtpub.com/submit-errata, click **Submit Errata**, and fill in the form.

Piracy: If you come across any illegal copies of our works in any form on the internet, we would be grateful if you would provide us with the location address or website name. Please contact us at copyright@packtpub.com with a link to the material.

If you are interested in becoming an author: If there is a topic that you have expertise in and you are interested in either writing or contributing to a book, please visit http://authors.packtpub.com/.

Share your thoughts

Once you've read *Building Neo4j-Powered Applications with LLMs*, we'd love to hear your thoughts! Scan the QR code below to go straight to the Amazon review page for this book and share your feedback.

https://packt.link/r/1836206232

Your review is important to us and the tech community and will help us make sure we're delivering excellent quality content.

Download a free PDF copy of this book

Thanks for purchasing this book!

Do you like to read on the go but are unable to carry your print books everywhere?

Is your eBook purchase not compatible with the device of your choice?

Don't worry, now with every Packt book you get a DRM-free PDF version of that book at no cost.

Read anywhere, any place, on any device. Search, copy, and paste code from your favorite technical books directly into your application.

The perks don't stop there, you can get exclusive access to discounts, newsletters, and great free content in your inbox daily.

Follow these simple steps to get the benefits:

1. Scan the QR code or visit the link below:

https://packt.link/free-ebook/9781836206231

2. Submit your proof of purchase.
3. That's it! We'll send your free PDF and other benefits to your email directly.

Part 1

Introducing RAG and Knowledge Graphs for LLM Grounding

This first part of the book sets the stage for building grounded, context-aware AI applications. We will start by introducing the fundamentals of **Large Language Models (LLMs)**, the challenges they face around factuality, and how **Retrieval-Augmented Generation (RAG)** helps address those limitations. Next, we break down RAG architectures with practical insights and implementation guidance. We conclude by establishing a foundational understanding of knowledge graphs—highlighting how Neo4j enables structured, semantically rich representations that enhance the grounding and reasoning capabilities of LLMs.

This part of the book includes the following chapters:

- *Chapter 1, Introducing LLMs, RAGs, and Neo4j Knowledge Graphs*
- *Chapter 2, Demystifying RAG*
- *Chapter 3, Building a Foundational Understanding of Knowledge Graph for Intelligent Applications*

Stay tuned

To keep up with the latest developments in the fields of Generative AI and LLMs, subscribe to our weekly newsletter, AI_Distilled, at `https://packt.link/Q5UyU`.

1

Introducing LLMs, RAGs, and Neo4j Knowledge Graphs

Artificial Intelligence (AI) is evolving beyond niche and specialized fields to become more accessible and able to assist with day-to-day tasks. One of the best examples is the explosive advent of **Generative AI (GenAI)**. In the last few years, GenAI has created a lot of excitement both for technology builders and regular users with its ease of use and ability to understand and answer questions the way humans can. The breakthroughs in **Large Language Models (LLMs)** have propelled GenAI to the forefront. This has opened up a lot of opportunities for businesses to change how they interact with their customers. Customers can ask a question in natural language and get an answer without needing a human to be available to understand the question or understand the data to extract intelligence from it. While GenAI has taken big strides in different fields with different modalities, such as text, audio, and video, our focus throughout this book remains on LLMs and their applications in business and industry use cases.

In this chapter, we will take a look at GenAI through the lens of LLMs, its impact, pitfalls, and ethical concerns. To set the stage for this book, we will briefly introduce techniques that can augment LLMs to make them more effective.

In this chapter, we are going to cover the following main topics:

- Outlining the evolution of GenAI through the lens of LLMs
- Understanding the importance of RAGs and knowledge graphs in LLMs
- Introducing Neo4j knowledge graphs

Outlining the evolution of GenAI through the lens of LLMs

In late 2022, OpenAI took the world by storm by releasing an AI engine called ChatGPT that could understand language like humans and interact with users in natural language. This was the best representation of GenAI in a long time. AI concepts started as rules-based systems and evolved into machine learning algorithms in the '90s. With the rise of deep learning and LLMs, the concept of GenAI became more popular. These AI systems could generate new content after being trained using existing content. OpenAI's GPT-3 LLM model was one of the first LLMs that captured the interest of the masses. GenAI can be used to get answers in a manner that feels like human interaction and it can also be used to generate images by providing a text description, describe an image as text content, generate videos using text content, and many other things. It can enhance creativity, accelerate research and development, enable a simple understanding of complex concepts, and improve personalization.

The evolution of LLMs is at the heart of GenAI's popularity. Let's take a look at LLMs and how they have propelled GenAI.

Introducing LLMs

An LLM is a machine learning model that is built for natural language processing and can understand language constructs and generate content in that language based on the training.

Before the popularity of GPT-3, a considerable amount of research had been conducted on LLMs fover several years. Some of the notable works that pioneered LLMs include Google's **Bidirectional Encoder Representations from Transformers (BERT** (`https://github.com/google-research/bert`)) and **Generative Pre-trained Transformer (GPT)** from OpenAI. LLM training requires a lot of parameters and computing power.

At their core, LLMs are a type of **Recurrent Neural Network (RNN)** architecture. Traditional RNNs struggle with long-term dependencies in sequential data. To address this, LLMs often leverage architectures such as **Long Short-Term Memory (LSTM)** networks or transformers. These architectures allow the model to learn complex relationships between words, even words that are separated by large distances within the training text.

Here is a simple illustration of a basic LLM architecture:

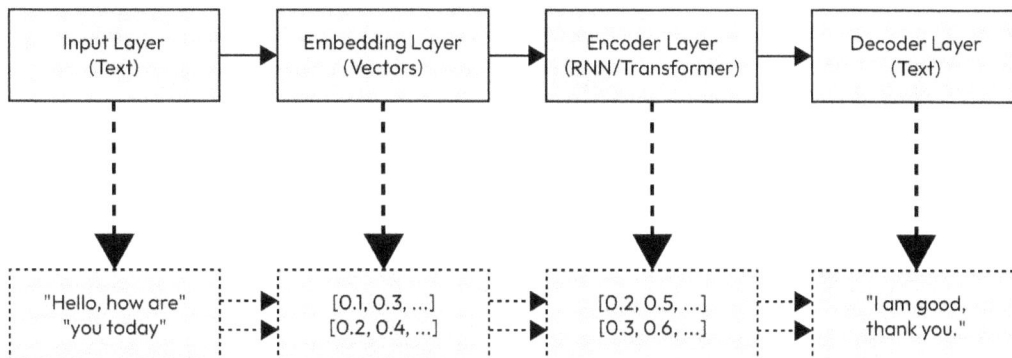

Figure 1.1 — Flowchart explaining a basic LLM architecture

Let's dissect this architecture

- **Input layer**: This layer receives the initial text prompt or sequence
- **Embedding layer**: Words in the input sequence are converted into numerical vectors, capturing their semantic meaning
- **Encoder**: This is a multi-layered RNN (e.g., LSTM) or transformer that processes the sequence of embedded words, capturing contextual information
- **Decoder**: The decoder utilizes the encoded representation to generate the output sequence one word at a time

You can read more about LLMs in this paper: `https://arxiv.org/pdf/2307.06435`.

Building an LLM requires a lot of effort and resources. Let's look at the number of parameters used by OpenAI to train each GPT model:

- **GPT-1**: This is the first model and used 117 million parameters.
- **GPT-2**: This model used 1.5 billion parameters to train.
- **GPT-3**: This model was the first general-purpose model released. 175 billion parameters were used to train this model.
- **GPT-4 series**: This is the latest model released by OpenAI. 170 trillion parameters were used to train this model.

These training figures demonstrate that with each new version, the number of parameters increased by several orders of magnitude. This means more and more computing power is needed to train these models. Similar training numbers can be observed for other LLM models too.

While GenAI is a great technology, there are pitfalls as well as legal and ethical concerns about the application of this technology. We will take a look at them next.

Understanding GenAI's pitfalls and ethical concerns

While LLMs are great at summarizing, generating context, and other use cases, they still do not understand the language per se. They recognize patterns based on the training text to generate new text. They also don't understand facts or understand emotions or ethics. They are simply predicting the next token and generating text. Because of these pitfalls, content generated by GenAI can have huge consequences.

To understand and address these aspects, we need to first identify any harmful or inaccurate content that is being generated and address it either by retraining the model or adding separate checks and balances to make sure this content is not used as output.

For example, there have been recent cases about using LLMs to generate legal briefs, where LLMs have created non-existent cases and generated a legal brief based on these cases. While technically it might have generated a solution that is requested, this is legally not correct. There have also been cases where LLMs are used to generate offensive images and videos and shared on the internet. Since it is difficult to identify content generated by AI, it is easy to be fooled by this content. This is neither socially, legally, or ethically acceptable. There are quite a few examples where LLMs simply make up facts.

This tutorial on the Microsoft site (`https://learn.microsoft.com/en-us/training/modules/responsible-ai-studio/`) provides a detailed explanation of these concerns and how we can identify them.

Retrieval-Augmented Generation (RAG) and **knowledge graphs** together can help address these issues, which we discuss next.

Understanding the importance of RAGs and knowledge graphs in LLMs

To address the pitfalls of GenAI, we can either fine-tune the model or ground the responses using other sources.

Fine-tuning involves training an existing model with additional information, which can result in high-quality responses. But this can be a complex and time-consuming process.

The **RAG approach** involves providing extra information when we are asking the LLM a question.

With this approach, you can integrate knowledge repositories into the generative process. In this scenario, LLM can leverage the extra information retrieved from other sources and tune the response to match the information provided, thus grounding the results.

These repositories and sources can include the following:

- **Publicly available structured datasets** (e.g., scientific databases such as PubMed or publicly accessible encyclopedic resources such as Wikipedia)
- **Enterprise knowledge bases** (e.g., internal company documentation, product catalogs, or compliance-related content with strict privacy and security requirements)
- **Domain-specific sources** (e.g., legal case records, medical guidelines, or technical manuals tailored to specific industries)

By incorporating relevant information from these repositories and sources, RAG empowers LLMs to generate output that is not only factually accurate but also contextually aligned with the task at hand. Unlike the static knowledge encoded in the LLM's training data, these additional data sources allow real-time retrieval of up-to-date and specialized information, addressing challenges such as data freshness, accuracy, and specificity. We will cover RAG in detail in *Chapter 2*.

Another source of information to enable RAG is knowledge graphs. Let's briefly talk about them and their role in the LLM landscape.

The role of knowledge graphs in LLMs

Knowledge graphs play a huge role in generating creative and contextually rich content for LLMs. They provide a structured, interconnected foundation and make information retrieval more relevant and insightful by grounding the AI results in a complex and multi-layered understanding of the data.

Representing the data as a graph opens up more avenues to understand the data. At the same time, a knowledge graph cannot be a static entity that represents data in only one dimension that's fixed. Its true power lies in its ability to be dynamic and multi-dimensional. It can capture temporal, spatial, or contextual information in real time through live data feeds.

Apart from being an important tool for storing information, knowledge graphs are the backbone of intelligent, context-aware AI.

There are several reasons why knowledge graphs are essential for GenAI:

- **Enhanced contextual understanding**: Knowledge graphs allow GenAI systems to retrieve relevant information based on relationships, not just isolated facts. For example, in health-care, a knowledge graph could link symptoms, diseases, and treatments, enabling GenAI to suggest more accurate diagnostic insights based on interconnected medical knowledge.

- **Efficient data retrieval**: Unlike traditional databases, knowledge graphs allow multi-hop reasoning, from which GenAI can draw insights across several degrees of separation. This is invaluable in fields such as finance, where GenAI can use knowledge graphs to reveal hidden relationships between entities such as customers, transactions, and market trends.

- **Integration of vector embeddings**: When combined with vector embeddings, knowledge graphs enable GenAI to understand and respond to more nuanced queries. Vector embed-dings capture semantic similarities between data points, which knowledge graphs then contextualize, creating a powerful blend of accuracy and relevance in responses.

- **Real-world impact**: Major organizations are already harnessing the power of knowl-edge graphs to enhance GenAI applications. For instance, companies in e-commerce use knowledge graphs to provide product recommendations that are not just relevant but contextually rich, drawing from diverse data sources such as customer reviews, purchase history, and product features.

By integrating knowledge graphs, GenAI models transcend traditional data limitations, helping to create smarter, more reliable applications across different fields.

Let's now talk about **Neo4j knowledge graphs**.

Introducing Neo4j knowledge graphs

A knowledge graph is dynamic and continues to evolve based on how data and relationships within the data evolve with time.

Neo4j is a database that excels with its ability to store data in graphs. For example, in a store, most products are laid out in a certain grouping and stay in those groups. But there is an exception to this arrangement. When a store wants to promote some products, they are placed at the front of the store. This kind of flexible thought process should be adapted for our knowledge graph implementation. As the semantics of data evolves the knowledge graph should be able to capture this change.

Neo4j, with its multiple labels for nodes and its optional schema approach, makes it easy to keep our graph relevant by helping us to persist (retain) our understanding of data as an extra label on the node, or a specific relationship that provides more relevant context between the nodes. We will take a deeper look at how we can build a Neo4j knowledge graph from the ground up in the upcoming chapters.

For now, let's see how a Neo4j knowledge graph works to enhance an LLM's response.

Using Neo4j knowledge graphs with LLMs

Suppose there is an LLM-based chatbot integrated with a Neo4j knowledge graph. This GenAI chatbot is designed to answer medical queries. *Figure 1.2* illustrates how a Neo4j knowledge graph can enhance this chatbot's medical reasoning by linking structured patient symptom records with unstructured insights from medical research papers and clinical trials.

The unstructured text undergoes embedding-based processing using models from providers such as **Ollama**, **OpenAI**, and **Hugging Face**, followed by **Named Entity Recognition** (NER), to extract key entities such as symptoms and treatments. This data is integrated into a Neo4j knowledge graph, where documents mention symptoms and treatments, patients show symptoms, and symptoms are linked to potential treatments. This enables **multi-hop reasoning**, allowing a chatbot to efficiently answer complex queries such as the following:

Which patients are showing symptoms similar to flu and also showed symptoms of COVID-19 in the past?

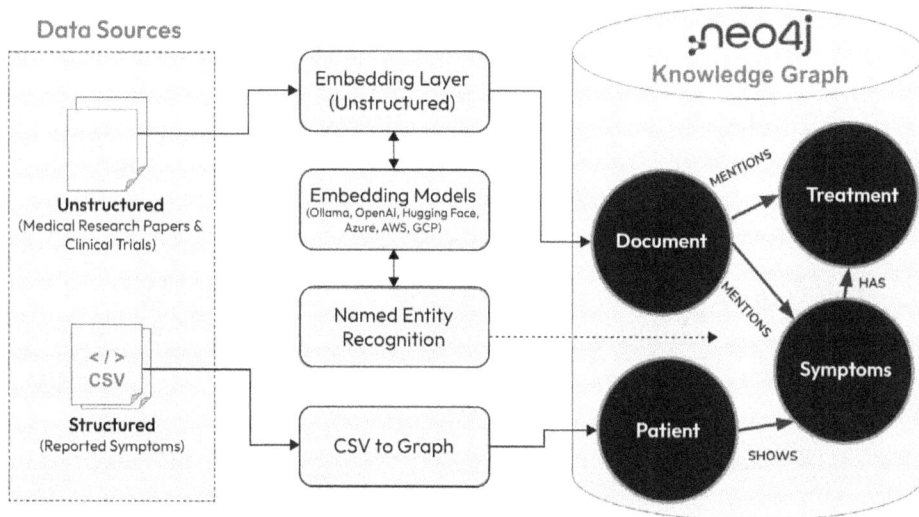

Figure 1.2 — Neo4j knowledge graph driven Gen-AI for healthcare

To retrieve the result of this query, a **multi-hop knowledge graph query path** (*Figure 1.2*) will be followed in this order:

1. Retrieve symptoms linked to flu from research documents.

2. Identify patients currently showing those symptoms.

3. Cross-reference past patient records for COVID-19 symptoms.

4. Return patients who match both conditions with supporting document sources.

With this approach, the LLM response can be grounded to generate factually correct, relevant, and up-to-date results to support medical decision-making.

A similar approach can be used to augment LLMs that support other applications.

We have now looked at how knowledge graphs enhance GenAI's ability to provide contextually rich, accurate insights. But how does this transformative power translate into concrete benefits in real life? We will continue this journey in the rest of the book.

Summary

In this chapter, we discussed the evolution of GenAI in the context of LLMs. We also looked at how RAG and knowledge graphs are key enablers of this transformation and help provide structure and context, improving an LLM's accuracy and reasoning.

Looking ahead, the next chapter dives deep into RAG — a technique that significantly enhances GenAI's accuracy by grounding responses in retrieved, verified information.

2

Demystifying RAG

In the previous chapter, we explored the evolution of LLMs and how they have changed the GenAI landscape. We also discussed some of their pitfalls. We will explore how we can avoid these pitfalls using **Retrieval-Augmented Generation (RAG)** in this chapter. We will take a look at what RAG means, what its architecture is, and how it fits into the LLM workflow in building improved intelligent applications.

In this chapter, we are going to cover the following main topics:

- Understanding the power of RAG
- Deconstructing the RAG flow
- Retrieving external information for your RAG
- Building an end-to-end RAG flow

Technical requirements

This chapter requires familiarity with the Python programming language (version 3.6 or higher is recommended) and basic concepts of deep learning.

We will be leveraging popular AI toolkits such as Hugging Face's Transformers library (https://huggingface.co/docs/transformers/en/index) to build and experiment with RAG. While not mandatory, having a basic understanding of Git version control can be helpful.

Git allows you to easily clone the code repository for this chapter and track any changes you make. Do not worry about finding or typing the code yourself! We have created a dedicated public repository on GitHub, `https://github.com/PacktPublishing/Building-Neo4j-Powered-Applications-with-LLMs/tree/main/ch2`, allowing you to easily clone it and follow along with the chapter's hands-on exercises.

This repository contains all the necessary scripts, files, and configurations required to implement the RAG model and integrate Neo4j with advanced knowledge graph capabilities.

To follow along, make sure you have the following Python libraries installed in your environment:

- **Transformers**: Install the Hugging Face Transformers library for handling model-related functionalities: `pip install transformers`.
- **PyTorch**: Install PyTorch as the backend for computation. Follow the instructions at `https://pytorch.org/get-started/locally/` to install the appropriate version for your system.
- **scikit-learn**: For similarity calculations, install `scikit-learn` using the `pip install scikit-learn` command.
- **NumPy**: Install NumPy for numerical operations: `pip install numpy`.
- **SentencePiece**: SentencePiece is required for text tokenization with certain models. You can install it using the instructions provided in the official GitHub repository: `https://github.com/google/sentencepiece#installation`. For most Python environments, install it via pip: `pip install sentencepiece`.
- **rank_bm25**: The `rank_bm25` library is required to implement the BM25 algorithm for keyword-based retrieval. You can install it using pip: `pip install rank_bm25`.
- **datasets**: The `datasets` library from Hugging Face provides efficient tools for loading, processing, and transforming datasets. It supports large-scale datasets with minimal memory usage. You can install it using `pip install datasets`.
- **pandas**: pandas is a powerful data analysis library in Python, used for manipulating tabular data. In this example, it helps preprocess the dataset by converting it into a DataFrame for easier manipulation. Install it using `pip install pandas`.
- **faiss-CPU**: `faiss-cpu` is a library for efficient similarity search and clustering of dense vectors. It is used in this example for building a retriever that fetches relevant passages during inference. Visit the Faiss GitHub repository (`https://github.com/facebookresearch/faiss`) for documentation and examples. Install it using pip: `pip install faiss-cpu`.

- **Accelerate**: Accelerate is a library by Hugging Face that simplifies distributed training and inference. It ensures optimal hardware utilization across CPUs, GPUs, and multi-node setups. Install it using `pip install accelerate`.

By ensuring your environment is configured with these tools, you can seamlessly explore the hands-on exercises provided in this chapter.

> **Note**
>
> All the sections in this chapter focus on the relevant code snippets. For the complete code, please refer to the book's GitHub repository: `https://github.com/PacktPublishing/Building-Neo4j-Powered-Applications-with-LLMs/tree/main/ch2`.

Understanding the power of RAG

RAG was introduced by Meta researchers in 2020 (`https://arxiv.org/abs/2005.11401v4`) as a framework that allows GenAI models to leverage external data that is not part of model training to enhance the output.

It is a widely known fact that LLMs suffer from hallucinations. One of the classic real-world examples of LLMs hallucinating is the case of Levidow, Levidow & Oberman, the New York law firm that was fined for submitting a legal brief containing fake citations generated by OpenAI's ChatGPT in a case against Colombian airline Avianca. They were subsequently fined thousands of dollars, and they are likely to have lost more in reputational damage. You can read more about it here: `https://news.sky.com/story/lawyers-fined-after-citing-bogus-cases-from-chatgpt-research-12908318`.

LLM hallucinations can arise from several factors, such as the following:

- **Overfitting to training data**: During training, the LLM might overfit to statistical patterns in the training data. This can lead the model to prioritize replicating those patterns over generating factually accurate content.
- **Lack of causal reasoning**: LLMs excel at identifying statistical relationships between words but may struggle to understand cause-and-effect relationships. This can lead to outputs that are grammatically correct but factually implausible.

- **Temperature configuration**: LLMs can be configured with a parameter called **tempera-ture**, a number between 0 and 1 that controls the randomness in text generation. Higher temperatures increase creativity but also the likelihood of hallucinations as the model deviates from expected responses.

- **Missing information**: If the information required to generate an accurate response is not included in the training data, the model might generate plausible sounding but incorrect answers.

- **Flawed or biased training data**: The quality of the training process plays a significant role. If the dataset contains biases or inaccuracies, the model may perpetuate these issues, leading to hallucinations.

While hallucinations are a significant challenge, several methods can help mitigate them to some extent:

- **Prompt engineering**: This involves carefully crafting and iteratively refining the instructions or queries given to the LLM to elicit consistent and accurate responses. For instance, asking an LLM

  ```
  List five key benefits of Neo4j for knowledge graphs
  ```

  provides more structure and precision compared to the broad query like:

  ```
  Tell me about Neo4j
  ```

  The former query specifies the expected output, leading the model to focus on a concise and relevant list of benefits, while the latter might yield a verbose or tangential response. Prompt engineering helps guide the model to stay within the desired scope of information and reduces the chances of it producing irrelevant or fabricated outputs. For a detailed exploration of prompt engineering techniques and best practices, check out this guide: https://cloud.google.com/discover/what-is-prompt-engineering.

- **In-context learning (few-shot prompting)**: In this method, examples are included within the prompt to guide the LLM toward accurate, task-specific responses. For instance, when asking for a product comparison, providing a few examples of properly structured comparisons within the prompt helps the model mimic the pattern. This approach leverages the model's capability to infer context and adjust its responses based on the given examples, making it effective for domain-specific tasks.

- **Fine-tuning**: This involves training an already pre-trained LLM further on a specific data-set to adapt it to specialized domains or tasks. This process enhances the model's ability to generate domain-specific, relevant, and accurate responses. One popular method for fine-tuning is **Reinforcement Learning with Human Feedback** (**RLHF**), where human evaluators guide the model by scoring its outputs. These scores are used to adjust the model's behavior, aligning it with human expectations. For example, fine-tuning an LLM on a company's internal documentation ensures it produces accurate and relevant outputs tailored to the organization's specific needs. If prompted with

  ```
  Explain the onboarding process for new hires
  ```

  a fine-tuned model might provide a detailed explanation consistent with the company's policies, whereas a general model might offer a vague or unrelated response. Let us take another example scenario to understand how using RLHF, you can improve responses.

  Suppose the LLM was initially asked:

  ```
  What are the benefits of using XYZ software?
  ```

  The response might include generic benefits that do not align with the software's unique features. With RLHF, human evaluators score the response based on accuracy, relevance, and completeness. For instance, the initial response could be:

  ```
  XYZ software improves productivity, enhances collaboration, and
  reduces costs.
  ```

  The feedback may be:

  ```
  Too generic; lacks specifics about XYZ software.
  ```

  After fine-tuning with human feedback, the result could be a more accurate and tailored response, as follows:

  ```
  XYZ software offers real-time data synchronization, customizable
  workflows, and advanced security features, making it ideal for
  enterprise resource planning.
  ```

  RLHF is especially valuable in reducing hallucinations because it emphasizes learning from human-curated feedback.

While these methods provide significant improvements, they still fall short in one critical area: enabling organizations to use domain-specific knowledge to rapidly build accurate, contextual, and explainable GenAI applications. The solution lies in **grounding** – a concept that ties the model's responses to real-world facts or data. This approach forms the foundation of a new paradigm in text generation called RAG. By dynamically retrieving factual information from reliable knowledge sources, RAG ensures outputs are both accurate and contextually aligned. RAG tries to address LLM hallucinations by incorporating relevant information from factual knowledge repositories.

The term retrieval-augmented generation, or RAG for short, was first introduced by researchers at **Facebook AI Research (FAIR)** in a paper titled *Retrieval-Augmented Generation for Knowledge-Intensive NLP Tasks*: https://arxiv.org/abs/2005.11401, submitted in May 2020.

The paper proposed RAG as a hybrid architecture (refer to *Figure 2.1*) that combines a neural retriever with a sequence-to-sequence generator. The **retriever** fetches relevant documents from an external knowledge base, which are then used as context for the generator to produce outputs grounded in factual data. This approach was shown to significantly improve performance on knowledge-intensive NLP tasks, such as open-domain question-answering and dialogue systems, by reducing the reliance on the model's internal knowledge and enhancing factual accuracy. RAG addresses the previously mentioned shortcomings of LLMs by introducing a critical element: the ability to retrieve relevant knowledge from supplementary or domain-specific data sources.

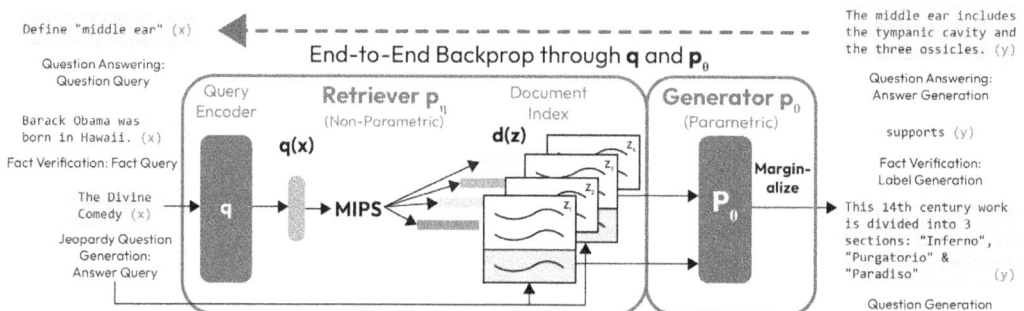

Figure 2.1 — RAG architecture proposed in the Retrieval-Augmented Generation for Knowledge-Intensive NLP Tasks research paper by FAIR

Additionally, RAG pipelines offer the potential to reduce model size while maintaining accuracy. Instead of embedding all knowledge within the model's parameters—which would require extensive resources—RAG allows the model to retrieve information dynamically, keeping it lightweight and scalable.

The next section in this chapter will delve deeper into the inner workings of RAG, exploring how it bridges the gap between raw generation and knowledge-grounded text production.

Deconstructing the RAG flow

Let us now deconstruct the building blocks of a RAG model and help you understand how it functions.

First, we will take a look at the regular LLM application flow. *Figure 2.2* illustrates this basic flow.

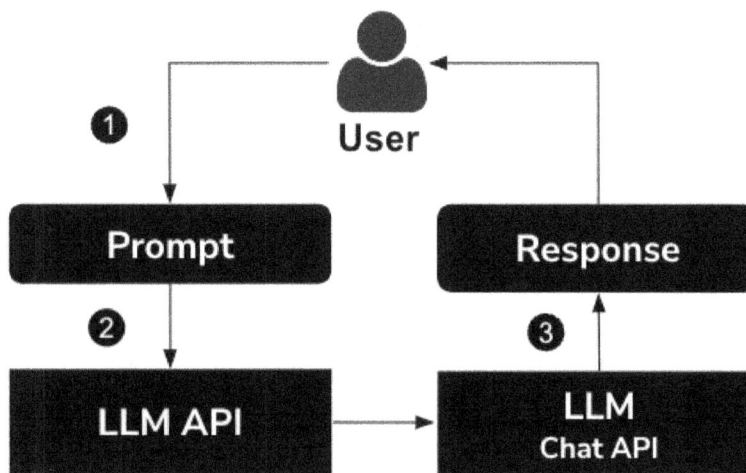

Figure 2.2 — The basic flow of information in a chat application with an LLM

Here is what happens when a user prompts an LLM

1. **User sends a prompt:** The process begins with a user sending a prompt to an LLM chat API. This prompt could be a question, an instruction, or any other request for information or content generation.

2. **LLM API processes the prompt:** The LLM chat API receives the user's prompt and transmits it to an LLM. LLMs are AI models trained on massive amounts of text data, allowing them to communicate and generate human-like text in response to a wide range of prompts and questions.

3. **LLM generates a response:** The LLM then processes the prompt and formulates a response. This response is sent back to the LLM chat API, which then transmits it to the user.

From this flow, we can see that the LLM is responsible for providing the answer and there is no other process in between. This is the most common usage without RAG in the request-response flow.

Now let us take a look at where RAG fits into this workflow.

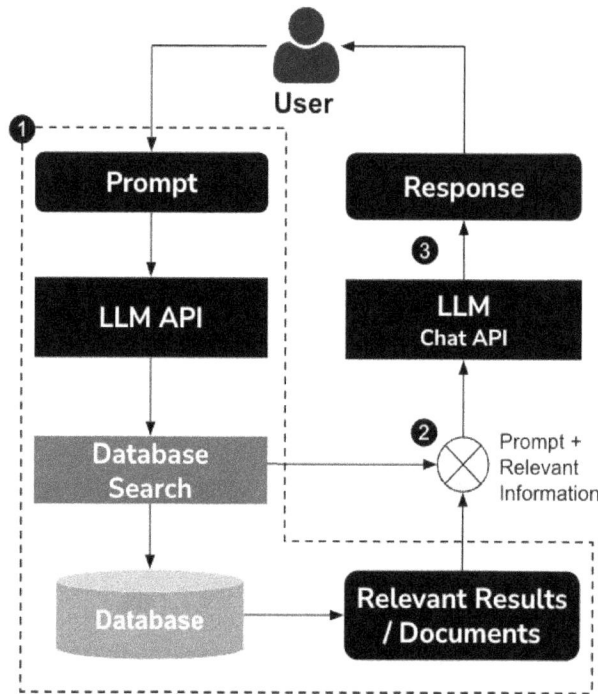

Figure 2.3 — The flow of information in a chat application with the RAG model

We can see from *Figure 2.3* that we have an intermediate data source before the actual LLM service invocation that can provide the context for the LLM request:

1. **User sends prompt**: The process starts with the user sending a prompt or question through a chat interface. This prompt could be anything the user wants information about or needs help with.

2. **RAG model processes prompt**: The prompt is received by a chat API, which then relays it to the RAG model. The RAG model has two main components working together: the *retriever* (discussed in Step 3) and the *encoder-decoder* (discussed in Step 4).

3. **Retriever**: This component searches through a knowledge repository, which may include unstructured documents, passages, or structured data such as tables or knowledge graphs. Its role is to locate the most relevant information needed to address the user's prompt.

   We will cover a simple example of the retriever component. You can review the full code available at `https://github.com/PacktPublishing/Building-Neo4j-Powered-Applications-with-LLMs/blob/main/ch2/dpr.py`

The following code snippet initializes a *context encoder model* and *tokenizer* from Hugging Face's Transformers library:

1. Let us define a set of documents that we want to store in a document store. We are using a few predefined sentences here for demonstration purposes:

```
documents = [
    "The IPL 2024 was a thrilling season with unexpected
results.",
    .....
    "Dense Passage Retrieval (') is a state-of-the-art
technique for information retrieval."
    ]
```

2. Next, we will store the content defined previously in a content store. Then we will generate an embedding for each of the documents and store them in the content store:

```
def encode_documents(documents):
    inputs = tokenizer(
        documents, return_tensors='pt',
        padding=True, truncation=True)
    with torch.no_grad():
        outputs = model(**inputs)
    return outputs.pooler_output.numpy()


document_embeddings = encode_documents(documents)
```

3. Now, let us define a method that retrieves the content from the document store based on query input. We will generate an embedding of the request and query the content store to retrieve the relevant result. We are leveraging vector search here to get the relevant results:

```
def retrieve_documents(query, num_results=3):
    inputs = tokenizer(query, return_tensors='pt',
        padding=True, truncation=True)
    with torch.no_grad():
        query_embedding = model(**inputs).pooler_output
                                          .numpy()
    similarity_scores = cosine_similarity(
```

```
        query_embedding, document_embeddings).flatten()
top_indices = similarity_scores.argsort()[-num_results:]
    [::-1]
top_docs = [
    (documents[i], similarity_scores[i])
    for i in top_indices]
return top_doc
```

We can see for a given query what kind of output we would receive as an example.

The following is sample input:

```
Query: What is Dense Passage Retrieval?
```

And here is the sample output:

```
Top Results:
Score: 0.7777, Document: Dense Passage Retrieval (') is a state-of-
the-art technique for information retrieval.
...
```

Note

Retriever implementations can be quite complex. They could involve using efficient search algorithms such as BM25, TF-IDF, or neural retrievers such as **Dense Passage Retrieval**. You can read more about it at https:// github.com/facebookresearch/.

4. **Encoder-decoder/augmented generation**: The encoder part of this component processes the prompt along with the retrieved information—whether structured or unstructured— to create a comprehensive representation. The decoder then uses this representation to generate a response that is accurate, contextually rich, and tailored to the user's prompt.

    This involves invoking the LLM API with the input query and context information. Let us take a look at an example of how this works. The following example shows how we can invoke a query with contextual information. This example showcases the use of T5Tokenizer model:

    1. Let us define an LLM first. We will be using the T5 model from Hugging Face:

        ```
        tokenizer = T5Tokenizer.from_pretrained('t5-small',
            legacy=False)
        ```

```
model = T5ForConditionalGeneration.from_pretrained(
    't5-small')
```

2. Define the query and documents for the RAG flow. Normally, we leverage a retriever for the RAG flow. We are going to use hardcoded values for demonstration purposes here:

```
query = "What are the benefits of solar energy?"
retrieved_passages = """
Solar energy is a renewable resource and reduces electricity
bills.
......
"""
```

3. We will define a method that takes the input query and the retrieved passages to use the LLM API to demonstrate the RAG approach:

```
def generate_response(query, retrieved_passages):
        input_text = f"Answer this question based on the
provided context: {query} Context: {retrieved_passages}"
    inputs = tokenizer(input_text, return_tensors='pt',
        padding=True,
        truncation=True, max_length=512
    ).to(device)
    with torch.no_grad():
        outputs = model.generate(
            **inputs,
            max_length=300,   # Allow longer responses
            num_beams=3,      # Use beam search for better
results
            early_stopping=True
        )
    return tokenizer.decode(outputs[0],
        skip_special_tokens=True)
```

Note

We are employing the **T5 model**'s beam search decoding to produce an accurate and contextually relevant response. **Beam search decoding** is a search algorithm used to find the most likely sequence of tokens (words) during text generation. Unlike greedy decoding, which selects the most probable token at each step, beam search maintains multiple potential sequences (called **beams**) and explores them simultaneously. This increases the chances of finding a high-quality result, as it avoids committing to suboptimal choices too early in the generation process. You can learn more about beam search in Transformers in this article: `https://huggingface.co/blog/constrained-beam-search`.

Now, let us invoke this method and review the response.

5. **Chat API delivers response**: The following code will invoke the generate_response method and deliver the chat response for the input query:

```
response = generate_response(query, retrieved_passages)
print("Query:", query)
print("Retrieved Passages:", retrieved_passages)
print("Generated Response:", response)
```

When we run this example, the outcome is as follows.

The following is sample input:

```
Query: What are the benefits of solar energy?
```

The retrieved passages are as follows:

```
Solar energy is a renewable resource and reduces electricity bills.
......
```

The following is the sample output:

```
Generated Response: it is environmentally friendly and helps combat
climate change
```

You can find the full code for this example at `https://github.com/PacktPublishing/Building-Neo4j-Powered-Applications-with-LLMs/blob/main/ch2/augmented_generation.py`.

6. **Integration and fine-tuning**: Now let us look at a code snippet that combines the retriever and the LLM invocation as the full RAG flow. The following code demonstrates this:

```
def rag_pipeline(query):
    retrieved_docs = retrieve_documents(query)
    response = generate_response(query, retrieved_docs)
    return response

query = "How does climate change affect biodiversity?"
generated_text = rag_pipeline(query)
print("Final Generated Text:", generated_text)
```

From the code, we can see that the flow is simple. We retrieve the documents needed to leverage the RAG flow using the retriever and pass the input query and the retrieved documents to the LLM API invocation.

In this deep dive into the RAG architecture, we focused on its mechanics and demonstrated the functioning of its core components. By combining efficient information retrieval with advanced language generation models, RAG produces contextually appropriate and knowledge-enriched responses. As we transition to the next section, we will discuss the **retrieval process**.

Retrieving external information for your RAG

Understanding how RAG leverages external knowledge is crucial for appreciating its ability to generate factually accurate and informative responses. This section discusses various **retrieval techniques**, strategies for integrating retrieved information, and practical examples to illustrate these concepts.

Understanding retrieval techniques and strategies

The success of a RAG model hinges on its ability to retrieve relevant information from a vast external knowledge base using one of the commonly used retrieval techniques. These retrieval methods are essential for sourcing relevant information from large datasets. Common techniques include traditional methods such as BM25 and modern neural approaches such as DPR. Broadly speaking, these techniques can be classified into three categories: **vector similarity search**, **keyword matching**, and **passage retrieval**. We will discuss each of them in the following subsections.

Vector similarity search

The text or query you pass to the LLM is converted into a vector representation called an **embedding**. The vector similarity search compares the vector embeddings to retrieve the closest match. The idea is that related and similar text will have similar embeddings. This technique works as follows:

1. Build an embedding of the input query. We tokenize the input query and generate the vector embedding representation of it:

```
query_inputs = question_tokenizer(query, return_tensors="pt")
with torch.no_grad():
  query_embeddings = question_encoder(
      **query_inputs
    ).pooler_output
```

2. Build the embeddings of the documents. We generate an embedding for each document using the tokenizer and associate each embedding with its document:

```
for doc in documents:
    doc_inputs = context_tokenizer(doc, return_tensors="pt")
    with torch.no_grad():
        doc_embeddings.append(
            context_encoder(**doc_inputs).pooler_output)
doc_embeddings = torch.cat(doc_embeddings)
```

3. Find similar documents using dot product calculation. This step uses the input query embedding and searches the document embeddings for results similar to the input query:

```
scores = torch.matmul(query_embeddings, doc_embeddings.T).squeeze()
```

4. Sort the documents by the relevancy score and return the results. The results contain the matching documents along with a score representing how similar it is to the input query. We will order the results in the order we want, most similar to least similar:

```
ranked_docs = sorted(
    zip(documents, scores), key=lambda x: x[1], reverse=True)
```

Let us run this example to see what the results would look like.

The following is a sample input query:

```
What are the benefits of solar energy?
```

The following is the sample output (ranked documents):

```
Document: Solar energy is a renewable source of power., Score: 80.8264
....
Document: Graph databases like Neo4j are used to model complex
relationships., Score: 52.8945
```

The preceding code demonstrates how to use DPR to encode a query and a set of documents into high-dimensional vector representations. By computing similarity scores, such as the dot product between the query vector and document vectors, the model evaluates the relevance of each document to the query. The documents are then ranked based on their similarity scores, with the most relevant ones appearing at the top. This process highlights the power of vector-based retrieval in effectively identifying contextually relevant information from a diverse set of documents, even when they include a mix of related and unrelated content.

The full version of this example is available in the GitHub repository: `https://github.com/PacktPublishing/Building-Neo4j-Powered-Applications-with-LLMs/blob/main/ch2/vector_similarity_search.py`.

Keyword matching

Keyword matching is a simpler approach that identifies documents containing keywords present in the user prompt. While efficient, it can be susceptible to noise and misses documents with relevant synonyms. BM25 is a keyword-based probabilistic retrieval function that scores documents based on the query terms appearing in each document, considering term frequency and document length. The flow of this approach looks as follows:

1. Build the BM25 corpus using the documents. We will tokenize documents and build a corpus from this. We will build the BM25 corpus:

   ```
   tokenized_corpus = [doc.split() for doc in corpus]
   # Initialize BM25 with the tokenized corpus
   bm25 = BM25Okapi(tokenized_corpus, k1=1.5, b=0.75)
   ```

2. Tokenize the query to search using it:

   ```
   tokenized_query = query.split()
   ```

3. Query the BM25 corpus using the tokenized query. This returns the scores for matching documents:

   ```
   scores = bm25.get_scores(tokenized_query)
   ```

4. We will take these scores, order the documents in the required order, and return them:

```
ranked_docs = sorted(zip(corpus, scores), key=lambda x: x[1],
    reverse=True)
```

When we run this example, the results would look like this for the given input.

The following is a sample input query:

```
quick fox
```

The following is the sample output:

```
Ranked Documents:
Document: The quick brown fox jumps over the lazy dog., Score: 0.6049
.....
Document: Artificial intelligence is transforming the world., Score:
0.0000
```

The BM25 algorithm ranks documents based on their relevance to a query. It relies on the term frequency (how often a keyword appears in a document) and document length, applying a probabilistic scoring function to evaluate relevance. Unlike vector similarity search, which represents both queries and documents as dense numerical vectors in high-dimensional space and measures similarity using mathematical functions such as the dot product, BM25 operates directly on discrete word matches. This means BM25 is efficient and interpretable but can struggle with semantic relationships, as it cannot recognize synonyms or contextual meanings. In contrast, vector similarity search, such as DPR, excels in identifying conceptual similarities even when exact keywords differ, making it more suitable for tasks requiring deep semantic understanding. This snippet illustrates BM25's utility for straightforward keyword-matching tasks where efficiency and explainability are critical.

The complete example is available in the GitHub repository: https://github.com/ PacktPublishing/Building-Neo4j-Powered-Applications-with-LLMs/blob/main/ch2/ keyword_matching.py.

Passage retrieval

Instead of retrieving entire documents, RAG can focus on specific passages within documents that directly address the user's query. This allows for more precise information extraction. The initial flow of this approach is very similar to the vector search approach. We get the ranked documents using the approach shown in vector search and then extract relevant passages as shown in the following code snippet:

```python
# Extract passages for the reader
passages = [doc for doc, score in ranked_docs]

# Prepare inputs for the reader
inputs = reader_tokenizer(
    questions=query,
    titles=["Passage"] * len(passages),
    texts=passages,
    return_tensors="pt",
    padding=True,
    truncation=True
)
# Use the reader to extract the most relevant passage
with torch.no_grad():
    outputs = reader(**inputs)

# Extract the passage with the highest score
max_score_index = torch.argmax(outputs.relevance_logits)
most_relevant_passage = passages[max_score_index]
```

When we run this example for the given input query, the results look as follows.

The following is a sample input query:

```
What are the benefits of solar energy?
```

The following is the sample output:

```
Ranked Documents:
Document: Solar energy is a renewable source of power., Score: 80.8264
.....
```

```
Document: It has low maintenance costs., Score: 57.9905

Most Relevant Passage: Solar panels help combat climate change and reduce
carbon footprint.
```

The preceding example illustrates the **passage-retrieval approach**, which is more granular than document-level retrieval, focusing on extracting specific passages that directly address the user's query. By leveraging a *reader model* in combination with a *retriever*, this approach enhances relevance and specificity, as it identifies not only the most relevant document but also the exact passage within it that best answers the query.

Even if a passage has a slightly lower retriever score, the reader may prioritize it because it evaluates relevance more precisely at the word and span levels, considering contextual nuances. The retriever typically calculates a similarity score using the dot product of the query and passage embeddings:

$$Score\ (q, p_i) = q.p_i = \sum_{j=1}^{d} q_j p_{ij}$$

Here, q is the query embedding, p_i is the passage embedding for the ith passage, and d is the dimensionality of the embeddings.

The reader, however, refines this further by analyzing the text content of each passage. It assigns a **relevance score** or **logit** (also known as **confidence score**) based on the likelihood that a given passage contains the answer. This relevance score is computed from the raw outputs (logits) of the reader model, which considers word-level and span-level interactions between the query and the passage. The formula for the relevance score can be expressed as follows:

$$Relevance\ Score(\ p_i) = softmax(logits(\ p_i))$$

Here, we have the following:

- logits(p_i) refers to the raw scores assigned to the passage, p_i, by the reader
- softmax converts these raw scores into probabilities, emphasizing the passage most likely to be relevant (https://pytorch.org/docs/stable/generated/torch.nn.Softmax.html)

By combining both stages, the system can identify passages that are not only semantically similar (*retriever stage*) but also contextually aligned with the query's intent (*reader stage*).

This dual-stage process highlights the strength of passage retrieval in generating highly targeted responses in information retrieval pipelines.

The complete example is available in the GitHub repository: `https://github.com/PacktPublishing/Building-Neo4j-Powered-Applications-with-LLMs/blob/main/ch2/passage_retrieval.py`.

Integrating the retrieved information

For the last step in the RAG flow, let us look at how we can combine the retriever information with the generation model in a way that synthesizes contextually relevant and coherent responses. Unlike earlier examples, this approach explicitly integrates multiple retrieved passages with the query. By doing so, it creates a single input for the generation model. This allows the model to synthesize a unified and enriched response that goes beyond merely selecting or ranking passages:

```python
def integrate_and_generate(query, retrieved_docs):
    # Combine query and retrieved documents into a single input
    input_text = f"Answer this question based on the following context:
{query} Context: {' '.join(retrieved_docs)}"

    # Tokenize input for T5
    inputs = t5_tokenizer(input_text, return_tensors="pt",
        padding=True, truncation=True, max_length=512)

    # Generate a response
    with torch.no_grad():
        outputs = t5_model.generate(**inputs, max_length=100)

    # Decode and return the generated response
    return t5_tokenizer.decode(outputs[0], skip_special_tokens=True)
```

The following is a sample input query:

```
What are the benefits of solar energy?
```

The following is the sample output:

```
Ranked Documents:
Document: Solar energy is a renewable source of power., Score: 80.8264
....
Document: It has low maintenance costs., Score: 57.9905
```

```
Most Relevant Passage: Solar panels help combat climate change and reduce
carbon footprint.
```

The preceding code snippet demonstrates how to integrate retrieved documents with a T5 model to generate a synthesized response. The generate() function processes the combined input (query and passages) through the encoder to produce contextual embeddings, h. These embeddings are then used by the decoder, which generates each token sequentially based on probabilities:

$$P(w_t \mid w < t, h) = Softmax (W \cdot h_t)$$

Here, w_t is the token at position t, h_t is the hidden state, and W is the model's weight matrix. Beam search ensures the selection of the most likely sequence by maximizing the overall probability across tokens. Unlike previous examples where individual passages were selected or ranked, this code explicitly combines multiple retrieved documents into a single input alongside the query. This enables the T5 model to process the combined context holistically and produce a coherent response that incorporates information from multiple sources, making it particularly effective for queries requiring synthesis or summarization across multiple passages.

To refer to the full version of this code, please refer: https://github.com/PacktPublishing/Building-Neo4j-Powered-Applications-with-LLMs/blob/main/ch2/integrate_and_generate.py

By exploring various retrieval techniques and their integration with generation models, we have seen how RAG architectures leverage external knowledge to produce accurate and informative responses.

In the next section, let us look at the holistic flow from reading input documents from a source and leveraging those documents for a retriever flow, instead of the simple hardcoded sentences we looked at in the examples in this section.

Building an end-to-end RAG flow

In the previous sections, we delved into the various steps in the RAG flow individually with simple data to demonstrate the usage. It would be a good idea to take a step back and use a real-world dataset, albeit a simple one, to complete the whole flow. For this, we will use the GitHub issues dataset (https://huggingface.co/datasets/lewtun/github-issues). We will look at how we can read this data and use it in the RAG flow. This would lay the foundation for the full end-to-end RAG flow implementation in later chapters.

In this example, we will load GitHub comments to be able to answer questions, such as how we can load data offline. We need to follow these steps to load the data and set up the retriever:

1. **Preparing the data**: First, we need to prepare our dataset. We will use the Hugging Face datasets library:

    ```
    # Load the GitHub issues dataset
    issues_dataset = load_dataset("lewtun/github-issues", split="train")


    # Filter out pull requests and keep only issues with comments
    issues_dataset = issues_dataset.filter(
        lambda x: not x["is_pull_request"] and len(x["comments"]) > 0)
    ```

2. **Select the relevant columns**: Keep only the columns required for analysis:

    ```
    # Define columns to keep
    columns_to_keep = ["title", "body", "html_url", "comments"]
    columns_to_remove = set(issues_dataset.column_names) - \
                            set(columns_to_keep)
    # Remove unnecessary columns
    issues_dataset = issues_dataset.remove_columns(columns_to_remove)
    ```

3. **Convert the dataset into a pandas DataFrame**: Convert the dataset into a pandas DataFrame for easier manipulation:

    ```
    # Set format to pandas and convert the dataset
    issues_dataset.set_format("pandas")
    df = issues_dataset[:]
    ```

4. **Explode comments, convert them back into a dataset, and process**: Flatten the comments into individual rows, convert the DataFrame back into a dataset, and compute the length of each comment. This step makes this data amenable to use with the retriever flow:

    ```
    # Explode comments into separate rows
    comments_df = df.explode("comments", ignore_index=True)


    # Convert the DataFrame back to a Dataset
    comments_dataset = Dataset.from_pandas(comments_df)


    # Compute the length of each comment
    comments_dataset = comments_dataset.map(
    ```

```
        lambda x: {"comment_length": len(x["comments"].split())},
        num_proc=1)


    # Filter out short comments
    comments_dataset = comments_dataset.filter(
        lambda x: x["comment_length"] > 15)
```

5. **Concatenate text for embeddings**: Let us prepare the document text by concatenating the relevant text fields. We will take individual fields from each row and prepare the text that represents the document text for that row. These documents are stored in an embedding store for retriever usage purposes:

```
    # Function to concatenate text fields
    def concatenate_text(examples):
        return {
            "text": examples["title"] + " \n " +
                    examples["body"] + " \n " +
                    examples["comments"]
        }


    # Apply the function to create a text field
    comments_dataset = comments_dataset.map(concatenate_text,
        num_proc=1)
```

6. **Load model and tokenizer**: Let us load the LLM that we will use to convert the documents into the embeddings and store them in an embedding store for the retriever flow:

```
    # Load pre-trained model and tokenizer
    model_ckpt = "sentence-transformers/all-MiniLM-L6-v2"
    tokenizer = AutoTokenizer.from_pretrained(model_ckpt)
    model = AutoModel.from_pretrained(model_ckpt).to("cpu")
```

7. **Define the embedding function**: Define the embedding function that leverages the model we defined previously to generate the embedding. We can invoke this method iteratively to generate the embeddings for all the documents we have, one document at a time:

```
    # Function to get embeddings for a list of texts
    def get_embeddings(text_list):
        encoded_input = tokenizer(text_list, padding=True,
            truncation=True, return_tensors="pt").to("cpu")
```

```
    with torch.no_grad():
        model_output = model(**encoded_input)
    return cls_pooling(model_output).numpy()
```

8. **Compute embeddings**: Compute embeddings for the dataset. Now that we have the embedding function defined, let us call it for all the documents we have in our comments dataset. Note that we are storing the embedding in a new column named embedding in the same dataset:

```
# Compute embeddings for the dataset
comments_dataset = comments_dataset.map(
    lambda batch: {"embeddings": [get_embeddings([text])[0]
        for text in batch["text"]]},
    batched=True,
    batch_size=100,
    num_proc=1
)
```

9. **Perform semantic search**: Let us perform the retriever flow for the question. This will retrieve all the questions related to the question we have asked. We can use these documents to refine the response as needed:

```
# Define a query
question = "How can I load a dataset offline?"

# Compute the embedding for the query
query_embedding = get_embeddings([question]).reshape(1, -1)
# Find the nearest examples
embeddings = np.vstack(comments_dataset["embeddings"])
similarities = cosine_similarity(
    query_embedding, embeddings
).flatten()

# Display the results
top_indices = np.argsort(similarities)[::-1][:5]
for idx in top_indices:
    result = comments_dataset[int(idx)]  # Convert NumPy integer to
native Python integer
    print(f"COMMENT: {result['comments']}")
```

```
    print(f"SCORE: {similarities[idx]}")
    print(f"TITLE: {result['title']}")
    print(f"URL: {result['html_url']}")
    print("=" * 50)
```

The preceding code showcases the complete flow, from how we load the data into a data store, which can form the basis for the retriever, to retrieving documents, which can be used to provide more context for the LLM when it is generating the answer.

Now let us see how the output looks when we run this application. We have the question hard-coded in the example code, and it is:

```
How can I load a dataset offline?.
```

The following is the sample output:

```
COMMENT: Yes currently you need an internet connection because the lib
tries to check for the etag of the dataset script ...
SCORE: 0.9054292969045314
TITLE: Downloaded datasets are not usable offline
URL: https://github.com/huggingface/datasets/issues/761
==================================================
COMMENT: Requiring online connection is a deal breaker in some cases ...
SCORE: 0.9052456782359709
TITLE: Discussion using datasets in offline mode
URL: https://github.com/huggingface/datasets/issues/824
==================================================
```

This hands-on example demonstrated the practical application of an end-to-end RAG architecture, leveraging powerful retrieval techniques to enhance language generation. The preceding code is adapted from the Hugging Face NLP course, available at https://huggingface.co/learn/nlp-course/chapter5/6?fw=tf.

The complete Python file, along with a detailed explanation of how to run it, is available at https://github.com/PacktPublishing/Building-Neo4j-Powered-Applications-with-LLMs/blob/main/ch2/full_rag_pipeline.py.

Summary

In this chapter, we deep-dived into the world of RAG models. We started by understanding the core principles of RAG and how they differ from traditional generative AI models. This foundational knowledge is crucial as it sets the stage for appreciating the enhanced capabilities that RAG brings to the table.

Next, we took a closer look at the architecture of RAG models, deconstructing their components through detailed code examples. By examining the encoder, retriever, and decoder, you gained insights into the inner workings of these models and how they integrate retrieved information to produce more contextually relevant and coherent outputs.

We then explored how RAG harnesses the power of information retrieval. These techniques help RAG effectively leverage external knowledge sources to improve the quality of a generated text. This is particularly useful for applications requiring high accuracy and context awareness. You also learned how to a simple RAG model using popular libraries such as Transformers and Hugging Face.

As we move forward to the next chapter, *Chapter 3*, we will build on this foundation. You will learn about graph data modeling and how to create knowledge graphs with Neo4j.

3

Building a Foundational Understanding of Knowledge Graph for Intelligent Applications

In the previous chapter, we looked at what RAG is and at a few simple examples of how we can implement RAG flow, along with LLMs. In this chapter, we will take a look at what knowledge graphs are and how graphs can make **Retrieval-Augmented Generation (RAG)** more effective. We will explore how to model knowledge graphs and how Neo4j can be used for this purpose. We will look at how data modeling with the Neo4j data persistence approach can help build more powerful knowledge graphs. We will also look at data store persistence approaches, from **Relational Database Management Systems (RDBMSs)** to Neo4j knowledge graphs, to get a better understanding of data using various data models.

We will embark on an exciting journey to understand how the fusion of RAG models and Neo4j's robust graph database capabilities enables the creation of intelligent applications that leverage structured knowledge bases for enhanced performance and results.

In this chapter, we are going to cover the following main topics:

- Understanding the importance of graph data modeling
- Combining the power of RAG and Neo4j knowledge graphs with GraphRAG
- Enhancing knowledge graph

Technical requirements

Before we dive into the practical aspects of building a knowledge graph for RAG integration with Neo4j, it is essential to set up the necessary tools and environments. Here are the technical requirements for this chapter:

- **Neo4j database**: You can use Neo4j Desktop for a local setup or Neo4j Aura for a cloud-based solution. Download Neo4j Desktop from the Neo4j download center: `https://neo4j.com/download/`. For Neo4j Aura, visit Neo4j Aura: `https://neo4j.com/product/neo4j-graph-database/`. Neo4j offers two primary cloud-based services – AuraDB and AuraDS:

  - **AuraDB** is a fully managed graph database service tailored for developers building intelligent applications. It supports flexible schemas, native storage of relationships, and efficient querying with the Cypher language. AuraDB offers a free tier, enabling users to explore graph data without incurring costs. Learn more about AuraDB at `https://neo4j.com/product/auradb/`.

  - **AuraDS** is a fully managed Neo4j Graph Data Science instance that can be used to build data science applications. You can learn more about it at `https://neo4j.com/docs/aura/graph-analytics/`.

- **DB Browser for SQLite**: This tool is used to query SQLite databases easily `https://sqlitebrowser.org/`.

- **Cypher query language**: Before starting with this chapter, you will need to familiarize yourself with Cypher, Neo4j's query language. Neo4j provides excellent Cypher tutorials. If you are unfamiliar with Cypher, Neo4j provides excellent tutorials and fundamental courses on GraphAcademy (`https://graphacademy.neo4j.com/`) to help you get started. You can also read this book to learn about Cypher in detail: Graph Data Processing with Cypher (`https://www.packtpub.com/en-us/product/graph-data-processing-with-cypher-9781804611074`).

- **Python environment**: Python 3.8 or higher is recommended. Ensure you have it installed. You can download it from the official Python website `https://www.python.org/downloads/`.

- **Neo4j Python Driver**: This allows you to interact with your Neo4j database from Python. Install it using `pip`:

  ```
  pip install neo4j-driver
  ```

- **GitHub repository**: All the code and resources for this chapter are available in the following GitHub repository: `https://github.com/PacktPublishing/Building-Neo4j-Powered-Applications-with-LLMs`. Navigate to the `ch3` folder for the specific content related to this chapter.

Ensure you have all these tools and libraries installed and configured before proceeding. This setup will enable you to follow along with the examples and exercises seamlessly.

Understanding the importance of graph data modeling

Before we go ahead with looking at how **GraphRAG flow** works with Neo4j, let us take a step back and understand how we can model knowledge graphs. We will take some simple data and try to look at how we model that data in RDBMSs and graphs. We will also see how this modeling differs depending on how we see that data.

Graphs force us to think in different ways and see the data from different perspectives depending on what we are trying to solve. While this might seem like a problem, it is actually opens a lot of doors. For a long time, we have been taught to think of the RDBMS storage approach in terms of **Entity-Relationship (ER)** diagrams. This approach was good for representing/persisting data when there were limitations in the technology, and storage costs were very high. With technologies evolving and hardware becoming cheaper, new avenues have opened and new approaches to model data are possible. Graphs are well suited to take advantage of this.

To think about new ways of modeling data, we might have to unlearn some of the ways we are used to representing data using ER diagrams. While this seems simple, in reality, it might be a bit difficult. The learning and unlearning process is similar to in the neural plasticity prism goggles experiment, depicted in the following figure.

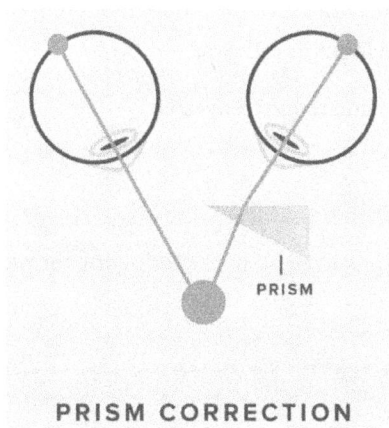

PRISM CORRECTION

Figure 3.1 — Neural plasticity prism goggles experiment

The experiment involves wearing prism goggles to perform a simple task. It takes some time for the mind to adjust to the shift in vision to perform the task correctly. When the participant takes off the goggles, it takes some time to be able to perform the same task again. It is the same with data modeling. We might have to unlearn a few of the approaches we used to rely on before we can build a better graph data model. You can read more about this experiment at `https://sfa.cems.umn.edu/neural-plasticity-prism-goggle-experiment`.

We will take a look at how we consume data in real life to understand whether there are any other approaches that can help us in building a good graph data model.

For example, let us consider a library or a bookstore to understand how our data or information consumption drives how the books are laid out. In a library, the books are laid out by category and last name of the author. This is similar to how we leverage indexes to find data. But there may be other sections at the entrance of the library that highlight new releases and popular books. This is done to make sure people can find these quickly. Trying to model these aspects in an RDBMS is difficult. But the graph database approach in Neo4j makes it quite easy to do this by leveraging multiple labels. This enables graph databases to help us build a data model that helps with the easy and efficient consumption of data. With graphs, we might have to try and change our thought process and try a few different data modeling approaches. Our initial approaches may not be completely correct, but we need to keep adjusting the data models to get to an acceptable data model that works for us. With RDBMSs and other technologies, the data model is rigid, and not getting it right can have a huge impact. This is where Neo4j stands out. Its optional flexible schema approach helps us get started with a data model that might not be optimal in the beginning, but we can tune it incrementally without needing to start from scratch.

We will take some small, simple data and look at data modeling with an RDBMS and graph. The data we will be trying to model looks as follows:

- A person with the following required details:

  ```
  firstName
  lastName
  ```

- Five rentals the person has lived at, in the following format:

  ```
  Address line 1
  City
  State
  zipCode
  ```

```
    fromTime
    tillTime
```

While this seems simple, it is enough for us to understand the nuances of how this data can be represented in an RDBMS and graph.

These are the questions we would like to answer using this data:

- What is the latest address the person named *John Doe* is living at?
- What is the first address the person named *John Doe* lived at?
- What is the third address the person named *John Doe* lived at?

Let's take a look at how this data can be modeled in an RDBMS.

RDBMS data modeling

In this section, we will take a look at the RDBMS data modeling aspects of the sample data we defined previously. The following figure represents the data model as an ER diagram:

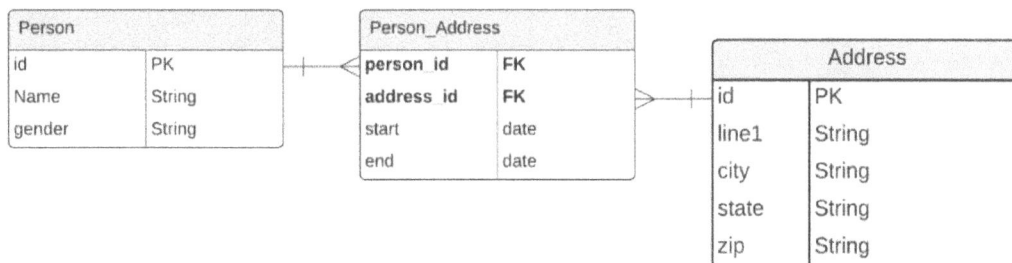

Figure 3.2 — ER diagram

There are three tables in this data model. The Person table contains the person details. The Address table contains the address details. The Person_Address table contains the rental details along with references to the Person and Address tables. We use this join table to represent the rental details, to avoid duplicating the data of Person or Address entities. We need to be extra sure of the details when we are building these data models, as changing them can be quite time-consuming, depending on how much we are changing. If we are splitting a table into multiple tables, then the data migration can be quite a task.

You can use this tutorial to create the SQLite database: https://datacarpentry.org/sql-socialsci/02-db-browser.html. We will use that SQLite database to load the data and validate queries to answer the questions we defined before.

The following SQL script creates the tables:

```sql
-- Person Table definition
CREATE TABLE IF NOT EXISTS person (
    id INTEGER PRIMARY KEY,
    name varchar(100) NOT NULL,
    gender varchar(20) ,
    UNIQUE(id)
) ;
-- Address table definition
CREATE TABLE IF NOT EXISTS address (
    id INTEGER PRIMARY KEY,
  line1 varchar(100) NOT NULL,
    city varchar(20) NOT NULL,
    state varchar(20) NOT NULL,
    zip varchar(20) NOT NULL,
    UNIQUE(id)
) ;

-- Person Address table definition
CREATE TABLE IF NOT EXISTS person_address (
    person_id INTEGER NOT NULL,
    address_id INTEGER NOT NULL,
    start varchar(20) NOT NULL,
    end varchar(20) ,
    FOREIGN KEY (person_id) REFERENCES person (id)
        ON DELETE CASCADE ON UPDATE NO ACTION,
    FOREIGN KEY (address_id) REFERENCES address (id)
        ON DELETE CASCADE ON UPDATE NO ACTION
) ;
```

The next SQL script inserts the data into the tables:

```
-- Insert Person Record
INSERT INTO person (id, name, gender) values (1, 'John Doe', 'Male') ;


-- Insert Address Records
INSERT INTO address (id, line1, city, state, zip) values (1, '1 first ln',
'Edison', 'NJ', '11111') ;

INSERT INTO address (id, line1, city, state, zip) values (2, '13 second
ln', 'Edison', 'NJ', '11111') ;

INSERT INTO address (id, line1, city, state, zip) values (3, '13 third
ln', 'Edison', 'NJ', '11111') ;

INSERT INTO address (id, line1, city, state, zip) values (4, '1 fourth
ln', 'Edison', 'NJ', '11111') ;

INSERT INTO address (id, line1, city, state, zip) values (5, '5 other ln',
'Edison', 'NJ', '11111') ;


-- Insert Person Address (Rental) Records
INSERT INTO person_address (person_id, address_id, start, end) values
(1,1,'2001-01-01', '2003-12-31') ;
INSERT INTO person_address (person_id, address_id, start, end) values
(1,2,'2004-01-01', '2008-12-31') ;
INSERT INTO person_address (person_id, address_id, start, end) values
(1,3,'2009-01-01', '2015-12-31') ;
INSERT INTO person_address (person_id, address_id, start, end) values
(1,4,'2016-01-01', '2020-12-31') ;
INSERT INTO person_address (person_id, address_id, start, end) values
(1,5,'2021-01-01', null) ;
```

Once we load the data, it will look like this.

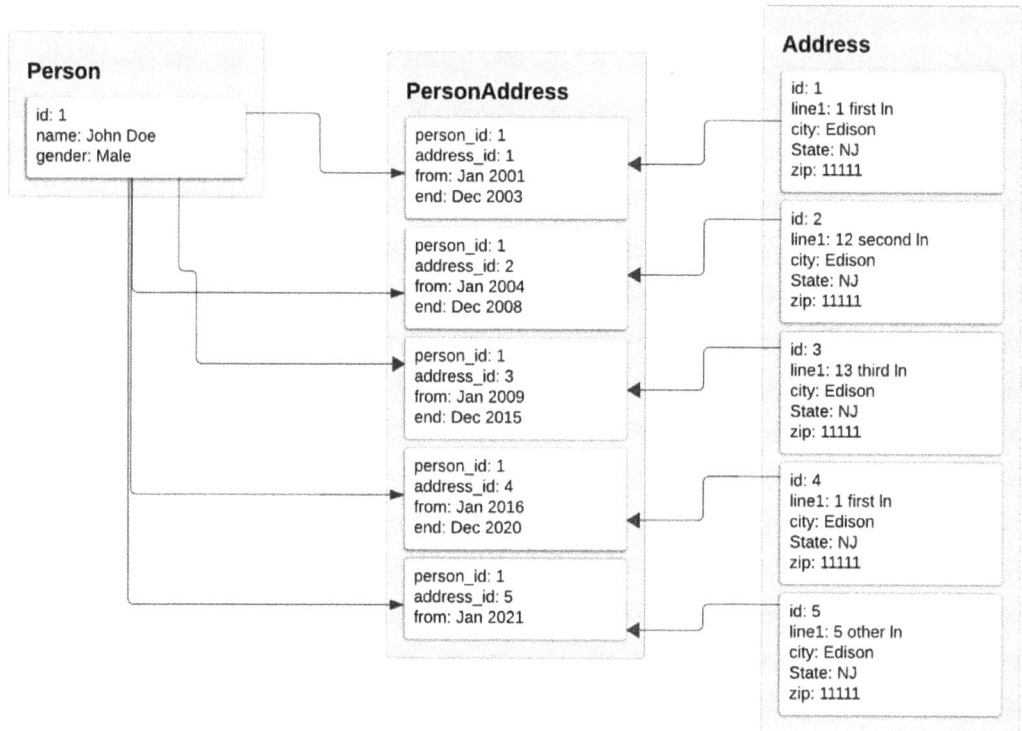

Figure 3.3 — Data stored in an RDBMS

We will now see how we can query data from the RDBMS:

- **Query 1 – Get the latest address**

    Let's take a look at the following SQL query to answer the first question:

    ```
    SELECT line1, city, state, zip from
    person p, person_address pa, address a
    WHERE p.name = 'John Doe'
        and pa.person_id = p.id
        and pa.address_id = a.id
        and pa.end is null
    ```

    From the query, we can see that we are relying on the end column value to be null to de-termine which is the latest address. This is the logic to determine what the last address is in the SQL query.

- **Query 2 – Get the first address**

We will take a look at the SQL query to answer the second question:

```
SELECT line1, city, state, zip from
person p, person_address pa, address a
WHERE p.name = 'John Doe'
    and pa.person_id = p.id
    and pa.address_id = a.id
ORDER BY pa.start ASC
LIMIT 1
```

From the query, we can see that we are relying on the search-sort-filter pattern to get to the data we want, with the logic in the SQL query.

- **Query 3 – Get the third address**

We will take a look at SQL query to answer the third question:

```
SELECT line1, city, state, zip from
person p, person_address pa, address a
WHERE p.name = 'John Doe'
    and pa.person_id = p.id
    and pa.address_id = a.id
ORDER BY pa.start ASC
LIMIT 2, 1
```

Again, in this query also we can see that we are relying on the pattern *Search-Sort-Filter* to get to the data we wanted.

We will now look at how this data can be modeled with graphs.

Graph data modeling: basic approach

For illustration purposes, we will use the most common and simplest way to model this data in a graph.

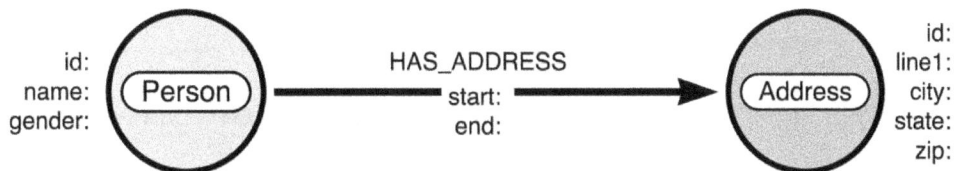

Figure 3.4 — Basic graph data model

This aligns with how we normally express the information in English:

Person *lives at* **Address**

In this sentence, the **nouns** are represented as **nodes**, and the **verb** is represented as a **relationship**. This data model approach is pretty simple and almost resembles the ER diagram of the RDBMS data model. The only difference here is that the join table that represents the rental is modeled as a relationship. The advantage of this type of data persistence is that it reduces the index lookup cost. In RDBMSs, the biggest cost in terms of data retrieval is the join table's index lookup cost. As the data size increases, that lookup cost keeps on increasing. We can reduce that cost with this approach.

> **Note**
>
> You can use this tutorial to create the Neo4j database if you are using Neo4j Desktop: https://neo4j.com/docs/desktop-manual/current/operations/create-dbms/.
>
> Alternatively, you can use this tutorial to create a database in the cloud: https://neo4j.com/docs/aura/auradb/getting-started/create-database/. There is a free option available. This would be optimal for those who may not or do not want to install Neo4j Desktop locally. Neo4j Aura is a fully managed graph-database-as-a-service solution.

Let's look at the following graph queries to understand this.

The following Cypher script sets up the indexes for faster data load and retrieval. This can be thought of as a schema:

```
CREATE CONSTRAINT person_id_idx FOR (n:Person) REQUIRE n.id IS UNIQUE ;
CREATE CONSTRAINT address_id_idx FOR (n:Address) REQUIRE n.id IS UNIQUE ;
CREATE INDEX person_name_idx FOR (n:Person) ON n.name ;
```

This Cypher script creates two unique constraints to make sure we don't have duplicate **Person** and **Address** nodes. We also added an index to speed up the person lookup using the name.

Once the schema is set up, we can use this Cypher script to load the data into Neo4j:

```
CREATE (p:Person {id:1, name:'John Doe', gender:'Male'})


CREATE (a1:Address {id:1, line1:'1 first ln', city:'Edison', state:'NJ',
zip:'11111'})
CREATE (a2:Address {id:2, line1:'13 second ln', city:'Edison', state:'NJ',
```

```
zip:'11111'})
CREATE (a3:Address {id:3, line1:'13 third ln', city:'Edison', state:'NJ',
zip:'11111'})
CREATE (a4:Address {id:4, line1:'1 fourth ln', city:'Edison', state:'NJ',
zip:'11111'})
CREATE (a5:Address {id:5, line1:'5 other ln', city:'Edison', state:'NJ',
zip:'11111'})


CREATE (p)-[:HAS_ADDRESS {start:'2001-01-01', end:'2003-12-31'}]->(a1)
CREATE (p)-[:HAS_ADDRESS {start:'2004-01-01', end:'2008-12-31'}]->(a2)
CREATE (p)-[:HAS_ADDRESS {start:'2009-01-01', end:'2015-12-31'}]->(a3)
CREATE (p)-[:HAS_ADDRESS {start:'2016-01-01', end:'2020-12-31'}]->(a4)
CREATE (p)-[:HAS_ADDRESS {start:'2021-01-01'}]->(a5)
```

Once we load the data, it looks like this in the graph.

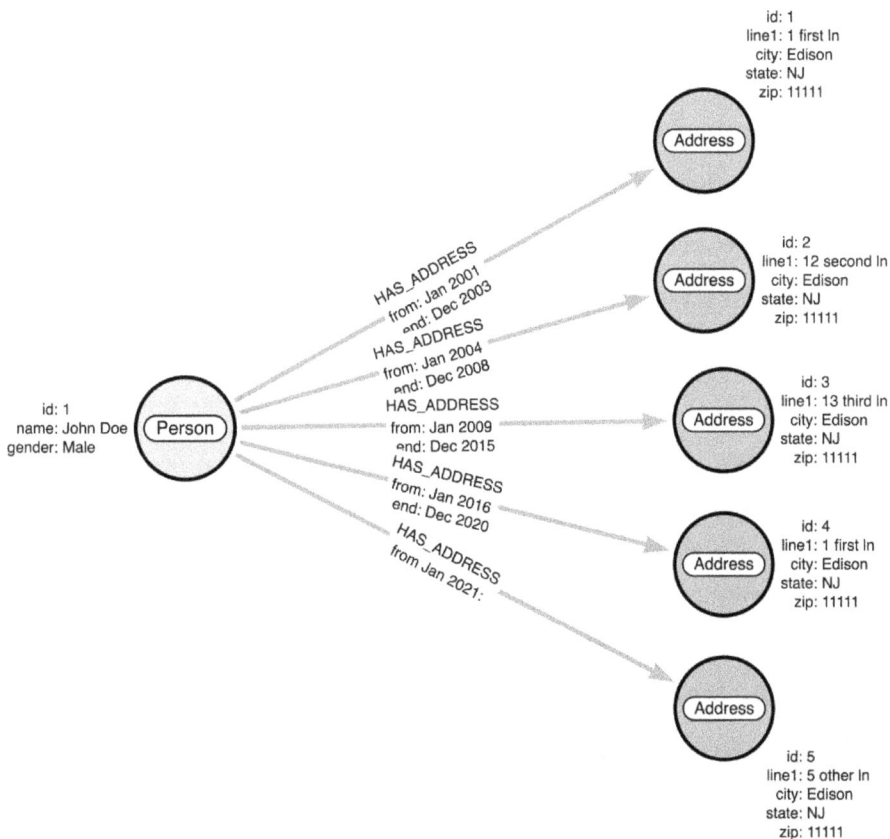

Figure 3.5 — Representation of Person Rentals using graph data modeling, basic approach

Now, we will create the Cypher queries analogous to the retrievals we performed with the RDBMS queries in the previous section:

- **Query 1 – Get the latest address**

   The following Cypher query gets us the latest address:

   ```
   MATCH (p:Person {name:'John Doe'})-[r:HAS_ADDRESS]->(a)
   WHERE r.end is null
   RETURN a
   ```

   If we look at this query, it is much simpler than the SQL query we saw earlier. Still, the result depends on how we mark the last address, by not having the end property set on the relationship. So, the logic to know what the last address is still part of the query, like in the SQL query. We can see that we are checking the values in the relationship and trying to use indexes, as shown in the following code, on the join table:

   ```
   and pa.person_id = p.id
   and pa.address_id = a.id
   ```

   Just avoiding these indexes itself can get us better performance.

- **Query 2 – Get the first address**

   This Cypher fetches us the first address:

   ```
   MATCH (p:Person {name:'John Doe'})-[r:HAS_ADDRESS]->(a)
   WITH r, a
   ORDER BY r.start ASC
   WITH r,a
   RETURN a
   LIMIT 1
   ```

   From the query, we can see that we are relying on the search-sort-filter pattern to get to the data we want, similar to the SQL query. The logic to determine what the first address is part of the Cypher query.

- **Query 3 – Get the third address**

   This Cypher gets us the third address:

   ```
   MATCH (p:Person {name:'John Doe'})-[r:HAS_ADDRESS]->(a)
   WITH r, a
   ORDER BY r.start ASC
   ```

```
WITH r,a
RETURN a
SKIP 2
LIMIT 1
```

Similar to the previous query, we had to rely on search-sort-filter to get to the data we wanted. The logic to determine what the third address is part of the Cypher query.

Next, we will dive into a more nuanced approach to graph data modeling.

Graph data modeling: advanced approach

We will look at this data differently and build a data model. This model is influenced by how we consume the data.

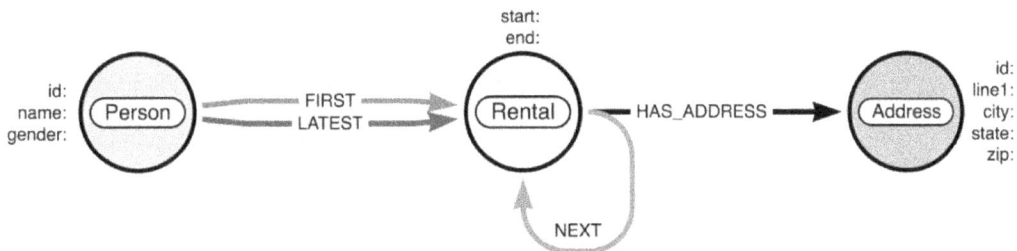

Figure 3.6 — Representation of Person Rentals using graph data modeling, consumption approach

At first look, this looks closer to the RDBMS ER diagram. We have **Person**, **Address**, and **Rental** nodes. That's where the similarity ends. We can see that **Person** is connected to the **Rental** node via a **FIRST** or **LATEST** relationship. **Rental** may have a **NEXT** relationship to another **Rental** node. The **Rental** node is connected to an **Address**, too. The model might look a bit complex. Once we load the data and see how it is connected, it makes more sense.

This Cypher script sets up the indexes for faster data load and retrieval:

```
CREATE CONSTRAINT person_id_idx FOR (n:Person) REQUIRE n.id IS UNIQUE ;
CREATE CONSTRAINT address_id_idx FOR (n:Address) REQUIRE n.id IS UNIQUE ;

CREATE INDEX person_name_idx FOR (n:Person) ON n.name ;
```

We can see the indexes are the same as in the previous model. We have not added any indexes or constraints to the **Rental** node.

This Cypher script loads the data into Neo4j:

```
CREATE (p:Person {id:1, name:'John Doe', gender:'Male'})
CREATE (a1:Address {id:1, line1:'1 first ln', city:'Edison', state:'NJ',
zip:'11111'})
CREATE (a2:Address {id:2, line1:'13 second ln', city:'Edison', state:'NJ',
zip:'11111'})
CREATE (a3:Address {id:3, line1:'13 third ln', city:'Edison', state:'NJ',
zip:'11111'})
CREATE (a4:Address {id:4, line1:'1 fourth ln', city:'Edison', state:'NJ',
zip:'11111'})
CREATE (a5:Address {id:5, line1:'5 other ln', city:'Edison', state:'NJ',
zip:'11111'})


CREATE (p)-[:FIRST]->(r1:Rental {start:'2001-01-01', end:'2003-12-31'})-
[:HAS_ADDRESS]->(a1)
CREATE (r1)-[:NEXT]->(r2:Rental {start:'2004-01-01', end:'2008-12-31'})-
[:HAS_ADDRESS]->(a2)
CREATE (r2)-[:NEXT]->(r3:Rental {start:'2009-01-01', end:'2015-12-31'})-
[:HAS_ADDRESS]->(a3)
CREATE (r3)-[:NEXT]->(r4:Rental {start:'2016-01-01', end:'2020-12-31'})-
[:HAS_ADDRESS]->(a4)
CREATE (r4)-[:NEXT]->(r5:Rental {start:'2021-01-01'})-[:HAS_ADDRESS]->(a5)
CREATE (p)-[:LATEST]->(r5)
```

Once the data is loaded, it will look like this in the graph (*Figure 3.7*).

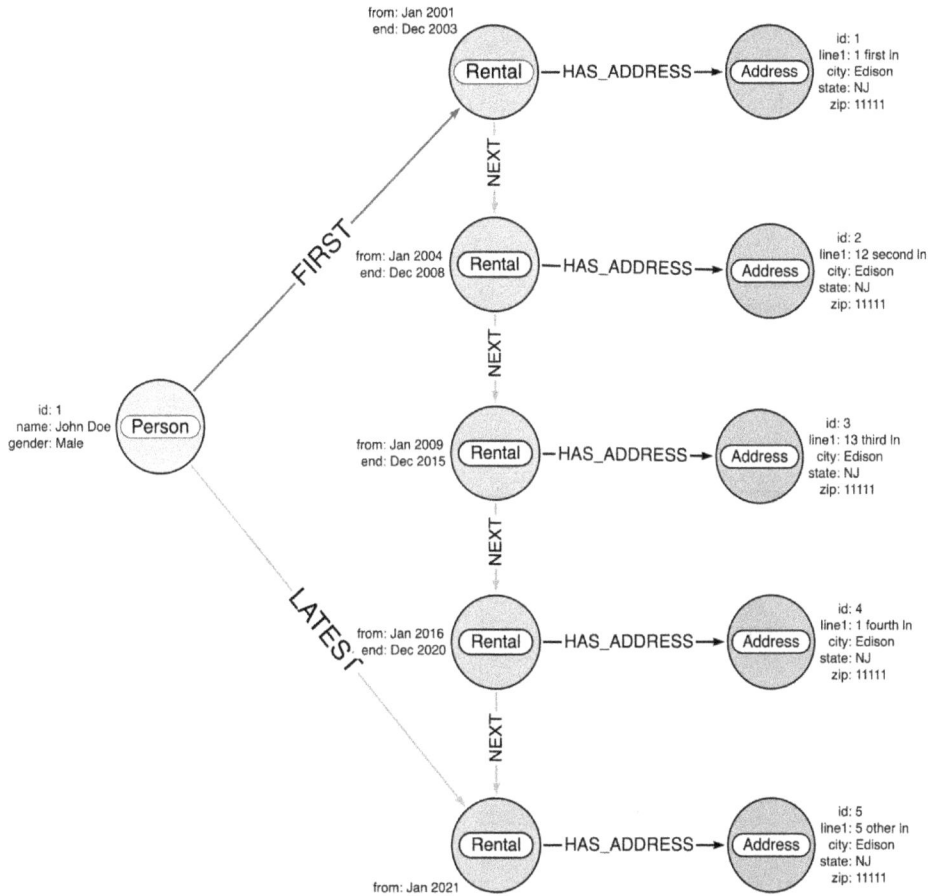

Figure 3.7 — Representation of Person Rentals with a Rental sequence graph

We can see that the data stored in the graph is way different from before. **Person** is connected to only the first and last rentals. Each of those rentals from first to last is connected via a **NEXT** relationship:

- **Query 1 – Get the latest address**

    This Cypher query gets us the latest address:

    ```
    MATCH (p:Person {name:'John Doe'})-[:LATEST]->()-[:HAS_ADDRESS]->(a)
    RETURN a
    ```

    We can see that this query is very different from the previous graph and SQL queries. In the previous graph model, the Cypher query was similar to the SQL query in determining what the last address is. Here, the query looks similar to a sentence in English (*Person's latest address*).

While the query looks simpler and easier to understand for most people, is it worth representing the data in this way? In this scenario, we will use more storage to be able to represent data in an elaborate manner. Let's profile the queries from the initial graph data model to this data model and see whether there is any advantage.

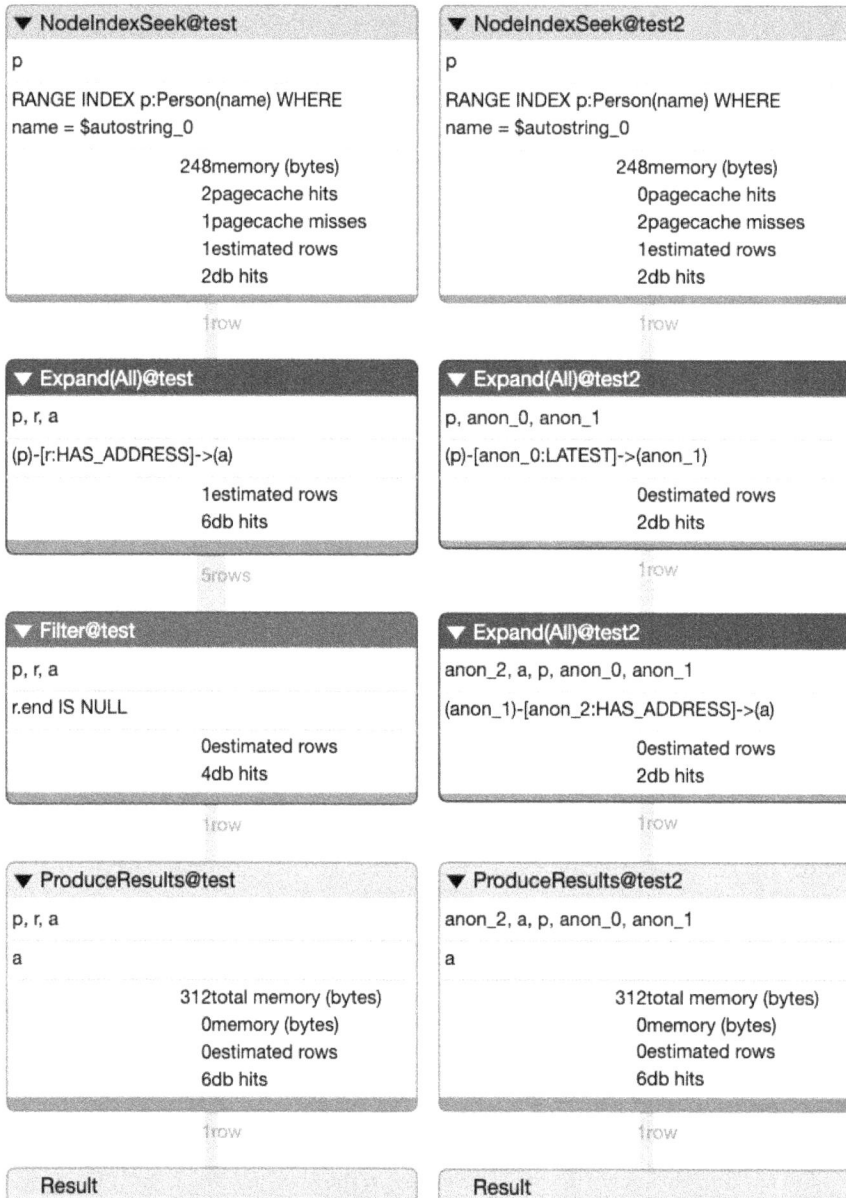

▼ NodeIndexSeek@test	▼ NodeIndexSeek@test2
p	p
RANGE INDEX p:Person(name) WHERE name = $autostring_0	RANGE INDEX p:Person(name) WHERE name = $autostring_0
248memory (bytes)	248memory (bytes)
2pagecache hits	0pagecache hits
1pagecache misses	2pagecache misses
1estimated rows	1estimated rows
2db hits	2db hits
1row	1row

▼ Expand(All)@test	▼ Expand(All)@test2
p, r, a	p, anon_0, anon_1
(p)-[r:HAS_ADDRESS]->(a)	(p)-[anon_0:LATEST]->(anon_1)
1estimated rows	0estimated rows
6db hits	2db hits
5rows	1row

▼ Filter@test	▼ Expand(All)@test2
p, r, a	anon_2, a, p, anon_0, anon_1
r.end IS NULL	(anon_1)-[anon_2:HAS_ADDRESS]->(a)
0estimated rows	0estimated rows
4db hits	2db hits
1row	1row

▼ ProduceResults@test	▼ ProduceResults@test2
p, r, a	anon_2, a, p, anon_0, anon_1
a	a
312total memory (bytes)	312total memory (bytes)
0memory (bytes)	0memory (bytes)
0estimated rows	0estimated rows
6db hits	6db hits
1row	1row

Result	Result

Figure 3.8 — Basic graph model versus advanced graph model – query 1 profiles

From the **query profiles**, we can see the initial graph data model took 18 **db hits** (accesses) and 312 bytes of memory to perform the operation. The current graph data model took 12 db hits and 312 bytes of memory to perform the operation. We can see the new data model is able to perform this query more optimally. As the data grows, the previous graph data model will take more time to perform the operation and the db hits will grow linearly with the number of relationships the person has. With the current data model, it would stay relatively constant.

Now let us look at query 2.

- **Query 2 – Get the first address**

This Cypher query gets us to the first address:

```
MATCH (p:Person {name:'John Doe'})-[:FIRST]->()-[:HAS_ADDRESS]->(a)
RETURN a
```

We can see that this query looks exactly like the previous one, except for the relationship we are traversing. We are not using the *search-sort-filter* pattern anymore here. This is the biggest advantage of this data model. This model also makes it easy for us to use a graph as a structure to retrieve the data. Also, it means the logic to determine what data we are looking at is not coded into the query in the form of some property comparisons. Let us compare the query profiles to see whether this gives us any advantage.

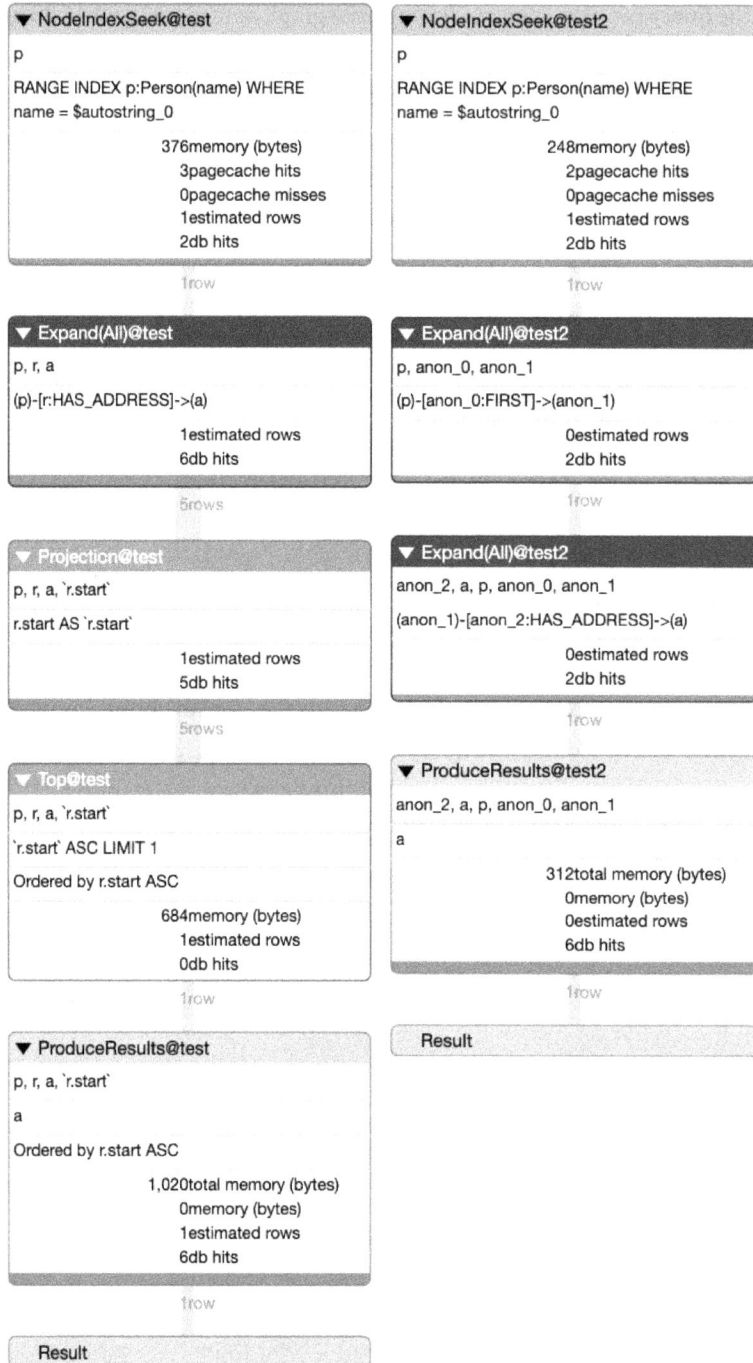

▼ NodeIndexSeek@test	▼ NodeIndexSeek@test2
p	p
RANGE INDEX p:Person(name) WHERE name = $autostring_0	RANGE INDEX p:Person(name) WHERE name = $autostring_0
376memory (bytes) 3pagecache hits 0pagecache misses 1estimated rows 2db hits	248memory (bytes) 2pagecache hits 0pagecache misses 1estimated rows 2db hits

1row   1row

▼ Expand(All)@test	▼ Expand(All)@test2
p, r, a	p, anon_0, anon_1
(p)-[r:HAS_ADDRESS]->(a)	(p)-[anon_0:FIRST]->(anon_1)
1estimated rows 6db hits	0estimated rows 2db hits

5rows   1row

▼ Projection@test	▼ Expand(All)@test2
p, r, a, `r.start`	anon_2, a, p, anon_0, anon_1
r.start AS `r.start`	(anon_1)-[anon_2:HAS_ADDRESS]->(a)
1estimated rows 5db hits	0estimated rows 2db hits

5rows   1row

▼ Top@test	▼ ProduceResults@test2
p, r, a, `r.start`	anon_2, a, p, anon_0, anon_1
`r.start` ASC LIMIT 1	a
Ordered by r.start ASC	
684memory (bytes) 1estimated rows 0db hits	312total memory (bytes) 0memory (bytes) 0estimated rows 6db hits

1row   1row

▼ ProduceResults@test		Result
p, r, a, `r.start`		
a		
Ordered by r.start ASC		
1,020total memory (bytes) 0memory (bytes) 1estimated rows 6db hits		

1row

Result

Figure 3.9 — Basic graph model versus advanced graph model – query 2 profiles

We can see the query execution plan for the initial graph data model is larger and more complex than the current data model. With the initial graph data model, it took 19 db hits and 1,020 bytes of memory to perform the operation. With the current data model, the plan is almost similar to query 1. It took 12 db hits and 312 bytes of memory. We can see that the ordering is causing us to use more memory and will consume more CPU cycles. As **Person** is connected to more addresses, the initial graph data model will take more memory and db hits as performance will slowly degrade. With the current data model, the performance will remain relatively constant.

- **Query 3 – Get the third address**

This Cypher query gets us the third address:

```
MATCH (p:Person {name:'John Doe'})-[:FIRST]->()-[:NEXT*2..2]->()-
[:HAS_ADDRESS]->(a)
RETURN a
```

We can see from the query that the way it is written is to traverse to the first rental and skip the next rental to get to the third rental. This is how we normally look at data and it feels natural to express the query this way to retrieve the data. Again, we are not relying on the *search-sort-filter* pattern. Let us compare the query profiles to see whether this gives us any advantage.

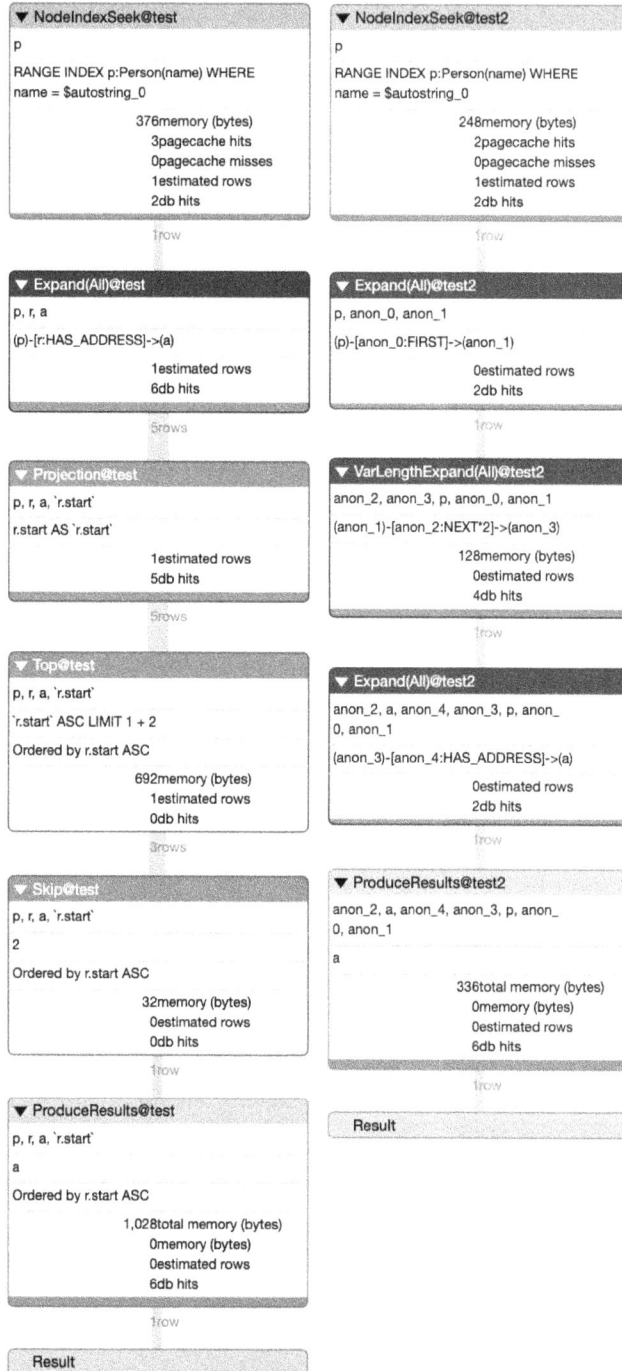

▼ NodeIndexSeek@test
p
RANGE INDEX p:Person(name) WHERE name = $autostring_0
376memory (bytes)
3pagecache hits
0pagecache misses
1estimated rows
2db hits

1row

▼ NodeIndexSeek@test2
p
RANGE INDEX p:Person(name) WHERE name = $autostring_0
248memory (bytes)
2pagecache hits
0pagecache misses
1estimated rows
2db hits

1row

▼ Expand(All)@test
p, r, a
(p)-[r:HAS_ADDRESS]->(a)
1estimated rows
6db hits

5rows

▼ Expand(All)@test2
p, anon_0, anon_1
(p)-[anon_0:FIRST]->(anon_1)
0estimated rows
2db hits

1row

▼ Projection@test
p, r, a, `r.start`
r.start AS `r.start`
1estimated rows
5db hits

5rows

▼ VarLengthExpand(All)@test2
anon_2, anon_3, p, anon_0, anon_1
(anon_1)-[anon_2:NEXT*2]->(anon_3)
128memory (bytes)
0estimated rows
4db hits

1row

▼ Top@test
p, r, a, `r.start`
`r.start` ASC LIMIT 1 + 2
Ordered by r.start ASC
692memory (bytes)
1estimated rows
0db hits

3rows

▼ Expand(All)@test2
anon_2, a, anon_4, anon_3, p, anon_0, anon_1
(anon_3)-[anon_4:HAS_ADDRESS]->(a)
0estimated rows
2db hits

1row

▼ Skip@test
p, r, a, `r.start`
2
Ordered by r.start ASC
32memory (bytes)
0estimated rows
0db hits

1row

▼ ProduceResults@test2
anon_2, a, anon_4, anon_3, p, anon_0, anon_1
a
336total memory (bytes)
0memory (bytes)
0estimated rows
6db hits

1row

▼ ProduceResults@test
p, r, a, `r.start`
a
Ordered by r.start ASC
1,028total memory (bytes)
0memory (bytes)
0estimated rows
6db hits

1row

Result

Result

Figure 3.10 — Basic graph model versus advanced graph model – query 3 profiles

We can see from these profiles that the current data model query profile is a bit more involved than the previous queries. The initial graph data model took 19 db hits and 1,028 bytes to perform the operation. The current graph data model took 16 db hits and 336 bytes to perform the operation.

> **Note**
>
> **Query profiling** is the best way to understand how the query works. If we are not happy with the query performance, profiling helps us understand which areas of the query execution we want to improve or change for better performance. You can read more about this at `https://neo4j.com/docs/cypher-manual/current/planning-and-tuning/`.

From analyzing the queries and data models, we can see that taking a fresher look at how the data models are defined can have a huge impact in terms of performance and cost to perform the same operations.

Another advantage of the current data model is that if we do want to track how the rentals are working from an address perspective, we can add just another relationship, say, **NEXT_RENTAL**, between the rentals for the same address. This would give us a different perspective of the same data. Trying to represent the data like this in an RDBMS or other data persistence layers would be difficult. This is where Neo4j with its flexibility to be able to persist relationships to avoid the join index cost and optional schema is better suited to build knowledge graphs.

A good graph data model makes the **retriever in RAG flow** more effective. It makes retrieving relevant data faster and easier, as we have explored here.

We will take a look at how we can use knowledge graphs as part of RAG flow next.

Combining the power of RAG and Neo4j knowledge graphs with GraphRAG

In the previous chapter, we looked at the **retriever**, which is the heart of RAG flows. The retriever leverages data stores to retrieve relevant information to provide to LLMs to get the best response to our question. Retrievers can work with various data stores as needed. The data store capabilities can greatly determine how useful, quick, and effective the information retrieved is. This is where graphs play a great role. That's how **GraphRAG** came into being.

Note

You can read more about GraphRAG and how it is effective at `https://www.`
`microsoft.com/en-us/research/blog/graphrag-unlocking-llm-discovery-`
`on-narrative-private-data/` and `https://microsoft.github.io/graphrag/`.
For a comprehensive understanding of GraphRAG, you can refer to Microsoft's research
paper titled *From Local to Global: A Graph RAG Approach to Query-Focused Summariza-*
tion (`https://arxiv.org/abs/2404.16130`). Additionally, Microsoft has made the
GraphRAG project available on GitHub (`https://github.com/microsoft/graphrag`),
providing resources and tools for implementing this approach.

The Neo4j graph database excels at persisting the data as a property graph with nodes and relationships. This makes it easy to store and retrieve data in an intuitive manner and serves the
data stores for RAG retrievers. This approach allows for more accurate, contextually aware, and
reliable AI-driven applications.

We will now build a GraphRAG flow that combines the power of RAG and knowledge graphs for
improved LLM responses.

GraphRAG: enhancing RAG models with Neo4j

In the previous chapter, we discussed the flow of information in a chat application with a RAG
model (refer to *Figure 3.5*).

Now we will see how this workflow can be augmented to generate improved responses for the
chat application. *Figure 3.11* shows the workflow of GraphRAG, where a user's prompt is processed
through an LLM API, retrieving relevant information from Neo4j, and then combined with the
prompt before being sent to an LLM API.

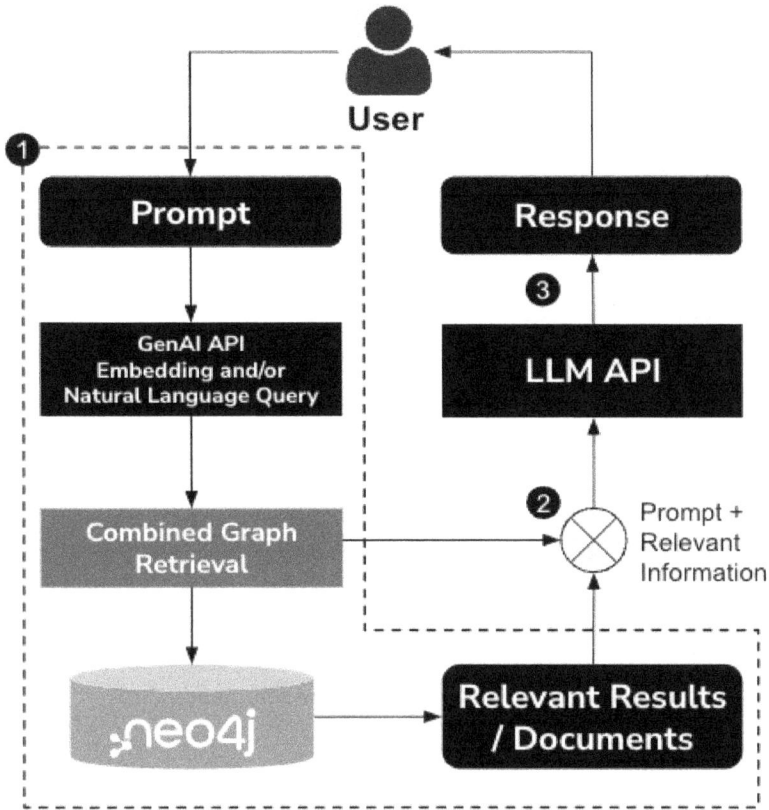

Figure 3.11 — Workflow of GraphRAG

The LLM API generates a response using both the prompt and the relevant information from the Neo4j knowledge graph, providing the user with accurate and contextually enriched results. By combining the capabilities of Neo4j and RAG models, GraphRAG enhances relevance with more domain context.

Let us build a simple graph to showcase this GraphRAG flow.

Building a knowledge graph for RAG integration

For this example, we will use limited data for demonstration purposes to build the graph, focusing on movies and their plots.

Python code example: Setting up a knowledge graph in Neo4j

By following along with the provided code example, you will learn how to set up a Neo4j database, define nodes and relationships, and perform basic queries using Cypher:

1. **Set up the Neo4j database**: Before running the code, ensure you have access to a Neo4j database. You can use either of the following:

    - **Neo4j Desktop**: Install and run it locally (download Neo4j Desktop: `https://neo4j.com/download/`)

    - **Neo4j AuraDB**: This is a cloud-hosted option (learn more about AuraDB at `https://neo4j.com/product/auradb/`)

2. Start your database instance and note the connection credentials (e.g., URI, username, and password).

3. **Install the necessary Python libraries**: You will need the following Python libraries:

    - **Neo4j Python Driver**: To interact with the database

    - **Pandas**: For handling data structures and analysis

    - Install these libraries using the following command:

        ```
        pip install neo4j pandas
        ```

4. **Connect to the database and set up the knowledge graph**: Once your Neo4j database is running and the required Python libraries are installed, you can use the following Python script to set up a simple knowledge graph. In this example, we will create a graph for IMDb movies and their plots, with nodes representing movies and plots and relationships indicating which plot belongs to which movie.

> **Note**
>
> We will not be using any external dataset, rather, we will be using a hardcoded data set to showcase the graph model and the GraphRAG flow. We will be exploring full-fledged data loading and the GraphRAG flow in *Chapters 4* and *5*. This example is to showcase the GraphRAG flow aspects only.

We will first build a simple graph. We will be using this simple graph to showcase where and how Neo4j fits in the GraphRAG flow:

1. Import the `GraphDatabase` library and define Neo4j connectivity and credentials:

```
from neo4j import GraphDatabase
uri = "bolt://localhost:7687"   # Replace with your Neo4j URI
username = "neo4j"              # Replace with your Neo4j username
password = "password"          # Replace with your Neo4j password
```

2. Let us create a few nodes:

```
def create_graph(tx):
    tx.run("CREATE (m:Movie {title: 'The Matrix', year: 1999})")
    ....

    # Create plot nodes
    tx.run("CREATE (p:Plot {description: 'A computer hacker learns
from mysterious rebels about the true nature of his reality and his
role in the war against its controllers.'})")
```

3. The next step is to create relationships:

```
    tx.run("""
    MATCH (m:Movie {title: 'The Matrix'}),
          (p:Plot {description: 'A computer hacker learns from
mysterious rebels about the true nature of his reality and his role
in the war against its controllers.'})
    CREATE (m)-[:HAS_PLOT]->(p)
    """)
```

4. If we visualize the data that we created, it would look as shown in *Figure 3.12*:

```
MATCH p=(:Movie)-[:HAS_PLOT]->()
RETURN p
LIMIT 5
```

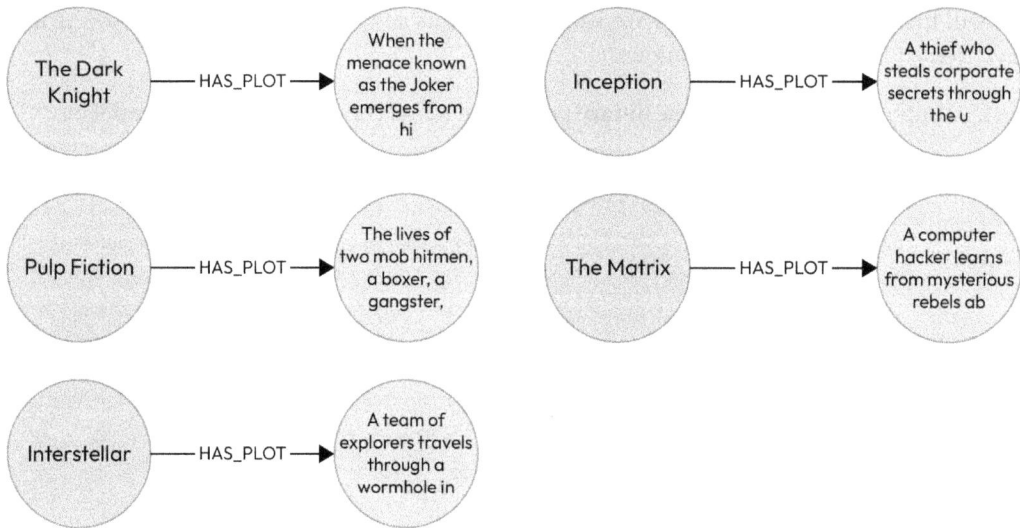

Figure 3.12 — Sample graph showing movies and plots

5. We will now retrieve the data using a Cypher query:

```
def query_graph(tx):
    # Query to retrieve movies and their plots
    result = tx.run("""
    MATCH (m:Movie)-[:HAS_PLOT]->(p:Plot)
    RETURN m.title AS movie, m.year AS year, p.description AS plot
    """)
    # Print the results
    for record in result:
        print(f"Movie: {record['movie']} ({record['year']}) - Plot:
{record['plot']}")
```

6. If we run this, we can see the output as shown here:

```
Movie: The Matrix (1999) - Plot: A computer hacker learns from
mysterious rebels about the true nature of his reality and his role
in the war against its controllers.
```

You can find the complete code at `https://github.com/PacktPublishing/Building-Neo4j-Powered-Applications-with-LLMs/blob/main/ch3/imdb_kg.py`.

Now that we have built the basic graph, let us use it in the GraphRAG flow.

Integrating RAG with your Neo4j knowledge graph

To integrate RAG models with Neo4j, you need to configure the models to query the graph database. This typically involves setting up an API or a middleware layer that facilitates communication between the RAG models and Neo4j.

An example integration workflow is provided here:

1. **User input:** The user provides a prompt. In the following code example, the prompt is predefined in the script as an example ("The Matrix"). Users can modify this to test other movies or prompts:

    ```
    prompt = "The Matrix"
    ```

2. **Query generation:** The prompt is processed, and a Cypher query is generated to retrieve relevant information from Neo4j. For example, the query might fetch the plot of the movie mentioned in the prompt:

    ```
    """
        Fetch relevant data (plots) for movies that match the user's
    prompt.
        """
        query = f"""
        MATCH (m:Movie)-[:HAS_PLOT]->(p:Plot)
        WHERE m.title CONTAINS '{prompt}'
        RETURN m.title AS title, m.year AS year, p.description AS plot
        """
    ```

3. **Data retrieval:** The Cypher query is executed, and the relevant data (e.g., the plot of *The Matrix*) is fetched from the knowledge graph:

    ```
    with driver.session() as session:
        result = session.run(query)
        records = [
            {
                "title": record["title"],
                "year": record["year"],
                "plot": record["plot"],
            }
            for record in result if record["plot"] is not None
    ```

```
    ]
    print(f"Retrieved Records: {records}")  # Debugging line
    return records
```

4. **RAG model processing**: The retrieved data is combined with the original prompt and passed to the RAG model for further processing, allowing the model to generate a richer and context-aware response:

```
    """

        Combine the user's prompt with relevant data from the graph
        and generate a focused, non-repetitive response using the RAG
    model.
        """

        relevant_data = get_relevant_data(prompt)

        if not relevant_data:
            return "No relevant data found for the given prompt."

        # Combine dictionaries in relevant_data into a single string
        combined_input = (
          f"Provide detailed information about: {prompt}. " +
          " ".join([
             f"{data['title']} ({data['year']}): {data['plot']}"
             for data in relevant_data
        ])

        print(f"Combined Input: {combined_input}")

        if not combined_input.strip():
            return "No relevant data to process for this prompt."

        # Tokenize the combined input with truncation
        max_input_length = 512 - 50  # Leave space for output
        tokenized_input = tokenizer(combined_input, truncation=True,
            max_length=max_input_length, return_tensors="pt")
```

5. **Response generation**: The RAG model generates a response using the enriched prompt (e.g., "The plot of *The Matrix* is: 'A computer hacker learns from mysterious rebels about the true nature of his reality and his role in the war against its controllers.'"):

```
# Generate response with tuned parameters
    outputs = model.generate(
        **tokenized_input,
        max_length=150,
        temperature=0.7,
        top_k=50,
        top_p=0.9,
        num_beams=5,
        no_repeat_ngram_size=3,
        early_stopping=True
    )

    # Decode the response with improved formatting
    response = tokenizer.decode(outputs[0],
        skip_special_tokens=True,
        clean_up_tokenization_spaces=True)
    return response
```

The following is a sample output:

```
Prompt: The Matrix
Response: : the matrix ( 1999 ) : a computer hacker learns from
mysterious rebels about the true nature of his reality and his role
in the war against its controllers.
```

The full version of the code in this chapter is placed at: https://github.com/PacktPublishing/Building-Neo4j-Powered-Applications-with-LLMs/blob/main/ch3/neo4j_rag.py.

This code snippet works only on numpy versions < 2. If you are running numpy versions > 2, use the following commands on the terminal to create a clean virtual environment to isolate the issue:

```
python3 -m venv my_env
source my_env/bin/activate
pip install numpy==1.26.4 neo4j transformers torch faiss-cpu datasets
```

With an understanding of how to build and query a basic knowledge graph, as well as how to integrate RAG models with Neo4j, you are now equipped with the foundational skills needed to create intelligent, context-aware applications. Next, we will take a look at a few approaches to enhance knowledge graphs. We will just be introducing these concepts here and will be exploring them in more detail upcoming chapters for building intelligent applications.

Enhancing knowledge graphs

We looked at building a graph and GraphRAG flow in the previous section. What we have looked at is a simple graph. There are a few approaches we can follow to make knowledge graphs more effective. Let us take a look at these approaches. We will be using these approaches to enhance our knowledge graphs in the upcoming chapters:

- **Ontology development**: An ontology can define the structure and the content of the graph. By having the ontology persisted in the graph, we might be able to explain the data and its connectivity in a more intuitive way. This ensures that the graph follows best practices and aligns with your domain-specific needs. Ontologies also help in maintaining uniformity across different datasets and in extending the graph over time. In *Chapter 5*, we would be enhancing the simple movie knowledge graph we created in this chapter If you want to learn more about ontologies, you can take a look at `https://neo4j.com/blog/ontologies-in-neo4j-semantics-and-knowledge-graphs/`.

- **Graph Data Science (GDS)**: While data loaded as a graph can be effective as a knowledge graph, there are a few other approaches that can make this graph much more effective. For example, we can perform some link prediction or perform community detection to create additional relationships between nodes that are inferred based on the existing data in the graph. This can help us enhance the intelligence stored in the graph to give us better answers when querying. We will be leveraging the KNN similarity and community detection algorithms in *Chapter 10* to enhance the graph to get more intelligence.

We have looked at a few approaches to enhance knowledge graphs. Let us now summarize our understanding of the concepts we have looked at.

Summary

In this chapter, we explored the foundational aspects of building a knowledge graph for RAG integration using Neo4j. We began by understanding the importance of Neo4j knowledge graphs and their role in GraphRAG. We also set up a Neo4j database, created nodes and relationships, and performed queries to retrieve relevant information.

We also covered the integration workflow of RAG models with Neo4j. You are now ready to move on to *Part 2, Integrating Haystack with Neo4j: A Practical Guide to Building AI-Powered Search*. In the next part, we will build on the foundation laid in this chapter and explore how to integrate Haystack with Neo4j to create powerful, AI-driven search capabilities. This next step will naturally extend your knowledge and skills, enabling you to develop sophisticated search applications that leverage the strengths of both Haystack and Neo4j.

Part 2

Integrating Haystack with Neo4j: A Practical Guide to Building AI-Powered Search

In the second part of the book, we move from concepts to hands-on implementation. We begin by modeling a real-world dataset—movies—into a well-structured Neo4j knowledge graph, preparing it for intelligent querying. Then, we integrate the Haystack framework with Neo4j to enable powerful, hybrid search experiences that combine semantic understanding with graph-based context. The final chapter takes this further by exploring advanced capabilities such as multi-hop reasoning and context-aware search, showcasing how to unlock deeper insights from your knowledge graph.

This part of the book includes the following chapters:

- *Chapter 4, Building Your Neo4j Graph with the Movies Dataset*
- *Chapter 5, Implementing Powerful Search Functionalities with Neo4j and Haystack*
- *Chapter 6, Exploring Advanced Knowledge Graph Capabilities*

Stay tuned

To keep up with the latest developments in the fields of Generative AI and LLMs, subscribe to our weekly newsletter, AI_Distilled, at `https://packt.link/Q5UyU`.

4

Building Your Neo4j Graph with Movies Dataset

In the previous chapters, we learned how knowledge graphs have emerged as a transformative tool, offering a structured way to connect diverse data points, enabling smarter search, recommendations, and inference capabilities across a wide range of domains.

Knowledge graphs excel at capturing complex relationships between entities, making them indispensable for applications that require deep contextual understanding.

Neo4j, with its state-of-the-art graph database technology, stands out as a leading platform for building and managing knowledge graphs. As we saw in the previous chapter, unlike traditional relational databases, Neo4j is designed to handle highly connected data with ease, allowing for more intuitive querying and faster retrieval of insights. This makes it an ideal choice for developers and data scientists looking to transform raw, unstructured data into meaningful insights that can drive AI-powered applications.

In this chapter, we are going to cover the following main topics:

- Design considerations for a Neo4j graph for an efficient search
- Utilizing a movies dataset
- Building your movie knowledge graph with code examples
- Beyond the basics: advanced Cypher techniques for complex graph structures

Technical requirements

To successfully work through the exercises in this chapter, you will need the following tools:

- **Neo4j AuraDB**: You can use Neo4j AuraDB, the cloud version of Neo4j, available at `https://neo4j.com/aura`.

- **Cypher query language**: Familiarity with the Cypher query language is essential, as we will be using Cypher extensively to create and query the graph. You can find out more about Cypher syntax in the Cypher query language documentation: `https://neo4j.com/docs/cypher/`.

- **Python**: You will need Python 3.x installed on your system. Python is used for scripting and interacting with the Neo4j database. You can download Python from the official Python website: `https://www.python.org/downloads/`.

- **Python libraries**:

  - **Neo4j Driver for Python**: Install the Neo4j Python driver to connect to the Neo4j database using Python. You can install it via `pip`:

    ```
    pip install neo4j
    ```

  - **pandas**: This library will be used for data manipulation and analysis. Install it via `pip`:

    ```
    pip install pandas
    ```

- **Integrated Development Environment (IDE)**: An IDE such as PyCharm, VS Code, or Jupyter Notebook is recommended for writing and managing your Python code efficiently.

- **Git and GitHub**: Basic knowledge of Git is required for version control. You will also need a GitHub account to access the code repository for this chapter.

- **Movies dataset: The Movie Database** (**TMDb**) is required, available on Kaggle: `https://www.kaggle.com/datasets/rounakbanik/the-movies-dataset/`.

- This dataset is a derivative of the **Movie Lens Datasets** (F. Maxwell Harper and Joseph A. Konstan. 2015. The MovieLens Datasets: History and Context. ACM Transactions on Interactive Intelligent Systems (TiiS) 5, 4: 19:1–19:19.`https://doi.org/10.1145/2827872`).

- Some of the data files, such as `credits.csv` and `ratings.csv`, may not be available on GitHub due to storage constraints. However, you can access all the raw data files from a GCS bucket.

All the code for this chapter is available in the following GitHub repository: `https://github.com/PacktPublishing/Building-Neo4j-Powered-Applications-with-LLMs/tree/main/ch4`.

The folder includes all the necessary files and scripts to help you build your Neo4j graph using the movies dataset and Cypher code.

Make sure to clone or download the repository to follow along with the code examples provided in this chapter.

The GitHub repository contains the path to GCS to access the raw data files.

Design considerations for a Neo4j graph for an efficient search

A well-designed Neo4j graph ensures that your search functionality is not only accurate but also efficient, enabling the quick retrieval of relevant information. The way data is organized in a graph directly impacts the performance and relevance of search results, making it crucial to understand the principles of effective graph modeling.

This section will delve into the importance of structuring your Neo4j graph correctly, how it influences the search process, and the key considerations you need to keep in mind while designing your graph model.

Considerations while defining node and relationship types

Recall from *Chapter 3* that the foundation of any Neo4j graph is built upon **nodes** and **relationships**. Nodes represent entities, such as movies or people (e.g., actors or directors), while relationships define how these entities are connected. The types of nodes and relationships you choose play a crucial role in determining the effectiveness of your search queries.

In a movies dataset, nodes could traditionally represent distinct entities such as Movies, Actors, Directors, and Genres. Relationships would then define how these nodes interact, such as ACTED_IN, DIRECTED, or BELONGS_TO. However, there is an alternative and often more efficient approach—consolidating similar entities under a single node type.

Instead of creating separate nodes for Actors and Directors, you can create a single Person node. The characteristic of each Person node—whether they are an actor, a director, or both—is then defined by the type of relationship it has with the Movie node. For example, a Person node connected to a Movie node by an ACTED_IN relationship signifies that the person is an actor in that movie. Similarly, a DIRECTED relationship indicates that the person directed the movie. We will be creating the complete graph in upcoming sections.

But first, let's talk about why this approach is better. As we demonstrated in *Chapter 3*, this approach results in the following:

- **Simplified data model**: By using a single Person node to represent both actors and directors, your data model becomes more streamlined. This reduces the complexity of the graph and makes it easier to understand and manage.

- **Enhanced query performance**: With fewer node types, the graph database can more efficiently traverse relationships during queries. This is because the database engine has fewer distinct entities to differentiate between, leading to faster query execution times.

- **Reduced redundancy**: A unified Person node eliminates the need to duplicate information. In cases where a person is both an actor and a director, you avoid creating two separate nodes with overlapping data, thus minimizing redundancy, and saving storage space.

- **Flexible relationship definitions**: This approach allows for more flexible and granular relationship definitions. If a person has multiple roles in different movies (e.g., acting in one and directing another), the relationships can clearly distinguish these roles without needing to create multiple nodes.

- **Easier maintenance and scalability**: As your dataset grows, maintaining a simpler node structure becomes increasingly important. Adding new roles or relationships becomes more straightforward when you are working with a unified node type.

By carefully selecting and defining these types and relationships, you create a graph structure that mirrors real-world connections. This makes your search queries more intuitive, the results more meaningful, and the overall system more efficient.

Applying indexing and constraints on search performance

As your Neo4j graph grows, the importance of **indexing** and applying **constraints** becomes paramount. **Indexes** allow Neo4j to quickly locate the starting points for queries, drastically improving search performance, especially in large datasets. Constraints, however, ensure data integrity by preventing the creation of duplicate nodes or invalid relationships.

In the context of our movies dataset, where we use a unified Person node for both actors and directors, indexing becomes even more crucial. You might **index** nodes based on properties such as person_name or role, ensuring that searches for specific people or their roles in movies return results swiftly. For example, you could index the role property on the relationships (e.g., ACTED_IN or DIRECTED) to quickly filter people by their involvement in a particular movie.

Constraints are also essential to maintaining the integrity of your graph. Let's look at some of these constraints. The constraints should be carefully designed based on the nature of your dataset and application requirements—they are not a one-size-fits-all solution.

The following are some example statements that demonstrate how to create constraints and indexes tailored for a movie dataset. These examples include common scenarios such as ensuring the uniqueness of person identifiers and optimizing search performance across node and relationship properties. Depending on your specific use case and data quality, you can adapt these patterns to enforce data integrity and improve query speed:

- Unique constraint on person_name (for a simplified use case). In many cases—such as our movie dataset, where we assume each person has a unique name—you might enforce a unique constraint on the person_name property to ensure that each individual is represented by a single node, even if they take on multiple roles (e.g., actor and director) across different movies. Here is how you can do this:

  ```
  CREATE CONSTRAINT unique_person_name IF NOT EXISTS
  FOR (p:Person)
  REQUIRE p.person_name IS UNIQUE;
  ```

  This helps prevent the accidental creation of duplicate nodes and keeps your graph clean and efficient.

- Unique constraint on a more reliable ID (e.g., person_id). The uniqueness constraint in the previous scenarios is based on assumptions about your data. In real-world scenarios, it is common to encounter different individuals with the same name.

  In such cases, you should use a more reliable identifier, such as a person_id value from an external source (e.g., **Internet Movie Database** (**IMDb**) or **TMDb**) to enforce uniqueness. The following Cypher code shows how to achieve this:

  ```
  CREATE CONSTRAINT unique_person_id IF NOT EXISTS
  FOR (p:Person)
  REQUIRE p.person_id IS UNIQUE;
  ```

- Index on person_name (for faster lookup if uniqueness is not enforced). If you're not enforcing uniqueness but still frequently search for people by name, an index on the person_name property can significantly improve query performance. This allows Neo4j to quickly locate Person nodes based on their names:

```
CREATE INDEX person_name_index IF NOT EXISTS
FOR (p:Person)
ON (p.person_name);
```

- Index on the title property of Movie. Movies are often queried by title—especially in recommendation systems or search functionalities. Indexing the title property ensures quick lookups when users search for specific movies:

```
CREATE INDEX movie_title_index IF NOT EXISTS
FOR (m:Movie)
ON (m.title);
```

- Index on the role property in the ACTED_IN relationship. If your application requires filtering actors by their specific roles in movies (e.g., lead or cameo), indexing the role property on the ACTED_IN relationship helps speed up those queries by avoiding full scans of all relationships:

```
CREATE INDEX acted_in_role_index IF NOT EXISTS
FOR ()-[r:ACTED_IN]-()
ON (r.role);
```

> **Note**
>
> Neo4j only supports relationship property indexes in version 5.x and above.

Properly implemented indexing and constraints make your graph more resilient and your search processes faster and more reliable. This not only enhances the user experience but also reduces the computational load on your system, allowing for more scalable solutions.

In the next section, we will explore how to harness the power of open data by utilizing a movies dataset to build your graph.

Utilizing a movies dataset

In this section, we will focus on utilizing **TMDb**, a comprehensive collection of metadata made available on Kaggle: `https://www.kaggle.com/datasets/rounakbanik/the-movies-dataset/`. This dataset includes a wide range of information about movies, such as titles, genres, cast, crew, release dates, and ratings. With over 45,000 movies and detailed information about the people involved in their creation, this dataset provides a robust foundation for building a Neo4j graph that captures the complex relationships within the film industry.

You will use this dataset to model the data as a knowledge graph, learning about data integration in a practical context. You will learn how to source, prepare, and import this data into Neo4j.

When working with large datasets such as TMDb, it is crucial to ensure that the data is clean, consistent, and properly structured before integrating it into your Neo4j graph. Raw data, while rich in information, often contains inconsistencies, redundancies, and complex structures that can hinder the performance and accuracy of your knowledge graph. This is where data normalization and cleaning come into play.

Why normalize and clean data?

Maintaining a clean and normalized dataset is crucial when building a Neo4j graph, as it directly impacts the quality and performance of your application. By normalizing and cleaning your data, you ensure consistency, improve efficiency, and create a scalable foundation for analysis. Here is why each of these steps matters:

- **Consistency**: Raw data can come with variations in how similar information is recorded. For example, movie genres might be listed in different formats or contain duplicates. Normalizing data ensures that similar data points are recorded in a consistent format, making it easier to query and analyze. However, tackling these issues in real-world datasets can be challenging. Neo4j helps address problems such as entity linkage and deduplication through powerful features such as Cypher pattern matching, APOC procedures for merging nodes and cleaning up duplicates, and the Graph Data Science library, which includes node similarity algorithms to identify and consolidate related entities. These capabilities enable you to build a clean, reliable graph that reflects the true structure of your data.

- **Efficiency**: Normalizing data reduces redundancy, which can improve the efficiency of your Neo4j graph. By organizing data into a standardized format, you minimize the storage requirements and optimize the performance of your queries.

- **Accuracy**: Cleaning data involves removing or correcting inaccurate records. This step is essential to ensure that the insights derived from your graph are based on accurate and reliable data.

- **Scalability**: A clean and normalized dataset is easier to scale. As your dataset grows, maintaining a standardized structure ensures that the graph remains manageable and performs well under increasing loads.

Let us move on to cleaning and normalizing CSV files next.

Cleaning and normalizing the CSV files

Now, we will clean and normalize each CSV file included in TMDb. The available CSV files in our dataset are as follows:

- `credits.csv`: This file contains detailed information about the cast and crew for each movie in our dataset, presented as a stringified JSON object. For our purposes, we will focus specifically on extracting the relevant details related to characters, actors, directors, and producers:

```
# Load the CSV file
df = pd.read_csv('./raw_data/credits.csv')

# Function to extract relevant cast information
def extract_cast(cast_str):
    cast_list = ast.literal_eval(cast_str)
    return [
        {
            'actor_id': c['id'],
            'name': c['name'],
            'character': c['character'],
            'cast_id': c['cast_id']
        }
        for c in cast_list
    ]

# Function to extract relevant crew information
def extract_crew(crew_str):
    crew_list = ast.literal_eval(crew_str)
    relevant_jobs = ['Director', 'Producer']
```

```
        return [
            {
                'crew_id': c['id'],
                'name': c['name'],
                'job': c['job']
            }
            for c in crew_list if c['job'] in relevant_jobs
        ]


    # Apply the extraction functions to each row
    df['cast'] = df['cast'].apply(extract_cast)
    df['crew'] = df['crew'].apply(extract_crew)


    # Explode the lists into separate rows
    df_cast = df.explode('cast').dropna(subset=['cast'])
    df_crew = df.explode('crew').dropna(subset=['crew'])


    # Normalize the exploded data
    df_cast_normalized = pd.json_normalize(df_cast['cast'])
    df_crew_normalized = pd.json_normalize(df_crew['crew'])


    # Reset index to avoid duplicate indices
    df_cast_normalized = df_cast_normalized.reset_index(drop=True)
    df_crew_normalized = df_crew_normalized.reset_index(drop=True)


    # Drop duplicate rows if any
    df_cast_normalized = df_cast_normalized.drop_duplicates()
    df_crew_normalized = df_crew_normalized.drop_duplicates()


    # Add the movie ID back to the normalized DataFrames
    df_cast_normalized['tmdbId'] = df_cast.reset_index(drop=True)['id']
    df_crew_normalized['tmdbId'] = df_crew.reset_index(drop=True)['id']


    # Save the normalized data with the updated column names
    df_cast_normalized.to_csv(
        os.path.join(output_dir, 'normalized_cast.csv'),
        index=False
```

```
    )
    df_crew_normalized.to_csv(
        os.path.join(output_dir, 'normalized_crew.csv'),
        index=False
    )


    # Display a sample of the output for verification
    print("Sample of normalized cast data:")
    print(df_cast_normalized.head())

    print("Sample of normalized crew data:")
    print(df_crew_normalized.head())
```

- keywords.csv: This file contains the movie plot keywords for each movie in the dataset. The keywords are essential for categorizing and identifying thematic elements within the movies, which can be used for various purposes, such as search, recommendation, and content analysis:

```
    # Load the CSV file
    df = pd.read_csv('./raw_data/keywords.csv')  # Update the path as
    necessary

    # Function to extract and normalize keywords
    def normalize_keywords(keyword_str):
        if pd.isna(keyword_str) or not isinstance(keyword_str, str):  #
    Check if the value is NaN or not a string
            return []

        # Convert the stringified JSON object into a list of
    dictionaries
        keyword_list = ast.literal_eval(keyword_str)
        # Extract the 'name' of each keyword and return them as a list
        return [kw['name'] for kw in keyword_list]

    # Apply the normalization function to the 'keywords' column
    df['keywords'] = df['keywords'].apply(normalize_keywords)

    # Combine all keywords for each tmdbId into a single row
```

```
df_keywords_aggregated = df.groupby('id', as_index=False).agg({
    'keywords': lambda x: ', '.join(sum(x, []))
})


# Rename the 'id' column to 'tmdbId'
df_keywords_aggregated.rename(
    columns={'id': 'tmdbId'}, inplace=True
)


# Save the aggregated DataFrame to a new CSV file
df_keywords_aggregated.to_csv(
    os.path.join(output_dir, 'normalized_keywords.csv'),
    index=False
)


# Display the first few rows of the aggregated DataFrame for
verification
print(df_keywords_aggregated.head())
```

- links.csv: This file contains essential metadata that links each movie in the full **Mov-ieLens dataset** to its corresponding entries in both TMDb and IMDB. This file serves as a crucial bridge for connecting the MovieLens dataset with external movie databases, enabling enriched data integration and further analysis. However, for this use case, we skipped processing the links.csv file, as it is not essential to our current analysis. Our focus will remain on other CSV files more directly relevant to our project's objectives. The data contained in links.csv can still be useful for future projects that require integration with external databases, but it will not be utilized in this instance.

- links_small.csv: This file contains the TMDb and IMDb IDs for a small subset of 9,000 movies from the full MovieLens dataset. While this file provides a streamlined version of the links for a smaller selection of movies, we will not be using this file, as we are already utilizing the full dataset from Kaggle, which includes all available movies. This file is typically useful for scenarios where a more manageable, smaller dataset is needed, but for our purposes, the full data set is preferred for comprehensive analysis and integration.

- movies_metadata.csv: This file is a comprehensive dataset containing detailed informa-tion on 45,000 movies featured in the full MovieLens dataset. This file includes various features such as posters, backdrops, budgets, revenue, release dates, languages, production countries, and companies, among others. To efficiently organize and analyze this data, we will normalize the `movies_metadata.csv` file into multiple CSV files, each representing a relevant node in our dataset. These nodes include genres, production companies, production countries, and spoken languages. By breaking down the data into these separate files, we can more easily manage and utilize the rich information contained within this dataset. Let's see how.

1. Begin with necessary imports.

    ```python
    import pandas as pd
    import ast


    # Load the CSV file
    df = pd.read_csv('./raw_data/movies_metadata.csv')  # Update
    the path as necessary
    ```

2. Extract and normalize genres, production companies, countries, and spoken languages. We will demonstrate this step for genres and production companies. The rest of the code is available on https://github.com/PacktPublishing/Building-Neo4j-Powered-Applications-with-LLMs/tree/main/ch4.

    ```python
    # Function to extract and normalize genres
    def extract_genres(genres_str):
        if pd.isna(genres_str) or not isinstance(
            genres_str, str
        ):
            return []
        genres_list = ast.literal_eval(genres_str)
        return [
            {'genre_id': int(g['id']), 'genre_name': g['name']}
            for g in genres_list
        ]


    # Function to extract and normalize production companies
    def extract_production_companies(companies_str):
        if pd.isna(companies_str) or not isinstance(
            companies_str, str
        ):
            return []
        companies_list = ast.literal_eval(companies_str)
    ```

```
        if isinstance(companies_list, list):
            return [
                {'company_id': int(c['id']),
                    'company_name': c['name']
                }
                for c in companies_list
            ]
        return []
```

3. Apply the extraction functions.

```
df['genres'] = df['genres'].apply(extract_genres)
df['production_companies'] = \
    df['production_companies'].apply(
        extract_production_companies
    )
df['production_countries'] = \
    df['production_countries'].apply(
        extract_production_countries
    )
df['spoken_languages'] = df['spoken_languages'].apply(
    extract_spoken_languages
)

# Explode lists into rows
df_genres = df.explode('genres').dropna(subset=['genres'])
df_companies = df.explode('production_companies').dropna(
    subset=['production_companies']
)
df_countries = df.explode('production_countries').dropna(
    subset=['production_countries']
)
df_languages = df.explode('spoken_languages').dropna(
    subset=['spoken_languages']
)
```

4. Normalize the exploded data. Let's do this for genres.

```
df_genres_normalized = pd.json_normalize(df_genres['genres'])
# Reset index to avoid duplicate indices
```

```
df_genres_normalized = \
    df_genres_normalized.reset_index(drop=True)
# Add the movie ID back to the normalized DataFrames as
'tmdbId'
df_genres_normalized['tmdbId'] = df_genres.reset_index(
    drop=True
)['id']
# Ensure that 'company_id' and similar fields are treated as
integers
df_genres_normalized['genre_id'] = \
    df_genres_normalized['genre_id'].astype(int)


# Save the normalized data with the updated column names
df_genres_normalized.to_csv(
    os.path.join(output_dir, 'normalized_genres.csv'),
    index=False
)
```

5. Next up, extract the collection name.

```
# For the movies, including "Belongs to Collection" within
the same CSV
# Extract only the "name" from "belongs_to_collection" and
include additional fields
def extract_collection_name(collection_str):
    if isinstance(collection_str, str):
        try:
            collection_dict = \
                ast.literal_eval(collection_str)
            if isinstance(collection_dict, dict):
                return collection_dict.get('name', "None")
        except (ValueError, SyntaxError):  # Handle cases
where string parsing fails
            return "None"
    return "None"


df_movies = df[
    [
        'id', 'original_title', 'adult', 'budget', 'imdb_id',
```

```
              'original_language', 'revenue', 'tagline', 'title',
              'release_date', 'runtime', 'overview',
              'belongs_to_collection'
        ]
    ].copy()

    df_movies['belongs_to_collection'] = \
        df_movies['belongs_to_collection'].apply(
            extract_collection_name
        )
    df_movies['adult'] = df_movies['adult'].apply(
        lambda x: 1 if x == 'TRUE' else 0
    )  # Convert 'adult' to integer

    # Rename 'id' to 'tmdbId'
    df_movies.rename(columns={'id': 'tmdbId'}, inplace=True)  #
    Rename 'id' to 'tmdbId'

    # Save the movies to a separate CSV, including the extracted
    fields
    df_movies.to_csv(
        './normalized_data/normalized_movies.csv', index=False
    )
```

- `ratings.csv`: This file is the full MovieLens dataset, consisting of 26 million ratings and 750,000 tag applications from 270,000 users on all 45,000 movies in this dataset. This comprehensive dataset provides detailed user interaction data, which we will use directly without the need for normalization. However, for this use case, we have decided to skip processing the `ratings.csv` file. While it provides extensive user interaction data, it is not essential to our current analysis and objectives. We are focusing on other CSV files that are more directly relevant to our project. The data in `ratings.csv` can still be valuable for future projects that require a deep dive into user ratings and interactions, but it will not be utilized in this instance.

- `ratings_small.csv`: This file is a smaller subset of the `ratings.csv` file, containing 100,000 ratings from 700 users on 9,000 movies. We will be using `ratings_small.csv` instead of focusing on the full dataset provided in `ratings.csv`.

Through this process, we have learned how to transform raw, unstructured data into clean, normalized datasets that are now primed for integration into your Neo4j graph. This preparation paves the way for constructing a robust, efficient, and effective AI-powered search and recommendation system. In the next section, we will take these normalized CSV files and use Cypher code to build a knowledge graph, unlocking the full potential of our dataset.

Building your movie knowledge graph with code examples

In this section, we will import your normalized datasets into Neo4j and transform them into a fully functional knowledge graph.

Setting up your AuraDB free instance

To start building your knowledge graph with Neo4j, you will first need to set up an AuraDB Free instance. AuraDB Free is a cloud-hosted Neo4j database that allows you to quickly get started without worrying about local installations or infrastructure management.

Follow these steps to create your instance:

1. Visit `https://console.neo4j.io`.
2. Log in with your Google account or with email.
3. Click **Create Free Instance**.
4. While the instance is being provisioned, a pop-up window will appear showing the connection credentials for your database.

Make sure to download and securely save the following details from the popup—these are essential for connecting your application to Neo4j:

```
NEO4J_URI=neo4j+s://<your-instance-id>.databases.neo4j.io
NEO4J_USERNAME=neo4j
NEO4J_PASSWORD=<your-generated-password>
AURA_INSTANCEID=<your-instance-id>
AURA_INSTANCENAME=<your-instance-name>
```

With your AuraDB Free instance set up, you are now ready to import your normalized datasets and start building your knowledge graph using Cypher code. In the following section, we will guide you through importing data and constructing relationships within your graph.

Importing your data into AuraDB

Now that your AuraDB Free instance is up and running, it is time to import your normalized datasets and build your knowledge graph. In this section, we will walk through preparing your CSV files, setting up indexes and constraints, importing data, and creating relationships—all through a Python script:

1. Prepare your CSV files for import.

2. Ensure that the CSV files you generated (e.g., `normalized_movies.csv`, `normalized_genres.csv`, etc.) are ready for import. These files should be clean, well structured, and hosted at accessible URLs. In this case, the `graph_build.py` script fetches files from public cloud storage (for example, `https://storage.googleapis.com/movies-packt/normalized_movies.csv`), so you do not need to upload them manually anywhere.

3. Add indexes and constraints to optimize graph query retrieval.

   Before loading data, it is critical to create unique constraints and indexes to ensure integrity and optimize query performance. The script includes Cypher commands to do the following:

   - Ensure uniqueness on IDs such as `tmdbId`, `movieId`, and `company_id`
   - Create indexes on properties such as `actor_id`, `crew_id`, and `user_id`

   Here is how you can create indexes and constraints:

```
"CREATE CONSTRAINT unique_tmdb_id IF NOT EXISTS FOR (m:Movie)
REQUIRE m.tmdbId IS UNIQUE;",
"CREATE CONSTRAINT unique_movie_id IF NOT EXISTS FOR (m:Movie)
REQUIRE m.movieId IS UNIQUE;",
"CREATE CONSTRAINT unique_prod_id IF NOT EXISTS FOR
(p:ProductionCompany) REQUIRE p.company_id IS UNIQUE;",
"CREATE CONSTRAINT unique_genre_id IF NOT EXISTS FOR (g:Genre)
REQUIRE g.genre_id IS UNIQUE;",
"CREATE CONSTRAINT unique_lang_id IF NOT EXISTS FOR
(l:SpokenLanguage) REQUIRE l.language_code IS UNIQUE;",
"CREATE CONSTRAINT unique_country_id IF NOT EXISTS FOR (c:Country)
REQUIRE c.country_code IS UNIQUE;",
"CREATE INDEX actor_id IF NOT EXISTS FOR (p:Person) ON (p.actor_
id);",
"CREATE INDEX crew_id IF NOT EXISTS FOR (p:Person) ON (p.crew_id);",
"CREATE INDEX movieId IF NOT EXISTS FOR (m:Movie) ON (m.movieId);",
"CREATE INDEX user_id IF NOT EXISTS FOR (p:Person) ON (p.user_id);"
```

4. Import data and create nodes.

    After adding constraints and indexes, the script loads the nodes from their respective CSVs:

    - `load_movies()` adds all movie metadata
    - `load_genres()`, `load_production_companies()`, `load_countries()`, and others create related nodes, such as `Genre`, `ProductionCompany`, `Country`, and `SpokenLanguage`
    - Person-related data is added using `load_person_actors()` and `load_person_crew()`

    Additional properties are added via `load_links()`, `load_keywords()`, and `load_ratings()`

    Take the following example:

    ```
    graph.load_movies('https://storage.googleapis.com/movies-packt/
    normalized_movies.csv', movie_limit)
    ```

5. Create relationships.

    As each loader function runs, it not only creates nodes but also establishes meaningful relationships:

    - `HAS_GENRE` between `Movie` and `Genre`
    - `PRODUCED_BY` between `Movie` and `ProductionCompany`
    - `HAS_LANGUAGE` between `Movie` and `SpokenLanguage`, `PRODUCED_IN` between `Movie` and `Country`, `ACTED_IN`, `DIRECTED`, `PRODUCED` between `Movie` and `Person`, and `RATED` between `Movie` and `User`, among others.

6. Run the full script.

    Before running the script, ensure you have the Neo4j Python driver installed. You can install it using `pip`.

    ```
    pip install neo4j
    ```

    To run the entire graph-building process, simply execute the following:

    ```
    python graph_build.py
    ```

    This script performs the following, in order:

    - Connects to your AuraDB instance using credentials from the `.env` file
    - Cleans up the database

- Adds indexes and constraints
- Loads all node data and relationships in bulk using hosted CSVs

Please refer to the complete script available here: `https://github.com/PacktPublishing/`
`Building-Neo4j-Powered-Applications-with-LLMs/blob/main/ch4/graph_build.py`.

Once complete, verify your import using Neo4j Browser:

```
MATCH (m:Movie)-[:HAS_GENRE]->(g:Genre)
RETURN m.title, g.genre_name
LIMIT 10;
```

Figure 4.1 illustrates a connected movie graph with over 90K nodes and 320K+ relationships. Nodes such as `Movie`, `Genre`, `Person`, and `ProductionCompany` are represented with distinct colors, while relationships such as `ACTED_IN`, `HAS_GENRE`, and `PRODUCED_BY` showcase the web of interconnected metadata.

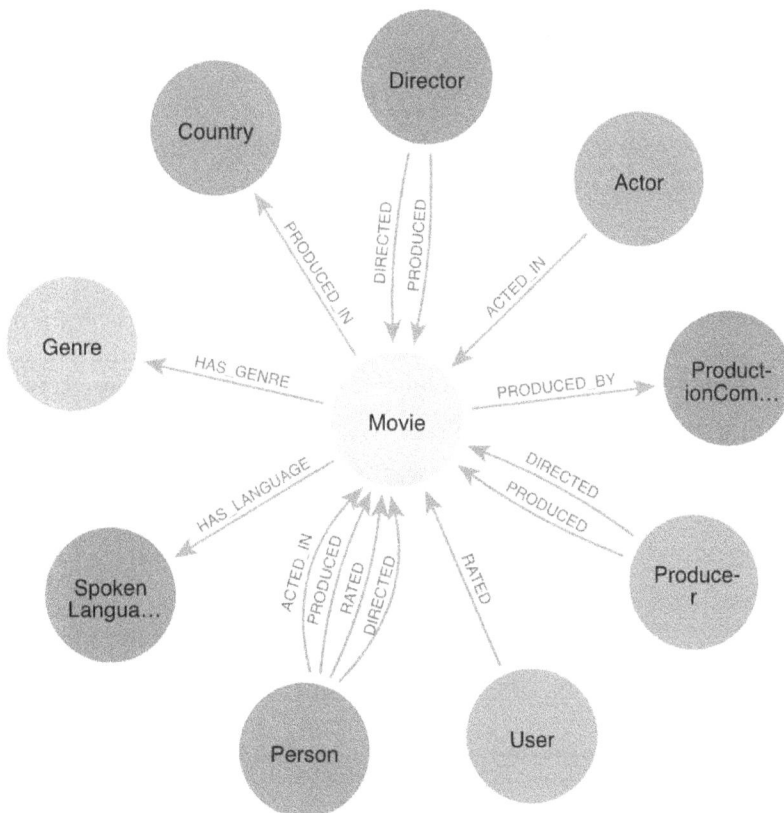

Figure 4.1 — Neo4j graph of movies dataset

With your data successfully imported and your knowledge graph fully constructed using Python and Cypher, you are now ready to dive into building a GenAI-powered search application in the next chapter. In the following section, we will dive into advanced Cypher techniques that empower you to handle intricate relationships and derive deeper insights from your data.

Beyond the basics: advanced Cypher techniques for complex graph structures

As your knowledge graph grows in size and complexity, so do the demands on your querying and data management capabilities. Cypher, Neo4j's powerful query language, offers a range of advanced features designed to handle complex graph structures and enable more sophisticated data analysis. In this section, we will explore these advanced Cypher techniques, including **path patterns**, **variable-length relationships**, subqueries, and graph algorithms. Understanding these techniques, will help you efficiently manage intricate relationships, perform deeper analyses, and unlock the full potential of your knowledge graph for advanced use cases.

Let us explore these key advanced Cypher techniques:

- **Variable-length relationships**: Variable-length relationships in Cypher allow you to match paths of varying lengths between nodes. This is particularly useful when exploring hierarchical structures or networks with multiple degrees of separation. An example is finding all movies connected to a specific actor within three degrees of separation:

  ```
  MATCH (a:Actor {name: 'Tom Hanks'})-[:ACTED_IN*1..3]-(m:Movie)
  RETURN DISTINCT m.title;
  ```

  - Here, *1..3 specifies that the relationship path can be between 1 and 3 steps long.
  - **Use cases**: Variable-length relationships are ideal for scenarios such as social network analysis, where you want to find all people within a certain degree of connection, or in hierarchical datasets where you want to explore parent-child relationships across multiple levels.

- **Pattern matching with path patterns**: You can create **named path patterns** as well as chain the paths in Neo4j.

  - **Defining path patterns**: Cypher allows you to define named path patterns that can be reused throughout your queries. This makes your queries more readable and allows you to encapsulate complex relationships in a single pattern. Take the following example:

    ```
    MATCH path = (a:Actor)-[:ACTED_IN]->(m:Movie)
    RETURN path;
    ```

    Here, path is a named path pattern that can be reused in subsequent operations or subqueries.

  - **Chaining path patterns**: Cypher allows you to combine multiple path patterns to perform complex traversals within the graph. This is especially useful when trying to uncover indirect relationships or discover multiple paths that satisfy specific criteria.

    An example is exploring collaborations in the movies dataset.

    Let's say we want to find movies where an actor has worked with a director they've previously collaborated with, possibly through another movie. This involves chaining paths from an actor to a movie, then to a director, and seeing whether there's another movie connecting the same actor-director pair:

    ```
    MATCH (a:Actor {name: "Tom Hanks"})-[:ACTED_IN]->(m1:Movie)<-
    [:DIRECTED_BY]-(d:Director) MATCH (a)-[:ACTED_IN]-
    >(m2:Movie)<-[:DIRECTED_BY]-(d)
    WHERE m1 <> m2
    RETURN a.name AS actor, d.name AS director, collect(DISTINCT
    m1.title) + collect(DISTINCT m2.title) AS movies
    ```

    This kind of pattern chaining is extremely helpful in identifying professional relationships, recurring collaborations, or analyzing indirect influence in networks.

- **Subqueries** and **procedural logic**: You can use subqueries and procedures to process complex queries. Here is how:

  - **Using subqueries for modular queries**: Subqueries in Cypher allow you to break down complex queries into modular, reusable components. This is particularly helpful when dealing with large graphs or when you need to perform multiple operations on the same dataset. Take the following example:

    ```
    CALL {
      MATCH (m:Movie)-[:HAS_GENRE]->(g:Genre {name: 'Action'})
      RETURN m
    }
    MATCH (m)-[:DIRECTED_BY]->(d:Director)
    RETURN d.name, COUNT(m) AS action_movies_directed;
    ```

    Here, the subquery retrieves all action movies, and the outer query matches these movies to their directors.

  - **Procedural logic with CALL**: The CALL clause in Cypher allows you to invoke procedures and use the results in further queries. This is essential for advanced data processing, such as running graph algorithms or invoking custom procedures.

    We've already applied this in our own implementation in the graph_build.py file, specifically in the load_ratings() function. Here, we use the CALL { ... } IN TRANSACTIONS pattern to efficiently load large datasets by processing them in chunks of 50,000 rows:

    ```
    LOAD CSV WITH HEADERS FROM $csvFile AS row
    CALL (row) {
      MATCH (m:Movie {movieId: toInteger(row.movieId)})
      WITH m, row
      MERGE (p:Person {user_id: toInteger(row.userId)})
      ON CREATE SET p.role = 'user'
      MERGE (p)-[r:RATED]->(m)
      ON CREATE SET r.rating = toFloat(row.rating), r.timestamp =
    toInteger(row.timestamp)
    } IN TRANSACTIONS OF 50000 ROWS;
    ```

    This approach allows us to handle massive CSV imports while maintaining performance and transactional integrity—just one of the many powerful use cases for CALL in real-world graph applications.

- **Working with nested queries:** In complex graph structures, you might need to **combine results from multiple queries**. Cypher allows you to nest queries, passing results from one query into another, which is useful for filtering or refining results based on multiple criteria. Take the following example:

```
MATCH (m:Movie)
WHERE m.revenue > 100000000
CALL {
  WITH m
  MATCH (m)-[:HAS_GENRE]->(g:Genre)
  RETURN g.name AS genre
}
RETURN m.title, genre;
```

Here, the nested query refines the results by filtering movies based on revenue and then finding their associated genres.

These Cypher techniques empower you to tackle complex graph structures, enabling deeper insights and more sophisticated analyses. You can refer to `https://neo4j.com/docs/cypher-manual/current/appendix/tutorials/advanced-query-tuning/` to explore some of these techniques further.

Summary

In this chapter, we worked on transforming raw, semi-structured data into clean, normalized datasets, ready for integration into our knowledge graph. We then explored the best practices in graph modeling, focusing on how to structure your nodes and relationships to enhance search efficiency and ensure your graph remains scalable and performant. Following this, we tackled other Cypher techniques, equipping you with the skills to handle variable-length relationships, pattern matching, subqueries, and graph algorithms. You are now well prepared to build a knowledge graph-driven search that can handle even the most intricate data relationships.

In the next chapter, we will take a step further by exploring how to integrate Haystack into Neo4j. This practical guide will show you how to build powerful search functionalities within your knowledge graph, allowing you to leverage the full potential of both Neo4j and Haystack for intelligent search solutions.

5

Implementing Powerful Search Functionalities with Neo4j and Haystack

In this chapter, we embark on a journey to integrate Haystack with Neo4j, combining the capabilities of LLMs and graph databases to build an AI-powered search system. **Haystack** is an open-source framework that enables developers to create AI-powered applications by leveraging modern NLP techniques, machine learning models, and graph-based data. For our intelligent search, Haystack will serve as a cohesive platform for orchestrating LLMs, search engines, and databases, delivering highly contextualized and relevant search results.

Building upon the work from the previous chapter—where we cleaned and structured our Neo4j data—we will start by generating embeddings using OpenAI's GPT models. These embeddings will enrich the graph, making it more powerful and capable of handling nuanced, context-aware search queries. Haystack will serve as the bridge between OpenAI's models and the Neo4j graph database, allowing us to combine the strengths of both.

In this chapter, you will learn how to set up and configure Haystack for seamless integration with Neo4j. We will walk you through building powerful search functionalities and finally deploying this fully functional search system, using Gradio on Hugging Face Spaces.

In this chapter, we are going to cover the following main topics:

- Generating embeddings with Haystack to enhance your Neo4j graph
- Connecting Haystack to Neo4j for advanced vector search
- Building powerful search experiences
- Fine-tuning your Haystack integration

Technical requirements

To successfully implement the integration of Haystack and Neo4j, and to build an AI-powered search system, you will need to ensure that your environment is properly set up. Here is a list of the technical requirements for this chapter:

- **Python:** You will need Python 3.11 installed on your system. Python is used for scripting and interacting with the Neo4j database. You can download Python from the official Python website: `https://www.python.org/downloads/`.

- **Neo4j AuraDB or local Neo4j instance:** You will need access to a Neo4j database to store and query your graph data. This can be either a locally installed Neo4j instance or a cloud-hosted Neo4j AuraDB instance. If you are following along from the previous chapter, where we talked about the `graph_build.py` script (`https://github.com/PacktPublishing/Building-Neo4j-Powered-Applications-with-LLMs/blob/main/ch4/graph_build.py`), you can continue using the same Neo4j instance that was set up and populated with data. This ensures continuity and allows you to build on top of the structured data that has already been imported.

- **Cypher query language:** Familiarity with the Cypher query language is essential, as we will be using Cypher extensively to create and query the graph. You can find out more about Cypher syntax in the Cypher query language documentation: `https://neo4j.com/docs/cypher/`.

- **Neo4j Python driver:** Install the Neo4j Python driver to connect to the Neo4j database using Python. You can install it via `pip`:

  ```
  pip install neo4j
  ```

- **Haystack:** We will be using Haystack v2.5.0.

  Install Haystack using pip:

  ```
  pip install haystack-ai
  ```

- **OpenAI API key**: To successfully generate embeddings using GPT-based models, you will need an OpenAI API key.

  Obtain the API key by signing up for an account at OpenAI (`https://platform.openai.com/signup`) if you do not have one.

  > **Note**
  >
  > A free-tier API key will not work for most use cases in this project. You will need an active paid OpenAI subscription to access the necessary endpoints and usage limits.

  Once you are logged in, navigate to the **API keys** section (`https://platform.openai.com/api-keys`) in your OpenAI dashboard and generate a new API key.

  You also need to install the OpenAI package using pip. Run the following command in your terminal:

  ```
  pip install openai
  ```

- **Gradio**: Gradio will be used to create a user-friendly chatbot interface. Install Gradio using pip:

  ```
  pip install gradio
  ```

- **Hugging Face account**: To host your chatbot on Hugging Face Spaces, you will need a Hugging Face account. If you do not have one, sign up on the Hugging Face website: `https://huggingface.co/`.
- **Google Cloud Storage (optional)**: If you are storing your CSV files on Google Cloud Storage, ensure that your file paths are properly configured in the script.
- **python-dotenv package**: Make sure to install the `python-dotenv` package to manage environment variables in your project:

  ```
  pip install python-dotenv
  ```

All the code for this chapter is available in the following GitHub repository: `https://github.com/PacktPublishing/Building-Neo4j-Powered-Applications-with-LLMs`.

Inside this repository, navigate to the folder named ch6 to access the code examples and resources related to this chapter. This folder contains all the necessary scripts, files, and configurations required to implement the Neo4j and Haystack integration, as well as build the AI-powered search system using the movies dataset.

Make sure to clone or download the repository so you can follow along with the code examples throughout this chapter.

Generating embeddings with Haystack to enhance your Neo4j graph

In this section, we will focus on generating embeddings for the movie plots that we added to our Neo4j graph in the previous chapter. **Embeddings** are a critical part of modern search systems, as they convert text into high-dimensional vectors that enable similarity search. This enables the search engine to understand the contextual relationships between words and phrases, improving the accuracy and relevance of search results.

We will integrate Haystack with OpenAI's GPT-based models to generate these embeddings and store them in your Neo4j graph. This will enable a more accurate and context-aware search functionality.

Initializing Haystack and OpenAI for embeddings

Before generating embeddings, you will need to ensure that Haystack is set up and integrated with OpenAI's API to retrieve embeddings from their GPT-based models. Follow these steps to set up Haystack:

1. Install the required libraries (if you have not already) by using the following command:

    ```
    pip install haystack haystack-ai openai neo4j-haystack
    ```

2. Next, configure your OpenAI API key and ensure that it is set up in your .env file:

    ```makefile
    OPENAI_API_KEY=your_openai_api_key_here
    ```

3. Initialize Haystack with OpenAI embeddings by creating a Python script that initializes Haystack and connects to OpenAI to generate the embeddings:

    ```
    # Initialize Haystack with OpenAI for text embeddings
    def initialize_haystack():
    ```

```
    # Initialize document store (In-memory for now, but you can
configure other stores)
    document_store = InMemoryDocumentStore()

    # Initialize OpenAITextEmbedder to generate text embeddings
    embedder = OpenAITextEmbedder(
        api_key=Secret.from_env_var("OPENAI_API_KEY"),
        model="text-embedding-ada-002"
    )
    return embedder
```

This configuration initializes Haystack with an in-memory document store and sets up the retriever using OpenAI embeddings.

Generating embeddings for movie plots

Next, we will generate embeddings for the movie plots stored in the Neo4j graph. The goal is to retrieve the plot descriptions, generate embeddings for them, and link these embeddings back to the respective movie nodes:

1. **Query movie plots from Neo4j:** First, you will need to query the movie plots from Neo4j. Use the following Cypher query to retrieve movie titles and plot summaries:

```
    # Retrieve movie plots and titles from Neo4j
    def retrieve_movie_plots():
        # The query retrieves the "title", "overview", and "tmdbId"
    properties of each Movie node
        query = """
        MATCH (m:Movie)
        WHERE m.embedding IS NULL
        RETURN m.tmdbId AS tmdbId, m.title AS title, m.overview AS
    overview
        """
        with driver.session() as session:
            results = session.run(query)
            # Each movie's title, plot (overview), and ID are retrieved
    and stored in the movies list
            movies = [
                {
                    "tmdbId": row["tmdbId"],
```

```
                "title": row["title"],
                "overview": row["overview"]
            }
            for row in results
        ]
    return movies
```

This will return the `tmdbId` value and overview (that is, the plot summary) for each movie in the graph.

2. **Generate embeddings using OpenAI and Haystack:** Once the plot summaries are retrieved, generate embeddings using Haystack's `OpenAITextEmbedder`:

```
#Parallel embedding generation with ThreadPoolExecutor
def generate_and_store_embeddings(embedder, movies, max_workers=10):
    results_to_store = []
    def process_movie(movie):
        title = movie.get("title", "Unknown Title")
        overview = str(movie.get("overview", "")).strip()
        tmdbId = movie.get("tmdbId")

        if not overview:
            print(f"Skipping {title} — No overview available.")
            return None

        try:
            print(f"Generating embedding for: {title}")
            embedding_result = embedder.run(overview)
            embedding = embedding_result.get("embedding")
            if embedding:
                return (tmdbId, embedding)
            else:
                print(f"No embedding generated for: {title}")
        except Exception as e:
            print(f"Error processing {title}: {e}")
        return None
```

3. **Store embeddings in Neo4j:** With the embeddings generated, the next step is to store them in your Neo4j graph. Each movie node will be updated with a property that stores its embedding:

```
# Store the embeddings back in Neo4j
def store_embedding_in_neo4j(tmdbId, embedding):

    query = """
    MATCH (m:Movie {tmdbId: $tmdbId})
    SET m.embedding = $embedding
    """

    with driver.session() as session:
        session.run(query, tmdbId=tmdbId, embedding=embedding)
    print(f"Stored embedding for TMDB ID: {tmdbId}")
```

This will store the embeddings as a property called embedding in each Movie node in the Neo4j graph.

4. **Verify the embedding storage in Neo4j:** Once the embeddings are stored, you can verify their presence in Neo4j by querying a few nodes to check the embedding property:

```
# Verify embeddings stored in Neo4j
def verify_embeddings():
    query = """
    MATCH (m:Movie)
    WHERE exists(m.embedding)
    RETURN m.title, m.embedding
    LIMIT 10
    """

    with driver.session() as session:
        results = session.run(query)
        for record in results:
            title = record["title"]
            embedding = np.array(record["embedding"])[:5]
            print(f" {title}: {embedding}...")
```

This query will return the titles and embeddings for a few movies, allowing you to verify that the embeddings were successfully stored.

Note

These are just the snippets of the code. The full version is available in the GitHub repository: `https://github.com/PacktPublishing/Building-Neo4j-Powered-Applications-with-LLMs/blob/main/ch5/generate_embeddings.py`.

We have now enriched our graph with these embeddings and thus added similarity search, which will allow us to perform more context-aware and intelligent queries. This step is crucial for enhancing the search experience and enabling advanced retrieval operations based on the meaning of text, rather than simple keyword matching.

Now that our Neo4j graph has been enriched with vector embeddings, the next step is to connect Haystack to Neo4j for advanced vector search. In the upcoming section, we will focus on how to use these embeddings to perform efficient and accurate vector searches within Neo4j, enabling us to retrieve movies or nodes based on their vector similarity.

Connecting Haystack to Neo4j for advanced vector search

With the movie embeddings now stored in Neo4j, we need to configure a vector index on the embedding property, which will allow us to efficiently search for movies based on their vector similarity. By creating a vector index in Neo4j, we enable rapid retrieval of nodes that are close in the high-dimensional embedding space, making it possible to perform sophisticated queries, such as finding movies with similar plot summaries.

Once the vector index has been created, it will be integrated with Haystack to perform vector-based retrieval from Neo4j. This search will be based on vector similarity mechanisms such as cosine similarity.

Creating a vector search index in Neo4j

You will first want to drop any existing vector index on the embedding property (if one exists) and then create a new one for performing vector searches. This is how you can do that using Cypher queries in your Python script:

```python
def create_or_reset_vector_index():
    with driver.session() as session:
        try:
            # Drop the existing vector index if it exists
```

```
        session.run("DROP INDEX overview_embeddings IF EXISTS ")
        print("Old index dropped")
    except:
        print("No index to drop")

    # Create a new vector index on the embedding property
    print("Creating new vector index")
    query_index = """
    CREATE VECTOR INDEX overview_embeddings IF NOT EXISTS
    FOR (m:Movie) ON (m.embedding)
    OPTIONS {indexConfig: {
        `vector.dimensions`: 1536,
        `vector.similarity_function`: 'cosine'}}
    """

    session.run(query_index)
    print("Vector index created successfully")
```

Performing similarity search with Haystack and a Neo4j vector index

After creating a vector index on the Neo4j graph, you can leverage Haystack to perform similarity search queries based on movie plot embeddings. This approach allows you to compare the similarity between a given movie plot or any text query and existing movie overviews, returning the most relevant results based on their embeddings. In this example, we use the OpenAITextEmbedder model from the Haystack library to convert the text query into an embedding and then use it to search the Neo4j graph for movies with similar plots.

This is how you generate the query embedding and perform the similarity search:

```
text_embedder = OpenAITextEmbedder(
    api_key=Secret.from_env_var("OPENAI_API_KEY"),
    model="text-embedding-ada-002"
)

# Step 1: Create embedding for the query
query_embedding = text_embedder.run(query).get("embedding")

if query_embedding is None:
    print("Query embedding not created successfully.")
```

```
        return

    print("Query embedding created successfully.")
```

Running a vector search query with Haystack and Neo4j

Once the vector index has been created and the embeddings are stored in Neo4j, you can perform a vector-based search by passing a query or a sample movie plot. The system will generate an embedding for the query, compare it with the embeddings stored in Neo4j, and return the most related results.

Here is an example of a vector search using Haystack that displays the most similar movie plots without Cypher:

```
# Step 2: Search for similar documents using the query embedding
    similar_documents = document_store.query_by_embedding(
        query_embedding, top_k=3
    )

    if not similar_documents:
        print("No similar documents found.")
        return

    print(f"Found {len(similar_documents)} similar documents.")

    print("\n\n")

    # Step 3: Displaying results
    for doc in similar_documents:
        title = doc.meta.get("title", "N/A")
        overview = doc.meta.get("overview", "N/A")
        score = doc.score
        print(
            f"Title: {title}\nOverview: {overview}\n"
            f"Score: {score:.2f}\n{'-'*40}"
        )
    print("\n\n")
```

Now, we will integrate Neo4j Cypher queries with Haystack to run a vector search, enabling the retrieval of similar movie plots.

Running a vector search query using Cypher and Haystack

To run a vector search, we will use Cypher's graph querying capabilities while performing similarity searches using vector embeddings generated by OpenAITextEmbedder.

Unlike directly querying the vector index using Haystack, this approach combines Cypher's flexibility to return more complex data, such as movie metadata (e.g., cast and genres), along with embeddings, while still maintaining the efficiency of vector similarity search.

Here are the steps involved in this process:

1. **Embed the query using OpenAITextEmbedder**: Convert the user's text query (e.g., a movie plot) into a high-dimensional vector embedding.

2. **Search using Neo4j and Cypher**: Use Cypher to retrieve similar movies by comparing the query embedding with movie plot embeddings stored in Neo4j's vector index.

3. **Return enriched data**: Fetch additional movie information, such as the title, overview, cast, genres, and score (similarity), for each result.

This is how you implement vector search:

1. **Define the Cypher query**: We start by defining a Cypher query that searches the Neo4j vector index (overview_embeddings) to retrieve the top_k most similar movies based on the cosine similarity between the query embedding and movie embeddings:

```
cypher_query = """
    CALL db.index.vector.queryNodes("overview_embeddings", $top_k,
$query_embedding)
    YIELD node AS movie, score
    MATCH (movie:Movie)
    RETURN movie.title AS title, movie.overview AS overview, score
"""
```

2. **Generate the query embedding**: Using OpenAITextEmbedder, we convert the user's input query (e.g., a movie plot) into an embedding. This embedding will be passed to the Neo4j vector index for comparison with the stored movie embeddings:

```
text_embedder = OpenAITextEmbedder(
    api_key= Secret.from_env_var("OPENAI_API_KEY"),
    model="text-embedding-ada-002"
)
```

3. **Run the vector search using the Haystack pipeline**: We set up the Haystack pipeline to manage the Haystack components:

- query_embedder generates embeddings from the user query
- retriever runs the Cypher query on Neo4j using the query embedding and returns the most similar movies:

```
retriever = Neo4jDynamicDocumentRetriever(
    client_config=client_config,
    runtime_parameters=["query_embedding"],
    compose_doc_from_result=True,
    verify_connectivity=True,
)

pipeline = Pipeline()
pipeline.add_component("query_embedder", text_embedder)
pipeline.add_component("retriever", retriever)
pipeline.connect(
    "query_embedder.embedding", "retriever.query_embedding"
)

result = pipeline.run(
    {
        "query_embedder": {"text": query},
        "retriever": {
            "query": cypher_query,
            "parameters": {
                "index": "overview_embeddings", "top_k": 3
            },
        },
    }
)
```

4. **Display the results**: Once the search is complete, we extract the results from the Neo4j graph and display the movie title, overview, and similarity score:

```
# Extracting documents from the retriever results
documents = result["retriever"]["documents"]
```

```
for doc in documents:
    # Extract title and overview from document metadata
    title = doc.meta.get("title", "N/A")
    overview = doc.meta.get("overview", "N/A")

    # Extract score from the document
    score = getattr(doc, "score", None)
    score_display = f"{score:.2f}" if score is not None else "N/A"

    # Print the title, overview, and score (or N/A for missing
score)
    print(
        f"Title: {title}\nOverview: {overview}\n"
        f"Score: {score_display}\n{'-'*40}\n"
    )
```

Using Cypher and Haystack offers several benefits, including the following:

- **Cypher's flexibility**: By combining Cypher with Haystack, we can not only query the embeddings but also retrieve additional graph-based information such as cast, genres, and relationships between entities.

- **Enriched results**: In addition to retrieving the most similar movies, you can easily extend the query to fetch related metadata (e.g., actors, genres, ratings) or refine the search with additional filtering conditions (e.g., release year, genre).

- **Optimized for large graphs**: Neo4j's vector index allows efficient querying of large datasets with complex relationships, while Haystack's embedding models provide an accurate understanding of movie plots.

Let's take a look at an example use case next.

Example use case

Consider finding movies with plots such as *A hero must save the world from destruction*. By using the pipeline we just created, you can retrieve relevant results:

```
Title: The Matrix
Overview: A computer hacker learns from mysterious rebels about the true
nature of his reality and his role in the war against its controllers.
Score: 0.98
----------------------------------------
```

```
Title: Inception
Overview: A thief who steals corporate secrets through dream-sharing
technology is given the inverse task of planting an idea into the mind of
a CEO.
Score: 0.96
-----------------------------------------
Title: The Dark Knight
Overview: Batman raises the stakes in his war on crime, with the help of
Lieutenant Jim Gordon and District Attorney Harvey Dent.
Score: 0.94
-----------------------------------------
```

This pipeline combines the best of both worlds—similarity search through vector embeddings and the rich data capabilities of graph querying with Cypher—allowing powerful, flexible searches over large datasets such as movies.

> **Note**
>
> These are just the snippets of the code. The full version is available in the GitHub repository: https://github.com/PacktPublishing/Building-Neo4j-Powered-Applications-with-LLMs/blob/main/ch5/vector_search.py.

We have now connected Haystack to Neo4j and enabled advanced vector search functionality. With the vector index in place, Neo4j can now efficiently search for similar movie nodes based on their embeddings similarity. Haystack's integration allows you to seamlessly perform these searches using Neo4jDynamicDocumentRetriever. This retriever performs a search for similar items in your graph by leveraging vector embeddings and Neo4j's graph capabilities.

In the next section, we will explore how to build a search-driven chatbot that leverages the power of Haystack and Neo4j to deliver rich, context-aware responses. Using Gradio, we will create an intuitive chatbot interface that can interact with users and perform advanced searches through natural language queries. This will bring together the strengths of LLMs, vector search, and Neo4j to create a user-friendly, AI-powered search experience.

Building a search-driven chatbot with Gradio and Haystack

In this section, we will integrate Gradio to build an interactive chatbot interface powered by Haystack and Neo4j. Gradio makes it easy to create a web-based interface for interacting with your chatbot. The chatbot will allow users to input queries, which will then trigger a vector-based search of movie embeddings stored in Neo4j. The chatbot will return detailed responses, including the movie titles, overviews, and similarity scores, providing an informative and user-friendly experience.

Setting up a Gradio interface

If you have not installed Gradio yet, do so by running the following:

```
pip install gradio
```

> **Note**
>
> The script in this chapter works fine with Gradio v 5.23.1.

Next, we will set up a basic Gradio interface that triggers our search pipeline and displays the results:

```
import gradio as gr

# Define the Gradio chatbot interface
def chatbot(user_input):
    return perform_vector_search_cypher(user_input)

# Create Gradio interface
chat_interface = gr.Interface(
    fn=chatbot,
    inputs=gr.Textbox(
        placeholder="What kind of movie would you like to watch?",
        lines=3,
        label="Your movie preference"
    ),
    outputs=gr.Textbox(
        label="Recommendations",
        lines=12
```

```
    ),
    title="AI Movie Recommendation System",
    description="Ask me about movies! I can recommend movies based on your
preferences.",
    examples=[
        ["I want to watch a sci-fi movie with time travel"],
        ["Recommend me a romantic comedy with a happy ending"],
        ["I'm in the mood for something with superheroes but not too
serious"],
        ["I want a thriller that keeps me on the edge of my seat"],
        ["Show me movies about artificial intelligence taking over the
world"]
    ],
    flagging_mode="never"
```

This interface allows users to input text queries, and the chatbot will use the perform_vector_
search_cypher() function to search for the most relevant movies.

Integrating with Haystack and Neo4j

To power the chatbot, we will connect it to Haystack's embedding generation and Neo4j's vector
search capabilities. We will be using OpenAITextEmbedder to generate the embeddings for both
the queries and the movie plots stored in Neo4j. The movie embeddings are stored in a vector
index inside Neo4j, which we query for the most similar movies.

This is how to integrate our chatbot with the previous Haystack setup:

```
# Conversational chatbot handler using Cypher-powered search and Haystack
def perform_vector_search(query):
    print("MESSAGES RECEIVED:", user_input)

    cypher_query = """
        CALL db.index.vector.queryNodes("overview_embeddings", $top_k,
$query_embedding)
        YIELD node AS movie, score
        MATCH (movie:Movie)
        RETURN movie.title AS title, movie.overview AS overview, score
    """

    # Embedder
```

```
    embedder = OpenAITextEmbedder(
        api_key=Secret.from_env_var("OPENAI_API_KEY"),
        model="text-embedding-ada-002"
    )

    # Retriever
    retriever = Neo4jDynamicDocumentRetriever(
        client_config=client_config,
        runtime_parameters=["query_embedding"],
        compose_doc_from_result=True,
        verify_connectivity=True,
    )

    # Pipeline
    pipeline = Pipeline()
    pipeline.add_component("query_embedder", embedder)
    pipeline.add_component("retriever", retriever)
    pipeline.connect(
        "query_embedder.embedding", "retriever.query_embedding"
    )
```

Connecting Gradio to the full pipeline

Now, connect this Gradio chatbot with the Haystack and Neo4j pipeline you have already set up.
The Gradio interface will call the `perform_vector_search_cypher()` function, which in turn
utilizes `Neo4jDynamicDocumentRetriever` to search for similar movies based on the user's query.

Update the `main()` function to initialize the chatbot:

```
# Main function to orchestrate the entire process
def main():
    # Step 1: Create or reset vector index in Neo4j AuraDB
    create_or_reset_vector_index()

    # Step 2: Launch Gradio chatbot interface
    chat_interface.launch()

if __name__ == "__main__":
    main()
```

Running the chatbot

To run the chatbot, simply execute your Python script. The Gradio interface will be launched in your browser, allowing you to interact with the chatbot in real time:

```
python search_chatbot.py
```

A Gradio interface will launch in your browser, allowing you to interact with the chatbot in real time. You can enter queries such as this:

```
"Tell me about a hero who saves the world."
```

The chatbot will return movie plots that are similar to this query based on the vector search.

> **Note**
>
> These are just the snippets of the code. The full version is available in the GitHub repository: `https://github.com/PacktPublishing/Building-Neo4j-Powered-Applications-with-LLMs/blob/main/ch5/search_chatbot.py`.

As we come to the end of this section, we have built a fully functional search-driven chatbot using Gradio, Haystack, and Neo4j. The chatbot leverages the embeddings stored in Neo4j to perform advanced vector-based searches, returning contextually relevant results to the user in the form of retrieving meaningful movie titles and actors from Neo4j in response to user queries.

However, this is just the beginning. In the next section, we will dive deeper into fine-tuning your Haystack integration and also explore advanced techniques such as optimizing search performance, adjusting retrieval models, and refining the chatbot's responses to create an even more seamless and efficient search-driven experience.

Fine-tuning your Haystack integration

It is now time to explore how to fine-tune this integration for improved performance and user experience. While the current setup provides rich, contextually aware responses, there are several advanced techniques, you can implement to optimize the search process, improve retrieval accuracy, and make the chatbot's interactions more seamless.

In this section, we will focus on adjusting key components of Haystack, including experimenting with different embedding models, optimizing Neo4j queries for faster results, and improving how the chatbot displays its responses. These enhancements will help you scale your chatbot to handle more complex queries, improve response times, and deliver even more relevant search results.

Experimenting with different embedding models

Currently, we are using OpenAI's `text-embedding-ada-002` model to generate embeddings. While this model has served as a reliable and performant choice across a wide range of tasks since its release, it's worth noting that OpenAI has recently introduced new models—such as `text-embedding-3-small` and `text-embedding-3-large`—that offer significant improvements in both performance and cost-efficiency. For example, `text-embedding-3-small` achieves better results in multilingual and English-language tasks, while also being up to five times more cost-effective than `text-embedding-ada-002`. Although we have not switched models in this project for consistency, readers who are implementing similar pipelines may consider using `text-embedding-3-small` to improve efficiency without compromising performance—especially if embedding generation is a frequent or large-scale operation.

However, Haystack supports various other models, and you can experiment with different ones to see which provides the most accurate or relevant results for your specific use case. For instance, you could switch to a more sophisticated OpenAI model with higher dimensions or try another embedding service supported by Haystack.

This is how you can easily switch to a different model:

```
embedder = OpenAITextEmbedder(
    api_key=Secret.from_env_var("OPENAI_API_KEY"),
    model="text-embedding-babbage-001"  # Experiment with different models
)
```

You can also explore other models from OpenAI or even integrate different embedding services to see which performs best for your movie chatbot.

Optimizing Neo4j for faster queries

While Neo4j is already efficient at handling graph-based queries, there are several optimizations you can apply, especially for large datasets. You can index additional properties to improve query performance.

Indexing additional properties

In addition to the vector index on the embedding property, you can index other frequently queried properties, such as `title` or `tmdbId`, to speed up retrieval. This will ensure that whenever you filter or retrieve movies based on these properties, the search is quicker and more efficient:

```
def create_additional_indexes():
    with driver.session() as session:
```

```
        session.run("CREATE INDEX IF NOT EXISTS movie_title_index FOR
(m:Movie) ON (m.title)")
        session.run("CREATE INDEX IF NOT EXISTS movie_tmdbId_index FOR
(m:Movie) ON (m.tmdbId)")
        print("Additional indexes created successfully")
```

By indexing these properties, you can optimize lookups when the search is not solely based on embeddings, such as when filtering by title or retrieving a specific movie.

To continuously improve the chatbot's search experience, you can log user queries and analyze them over time. Let's talk about this in detail.

Logging and analyzing queries

Logging helps you track the most common search patterns. Based on logs of user queries and their analysis, you can adjust the indexing strategy, optimize the retriever, or tweak the embedding model for better accuracy.

This is how to implement a simple logging mechanism:

```
import logging

logging.basicConfig(filename='chatbot_queries.log', level=logging.INFO)

def log_query(query):
    logging.info(f"User query: {query}")
```

Every time a user inputs a query, it will be logged for future analysis. You can then analyze these logs to make informed adjustments to the system, ensuring that it becomes more responsive and accurate over time.

These techniques can help you significantly enhance the performance, accuracy, and user experience of your search-driven chatbot. Whether it is experimenting with different embedding models, optimizing Neo4j queries, or improving how the results are formatted, each adjustment brings you closer to a seamless and powerful user interaction.

These advanced techniques allow your chatbot to scale effectively, handle more complex queries, and return even more relevant and engaging results.

Summary

In this chapter, we successfully built a fully functional search-driven chatbot by integrating Gradio, Haystack, and Neo4j. We began by enriching our Neo4j graph with movie embeddings generated by OpenAI's models, enabling advanced vector-based search functionality. From there, we connected Haystack to Neo4j, allowing us to perform similarity searches on the embeddings stored in the graph. Finally, we wrapped it all up by creating a user-friendly chatbot interface with Gradio, which dynamically retrieves movie details such as titles and actors based on user queries.

In the next chapter we will focus on advanced search capabilities and search optimization with Haystack. We will also discuss query optimization for large graphs.

6

Exploring Advanced Knowledge Graph Capabilities with Neo4j

By building on the foundational knowledge from the previous chapter, where we introduced basic search functionalities, we will now explore more sophisticated techniques for knowledge exploration, graph reasoning, and performance optimization. In this chapter, we will utilize the advanced capabilities of Neo4j, focusing on integrating these capabilities with Haystack to create a more intelligent, AI-powered search system.

By the end of this chapter, you will be able to unlock deeper insights from your knowledge graph, leverage advanced search functionalities, and ensure your AI-powered search system is both performant and sustainable.

In this chapter, we are going to cover the following main topics:

- Exploring advanced Haystack functionalities for knowledge exploration
- Graph reasoning with Haystack
- Scaling your Haystack and Neo4j integration
- Best practices for maintaining and monitoring your AI-powered search system

Technical requirements

Before diving into this chapter, ensure that your development environment is set up with the necessary technologies and tools. Also, your Neo4j instance should be loaded with the data from Ch4 and embeddings from Ch5. Here are the technical requirements for this chapter:

- **Neo4j (v5.x or higher)**: You will need Neo4j installed and running on your local machine or server. You can download it from `https://neo4j.com/download/`.

- **Haystack (v1.x)**: We will be using the Haystack framework for integrating AI-powered search capabilities. Make sure to install Haystack by following the instructions at `https://docs.haystack.deepset.ai/docs/installation`.

- **Python (v3.8 or higher)**: Ensure that you have Python installed. You can download it from `https://www.python.org/downloads/`.

- **OpenAI API key**: To successfully generate embeddings using GPT-based models, you will need an OpenAI API key:

  - Obtain the API Key by signing up for an account at OpenAI (`https://platform.openai.com/signup`) if you do not have one

    Note

    A free-tier API key will not work for most use cases in this project. You will need an active paid OpenAI subscription to access the necessary endpoints and usage limits.

  - Once logged in, navigate to the API Keys section (`https://platform.openai.com/api-keys`) in your OpenAI dashboard and generate a new API key

If you have followed the setup from the previous chapters, you can skip these requirements, as they will have already been installed.

All the code for this chapter is available in the following GitHub repository: `https://github.com/PacktPublishing/Building-Neo4j-Powered-Applications-with-LLMs/tree/main/ch6`.

This folder contains all the necessary scripts, files, and configurations required to implement the Neo4j and Haystack integration with advanced knowledge graph capabilities.

Make sure to clone or download the repository so you can follow along with the code examples throughout this chapter.

Exploring advanced Haystack functionalities for knowledge exploration

In this section, we will dive into more advanced search capabilities using Haystack. You integrated embeddings into your Neo4j graph in *Chapter 5*. It is now time to explore how to enhance search beyond basic similarity matching. The goal here is to move from simple retrieval-based embeddings to a more nuanced, multi-layered exploration of knowledge in your graph.

We will explore techniques such as context-based reasoning and optimizing your search functionalities for specific use cases to deliver highly relevant and intelligent results.

Let us first talk about context-based reasoning.

Context-aware search

Now, we will build on the embedding-based approach in the *Connecting Haystack to Neo4j for advanced vector search* section of the previous chapter, by integrating multi-hop reasoning across the Neo4j graph with Haystack's similarity search capabilities. This approach allows the search engine to traverse multiple relationships between nodes while utilizing advanced AI-based retrieval methods. Instead of simply retrieving nodes or documents based on direct matches, we will leverage Haystack to explore paths between related nodes, adding layers of context and uncovering deeper insights. This combination of graph-based reasoning and similarity understanding enables more intelligent and relevant search results.

In the following code snippet, the query attempts to retrieve all movies directed by the same director who directed the movie *Inception*.

> **Note**
>
> The title is being passed as the value of the `title` variable in the main program.

After retrieving these related movies, Haystack is used to analyze and rank the results based on a similar query, demonstrating a multi-hop search that combines graph-based relationships with advanced similarity retrieval:

```
def fetch_multi_hop_related_movies(title):
    query = """
    MATCH (m:Movie {title: $title})<-[:DIRECTED]-(d:Director)-[:DIRECTED]-
>(related:Movie)
    RETURN related.title AS related_movie, related.overview AS overview
```

```python
    """

    with driver.session() as session:
        result = session.run(query, title=title)
        documents = [
            {
                "content": record["overview"],
                "meta": {"title": record["related_movie"]}
            }
            for record in result
        ]
    return documents


def perform_similarity_search_with_multi_hop(query, movie_title):
    # Fetch multi-hop related movies from Neo4j
    multi_hop_docs = fetch_multi_hop_related_movies(movie_title)

    if not multi_hop_docs:
        print(f"No related movies found for {movie_title}")
        return

    # Write these documents to the document store
    document_store.write_documents(multi_hop_docs)

    # Generate embedding for the search query (e.g., "time travel")
    query_embedding = text_embedder.run(query).get("embedding")

    if query_embedding is None:
        print("Query embedding not created successfully.")
        return

    # Perform vector search only on the multi-hop related movies
    similar_docs = document_store.query_by_embedding(
        query_embedding, top_k=3
    )

    if not similar_docs:
        print("No similar documents found.")
```

```
            return

        for doc in similar_docs:
            title = doc.meta.get("title", "N/A")
            overview = doc.meta.get("overview", "N/A")
            score = doc.score
            print(
                f"Title: {title}\nOverview: {overview}\n"
                f"Score: {score:.2f}\n{'-'*40}"
            )
        print("\n\n")
```

However, since we imported only a fraction of the original dataset, it does not have one-to-many relationships. Where a director has directed multiple movies, the search will likely result in output such as No related movies found for Inception.

You may try updating the script to import the entire dataset (after upgrading from AuraDB Free to AuraDB Professional or AuraDB Business Critical or in the Neo4j Desktop version) and see how multi-hop reasoning is performed.

Dynamic search queries with flexible search filters

One of the strengths of a knowledge graph is the ability to apply filters dynamically during search queries.

In the following code snippet, we will demonstrate how to incorporate filters and constraints into your Haystack queries, allowing users to refine search results based on specific parameters (e.g., time range, categories, or relationships between entities). This flexibility is crucial for building more interactive and contextually rich search systems:

```
def perform_filtered_search(query):
    pipeline = Pipeline()
    pipeline.add_component("query_embedder", text_embedder)
    # pipeline.add_component("retriever", retriever)
    pipeline.add_component(
        "retriever",
        Neo4jEmbeddingRetriever(document_store=document_store)
    )
    pipeline.connect(
        "query_embedder.embedding", "retriever.query_embedding"
```

```python
    )
    result = pipeline.run(
        data={
            "query_embedder": {"text": query},
            "retriever": {
                "top_k": 5,
                "filters": {
                    "field": "release_date", "operator": ">=",
                    "value": "1995-11-17"
                },
            },
        }
    )


    # Extracting documents from the retriever results
    documents = result["retriever"]["documents"]
    for doc in documents:
        # Extract title and overview from document metadata
        title = doc.meta.get("title", "N/A")
        overview = doc.meta.get("overview", "N/A")
        # Extract score from the document (not from meta)
        score = getattr(doc, "score", None)
        # Format score if it exists, else show "N/A"
        score_display = f"{score:.2f}" if score is not None else "N/A"
        # Print the title, overview, and score (or N/A for missing score)
        print(
            f"Title: {title}\nOverview: {overview}\n"
            f"Score: {score_display}\n{'-'*40}\n"
        )
```

This snippet demonstrates how to apply dynamic filters, such as release_date, to refine search results. By incorporating these filters, you can add constraints on specific fields—for instance, showing only documents from a certain date onward or filtering by specific attributes such as category or rating. This capability allows you to narrow down results to what is most relevant to them, effectively enhancing the search functionality. Using this approach, you can easily extend or modify filters to suit different needs, offering a flexible and powerful way to interact with data in the knowledge graph.

Search optimization: tailoring search for specific use cases

Not all search systems are built the same. Whether you are building a recommendation engine or a domain-specific search tool, different optimizations are required. In this section, we will explore how to tailor Haystack's search configuration for your unique use case, ensuring the best performance and relevance for your specific data. We will also cover the importance of tuning models and indexing for high-scale environments.

Have a look at the following code block:

```python
def perform_optimized_search(query, top_k):
        optimized_results = document_store.query_by_embedding(
            query_embedding=text_embedder.run(query).get("embedding"),
            top_k=top_k
        )

    for doc in optimized_results:
        title = doc.meta["title"]
        overview = doc.meta.get("overview", "N/A")
        print(f"Title: {title}\nOverview: {overview}\n{'-'*40}")
```

This code shows how to adjust parameters, such as top_k, to fine-tune the number of top results returned by the search query—not the model itself. The top_k parameter determines how many top results are retrieved based on vector similarity.

> **Note**
>
> These are just the snippets of the code. The full version is available in the GitHub repository: https://github.com/PacktPublishing/Building-Neo4j-Powered-Applications-with-LLMs/blob/main/ch6/beyond_basic_search.py.

With Haystack's similarity retrieval capabilities (such as context-aware search methods to dynamic filtering), you can now create more accurate AI-powered search systems and better search optimization. However, *search* is just the beginning.

In the next section, we will move beyond search to graph-based reasoning by utilizing the reasoning power of Haystack and relationships within the Neo4j knowledge graph.

Graph reasoning with Haystack

In this section, we will explore how to extend Haystack's capabilities beyond basic search by integrating it with the powerful graph reasoning features of Neo4j. While traditional search methods retrieve results based on text similarity, graph reasoning allows you to uncover deeper insights by leveraging the rich relationships between entities in your knowledge graph. By combining the similarity understanding of Haystack with the structured data in Neo4j, you can perform more complex queries that traverse multiple connections, reveal hidden patterns, and unlock contextually enriched insights.

This section will guide you through the process of building these advanced reasoning capabilities, transforming your search system into an intelligent, knowledge-driven tool.

Traversing multiple relationships to reveal hidden insights

While graph traversal helps discover connections between entities, traversing across multiple relationships and different types of relationships can reveal hidden patterns in your knowledge graph. By moving across various paths in Neo4j—whether it is between movies, actors, directors, or genres—you can generate deeper insights that go beyond direct relationships. This multi-step traversal allows you to explore data in ways that basic search cannot, revealing connections that might otherwise be overlooked.

We will now explore how to use multiple relationship types and multi-hop queries to retrieve more complex results. We will then combine them with Haystack's similarity search capabilities for refinement and ranking.

Here is an example; you want to find movies that have both the same actors and director as *Jurassic Park*, allowing you to uncover not just direct collaborations but also indirect connections:

```
def fetch_multi_hop_related_movies(title):
    query = """
    MATCH (m:Movie {title: $title})<-[:ACTED_IN|DIRECTED]-(p)-
        [:ACTED_IN|DIRECTED]->(related:Movie)
    WITH related.title AS related_movie, p.name AS person,
        CASE
            WHEN (p)-[:ACTED_IN]->(m) AND (p)-[:ACTED_IN]->(related) THEN
'Actor'
            WHEN (p)-[:DIRECTED]->(m) AND (p)-[:DIRECTED]->(related) THEN
'Director'
            ELSE 'Unknown Role'
```

```
            END AS role,
            related.overview AS overview, related.embedding AS embedding
        RETURN related_movie, person, role, overview, embedding
        """


    with driver.session() as session:
        result = session.run(query, title=title)
        documents = []
        for record in result:
            documents.append(
                Document(
                    content=record.get("overview", "No overview
available"),  # Store overview in content
                    meta={
                        "title": record.get("related_movie", "Unknown
Movie"),  # Movie title
                        "person": record.get("person", "Unknown
Person"),        # Actor/Director's name
                        "role": record.get("role", "Unknown
Role"),               # Actor or Director
                        "embedding": record.get("embedding", "No embedding
available")  # Retrieve the precomputed embedding
                    },
                )
            )
    return documents
```

Unlocking insights through path queries

Another powerful feature of graph reasoning is the ability to query for specific paths between nodes. For instance, finding out how two movies are connected through a series of collaborations can reveal surprising insights.

Have a look at the following query:

```
MATCH path = (m1:Movie {title: "Inception"})-[:ACTED_IN*3]-(m2:Movie)
RETURN m1.title, m2.title, path
```

This query finds how *Inception* and another movie are connected by shared actors, spanning three levels of relationships.

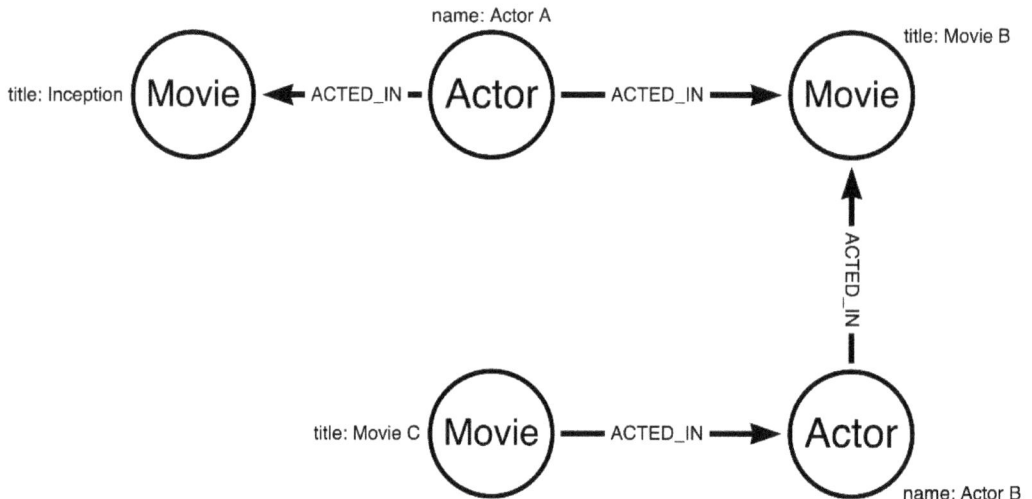

Figure 6.1 — Illustration of a three-hop path traversal in a movie graph

The illustration in this figure shows a three-hop path traversal in a movie graph, starting from the movie *Inception* and reaching *Movie C* through a chain of actor collaborations. This path is the result of a Cypher query that explores connections between movies using the ACTED_IN relationship repeated three times. In the depicted example, *Inception* is connected to *Movie B* via *Actor A*, and *Movie B* is further linked to *Movie C* through *Actor B*. Each hop represents a transition from a movie to an actor, or vice versa, forming a three-hop undirected traversal. This visualization highlights how multi-hop reasoning in Neo4j can uncover deeper, indirect relationships—valuable for applications such as content discovery, recommendation systems, and collaboration network analysis.

Note

These are just the snippets of the code. The full version is available in the GitHub repository at https://github.com/PacktPublishing/Building-Neo4j-Powered-Applications-with-LLMs/blob/main/ch6/graph_reasoning.py.

By combining Neo4j's graph reasoning and Haystack's similarity understanding, we have been able to capture meaningful connections in our data, such as relationships between movies and actors, understanding multi-hop director collaborations, and uncovering complex paths between entities.

Next, we will explore how to optimize these processes to ensure high performance as your graph grows in complexity and scale.

Scaling your Haystack and Neo4j integration

As your system scales, so do the demands on both Haystack and Neo4j. Optimizing performance becomes crucial, especially when dealing with larger datasets, more complex graph structures, and advanced search capabilities.

In this section, we will focus on best practices and techniques to ensure that your Haystack and Neo4j integration can handle increased loads efficiently. We will look into query optimization, caching strategies, indexing improvements, and techniques for scaling out your infrastructure to meet performance needs without sacrificing speed or accuracy in the following subsections.

Optimizing Neo4j queries for large graphs

As your Neo4j graph grows in size and complexity, query performance can degrade, especially when traversing multiple relationships or working with large datasets. Here are a few techniques to improve the performance of your Neo4j queries:

- **Use indexes and constraints**: Ensure that frequently queried properties such as title and name are indexed. Indexing speeds up node lookups and makes traversal more efficient:

  ```
  CREATE INDEX FOR (m:Movie) ON (m.title);
  CREATE INDEX FOR (p:Person) ON (p.name);
  ```

- **Profile and optimize queries**: Use Neo4j's PROFILE or EXPLAIN keywords to analyze the performance of your queries. This helps you understand which parts of the query are slowing down and where you can optimize:

  ```
  PROFILE MATCH (m:Movie {title: "Inception"}) RETURN m;
  ```

- **Limit Results Early**: If you are dealing with large result sets, limit the number of returned nodes early in the query to avoid over-fetching data:

  ```
  MATCH (m:Movie)-[:ACTED_IN]->(a:Actor) RETURN m.title LIMIT 10;
  ```

Caching embeddings and query results

When scaling Haystack and Neo4j, caching can help reduce redundant computations and network calls, significantly boosting performance. By caching both embeddings and query results, you can enhance the efficiency of your search system, especially when handling high volumes of queries. Here is how these caching strategies can make a difference:

- **Cache embeddings:** Store embeddings generated by Haystack in Neo4j or a separate cache layer (such as Redis). By caching embeddings, you avoid recomputing them for frequently asked queries:

```python
# Example of caching embeddings
embedding_cache = {}  # Simple in-memory cache, replace with Redis
for larger setups

def get_cached_embedding(query):
    if query in embedding_cache:
        return embedding_cache[query]
    else:
        embedding = text_embedder.run(query).get("embedding")
        embedding_cache[query] = embedding
        return embedding
```

- **Cache query results:** For frequently executed Neo4j queries, consider caching query results in memory or using a cache such as Redis or Memcached. This reduces the load on Neo4j by returning cached results for popular queries:

```python
# Example using a Redis cache for Neo4j query results
import redis
cache = redis.Redis()

def get_cached_query_result(query):
    cached_result = cache.get(query)
    if cached_result:
        return cached_result
    else:
        # Run the query against Neo4j
        result = run_neo4j_query(query)
        cache.set(query, result)
        return result
```

Efficient use of vector indexing

As your vector-based search capabilities expand, optimizing vector indexes in Neo4j is critical for maintaining performance. You can do this as follows:

- **Configure vector indexes for high performance**: Ensure that your vector index in Neo4j is configured optimally, based on your embedding dimensions and search requirements:

```
CREATE VECTOR INDEX overview_embeddings IF NOT EXISTS
FOR (m:Movie) ON (m.embedding)
OPTIONS {
    indexConfig: {
        `vector.dimensions`: 1536,
        `vector.similarity_function`: 'cosine'
    }
}
```

- **Batch write operations**: When writing many embeddings into Neo4j, use batch operations to reduce the overhead of individual writes:

```
document_store.write_documents(embeddings_list, batch_size=100)
# Batch size optimized for performance
```

Load balancing and horizontal scaling

To handle increased traffic and load on both Haystack and Neo4j, horizontal scaling and load balancing are essential. By implementing load balancing and horizontal scaling, you can ensure your system remains responsive and resilient under heavy traffic. Here is how each approach contributes to scalability:

- **Scale Neo4j**: Leveraging Neo4j AuraDB or a Neo4j cluster enables you to distribute your database workload across multiple instances, enhancing read and write capabilities. This is especially beneficial for applications requiring fast data retrieval and processing at scale.

- **Load balance Haystack**: Distributing incoming search queries across multiple Haystack instances with a load balancer prevents any single instance from being overwhelmed. This approach maintains consistent performance and ensures high availability, even as the demand grows.

- **Use Kubernetes:** Deploying Haystack on Kubernetes with containerized instances allows you to scale effortlessly by adjusting the number of replicas based on traffic. Kubernetes orchestrates these replicas dynamically, ensuring that resources align with demand and that your system can efficiently handle peaks in usage. Here is an example of a Kubernetes deployment configuration to scale Haystack, where multiple replicas are created to handle increased traffic efficiently:

```
apiVersion: apps/v1
kind: Deployment
metadata:
  name: haystack-deployment
spec:
  replicas: 3  # Number of replicas to scale based on traffic
  selector:
    matchLabels:
      app: haystack
  template:
    metadata:
      labels:
        app: haystack
    spec:
      containers:
      - name: haystack
        image: haystack:latest
```

By implementing these optimization strategies, you can ensure that your Haystack and Neo4j integration remains performant and scalable as your data and query complexity grow. Whether through caching, efficient indexing, or scaling infrastructure horizontally, these techniques will help you maintain speed and accuracy under increasing loads. As your system grows, optimizing performance is essential, but maintaining and monitoring the health of your AI-powered search system is just as critical.

Note

Interested in understanding how Neo4j achieves industry-leading speed and scalability, especially as your data and query complexity grow? Explore this blog post: *Achieve Unrivaled Speed and Scalability with Neo4j* (`https://neo4j.com/blog/machine-learning/achieve-unrivaled-speed-and-scalability-neo4j/`).

In the next section, we will explore best practices for keeping your system running smoothly over time, focusing on how to monitor performance, set up alerts, and ensure long-term stability and reliability beyond the code.

Best practices for maintaining and monitoring your AI-powered search system

Building a powerful AI-driven search system is only the beginning. To ensure its long-term success, you need to go beyond the initial setup and focus on maintaining and monitoring your system over time. Regular performance checks, proactive monitoring, and a solid logging strategy are essential for identifying bottlenecks, preventing system failures, and optimizing resource usage.

We now talk about the best practices for keeping your Haystack and Neo4j integration running smoothly, including monitoring key performance metrics, setting up alerts for critical issues, and implementing a sustainable maintenance routine to ensure that your search system remains reliable and efficient, even as it scales.

Performance optimization is not a one-time activity. We need to continuously monitor and collect metrics to identify bottlenecks and areas for improvement. Let us see how we can achieve this.

Monitoring Neo4j and Haystack performance

Regularly tracking query response times, database performance, and overall system health is essential for maintaining an AI-powered search system. Set up monitoring for Neo4j and Haystack to track key metrics, identify bottlenecks, and ensure smooth operation:

- **Neo4j monitoring**: Leverage Neo4j's built-in metrics and integration with tools such as Prometheus and Grafana to visualize query performance and monitor system load.
- **Haystack monitoring**: Use Grafana and Prometheus to monitor query throughput, latency, and response times in Haystack.

  Here is an example of monitoring the query response time:

  ```
  # Example: Monitor response time of a query in Haystack
  import time

  start_time = time.time()
  result = retriever.retrieve(query)
  ```

```
end_time = time.time()

response_time = end_time - start_time
print(f"Query response time: {response_time} seconds")
```

Setting up alerts for critical issues

Setting up automated alerts ensures you are notified when performance or system failures occur. By using Prometheus with Alertmanager or Grafana, you can set threshold-based alerts for slow queries, failed searches, or increased load.

For instance, you can create alerts that trigger when Neo4j query response times exceed a certain threshold or when Haystack's search latency increases beyond acceptable limits.

You can read more on Neo4j monitoring and alerts here: `https://neo4j.com/docs/operations-manual/current/monitoring/`.

Implementing a logging strategy

Detailed logs help troubleshoot issues and understand the root cause of failures or performance degradation. Implement logging in both Haystack and Neo4j, including logging query execution times, failures, and system resource usage.

Read more on Neo4j logging at `https://neo4j.com/docs/operations-manual/current/logging/`. For more on Haystack logging and debugging, visit `https://docs.haystack.deepset.ai/docs/debug`.

Establishing a regular maintenance routine

Regularly scheduled maintenance ensures your AI-powered search system continues to perform optimally over time. This includes the following:

- **Neo4j**: Perform regular index rebuilding, data consistency checks, and disk space monitoring. Read more on Neo4j maintenance here: `https://neo4j.com/docs/operations-manual/current/backup-restore/maintenance/`.
- **Haystack**: Monitor embedding quality, update models as needed, and manage document store growth to avoid performance degradation. Read more on Haystack optimization and maintenance here: `https://docs.haystack.deepset.ai/docs/pipelineoptimization`.

By implementing these best practices, you ensure that your AI-powered search system remains robust, reliable, and adaptable to changing demands. Proactive monitoring, effective logging, and regular maintenance allow you to identify issues before they impact performance and ensure smooth operation as your data and query loads grow. These strategies not only prevent downtime and inefficiencies but also allow your system to evolve and scale seamlessly. As you continue to build and refine your AI-driven search, ongoing attention to monitoring and maintenance will be the key to sustaining its long-term success.

Summary

In this chapter, we explored how to optimize the performance of your Haystack and Neo4j integration and established best practices for maintaining and monitoring your AI-powered search system. You learned about key strategies for caching, efficient indexing, query optimization, and scaling your infrastructure to handle growing data and query loads. We also emphasized the importance of monitoring system performance, setting up alerts, and implementing a solid logging strategy to keep your system running smoothly over time. This knowledge is a crucial first step to creating a fast, reliable, and scalable search system as your data and complexity increase.

As we wrap up the Haystack portion of this journey, the next part of this book will shift focus to integrating Spring AI frameworks and LangChain4j with Neo4j. In the following chapters, you will explore how these technologies can come together to build sophisticated recommendation systems, further enhancing the capabilities of your AI-powered applications.

Part 3

Building an Intelligent Recommendation System with Neo4j, Spring AI, and LangChain4j

In this third part of the book, we'll look at building a recommendation application using the Spring AI and LangChain4j frameworks. We will look at leveraging LLMs and GraphRAG to enhance the graph to lay the foundation for building better recommendation applications. We will further enhance the graph by leveraging Graph Data Science algorithms such as KNN similarity and community detection to augment the graph to deliver better recommendations. We will also take a look at how using these algorithms is the better approach over basic vector search. This part of the book includes the following chapters:

This part of the book includes the following chapters:

- *Chapter 7, Introducing the Neo4j Spring AI and LangChain4j Frameworks for Building Recommendation Systems*
- *Chapter 8, Constructing a Recommendation Graph with the H&M Personalization Dataset*
- *Chapter 9, Integrating LangChain4j and Spring AI with Neo4j*
- *Chapter 10, Creating an Intelligent Recommendation System*

Stay tuned

To keep up with the latest developments in the fields of Generative AI and LLMs, subscribe to our weekly newsletter, AI_Distilled, at `https://packt.link/Q5UyU`.

7

Introducing the Neo4j Spring AI and LangChain4j Frameworks for Building Recommendation Systems

We looked at Haystack and Python-based intelligent applications in the previous chapters. While Python is the favored language framework of data scientists, there are scenarios where we might need other frameworks to build solutions. One other popular language framework that comes to mind is Java. Java is faster than Python, provides integration to various data sources in a seamless manner, and is the most used language to build web-based applications along with the Spring Framework. For this purpose, we will look at how we can build intelligent applications based on **Large Language Models (LLMs)** and Neo4j in the next few chapters.

Also, we have been concentrating on leveraging LLM capabilities to build intelligent search applications. This is just one aspect, though; LLMs can also be great tools in building and using knowledge graphs to power better recommendation systems. In this chapter, we will understand recommendation systems and why personalized recommendations are important. We will briefly touch upon the traditional rule-based approach for recommendation systems and also talk about some of their shortcomings. We will then introduce you to the LangChain4j and Spring AI frameworks and how they can support you in building intelligent recommendation systems.

In this chapter, we are going to cover the following main topics:

- Understanding extended Neo4j capabilities to build intelligent applications
- Personalizing recommendations
- Introducing Neo4j's LangChain4j and Spring AI frameworks
- Overview of an intelligent recommendation system in Neo4j GenAI ecosystem

Technical requirements

While this chapter focuses on personalized recommendations and introduces the LangChain4j and Spring AI frameworks, there are no specific technical requirements for this section.

However, if you are new to Spring applications, you can follow the documentation available at `https://spring.io/guides/gs/spring-boot` to get yourself warmed up with Spring Boot. We will be using a Spring Boot application with a built-in web framework in the upcoming chapters. You also need Java installed on your system. Java 17 or 19 is recommended for the coming chapters.

Understanding extended Neo4j capabilities to build intelligent applications

In earlier chapters, we looked at using LLMs and Neo4j to build good search applications. While knowledge graphs provide great context for building intelligent search applications, they can also be a great foundation for building personalized recommendation applications.

To extract intelligence from the data and build better, more intelligent applications that go beyond basic flow-based analytics, we would need more than graph database capabilities. This is where Neo4j's capabilities as a database can help with building better applications.

Some of these capabilities are listed here:

- **Scalability**: Neo4j enables us to build large graphs, using sharding to build federated graphs to handle large datasets. It can scale to meet data growth and business needs while minimizing costs. You can read more about these capabilities at `https://neo4j.com/docs/operations-manual/current/database-administration/composite-databases/concepts/`.
- **Security**: Neo4j, by leveraging roles, enables data security. There are roles that enable security at a high level, such as who can read or write to the database. It also provides more granular security controls defining what data can be read based on the roles. Using this approach, one user might be looking at one part of the graph and another user

looking at a different part of the graph based on the roles they are assigned. You can read more about these capabilities at `https://neo4j.com/docs/operations-manual/current/authentication-authorization/`.

- **Flexible deployment architecture**: Neo4j's clustering architecture provides multiple options that can be deployed to scale horizontally to handle a higher volume of reads and localize reads to different servers, to minimize the cost of ownership even as data grows. You can read more about Neo4j's clustering capabilities at `https://neo4j.com/docs/operations-manual/current/clustering/introduction/`.

- **Graph Data Science algorithms**: Neo4j Graph Data Science algorithms unlock hidden insights from the connected data. These algorithms range from pathfinding, node similarity, centrality, and community detection to machine learning aspects such as link prediction and node classifications. You can read more about Neo4j Graph Data Science's capabilities at `https://neo4j.com/docs/graph-data-science/current/`.

- **Vector indexes**: Neo4j provides vector index capabilities, to index embeddings to be able to look up similar nodes and then leverage graph traversal to provide more accurate results. You can read more about its vector index capabilities at `https://neo4j.com/docs/cypher-manual/current/indexes/semantic-indexes/vector-indexes/`.

Neo4j as a graph database makes it easy to work with connected data easily, and the preceding capabilities go beyond connected data to help us build intelligent applications that are scalable and complex.

> **Note**
>
> If you want to read more about how search and recommendation systems differ, these articles may be helpful:
>
> What's the difference between search and recommendation: `https://medium.com/understanding-recommenders/whats-the-difference-between-search-and-recommendation-c32937506a29`
>
> How are search and recommendations the same, and how are they different?: `https://gist.github.com/veekaybee/2cf54ebcbd72aa73bfe482f20866c6ef`

We will utilize Neo4j capabilities to build an intelligent recommendation system in upcoming chapters. Before that, let's discuss what a recommendation engine is and how personalization can help create intelligent recommendation systems.

Personalizing recommendations

A **recommendation system** is an application that recommends products to users based on their buying and search preferences. This aspect is not limited to just product placement but is also used in medical diagnostics and treatment. For example, recommendations may help with understanding how patients respond to medication and what kind of treatment sequence is more effective.

As the data grows and the number of products available increases, the ability to understand user behavior and provide the most personal recommendations becomes more and more important.

These strategies can be used to build personalized experiences. Some of these strategies are mentioned here:

- **Building user profiles**: We can build custom user profiles by understanding user behavior. Behavior patterns can include the order of transactions made by users for a given time period or outcomes of events that occurred, along with other attributes such as age, race, and gender. We can use these aspects to segment users into various groups and create profiles for each of the groups.

- **Provide contextual support**: Once the user profiles are available, we should be able to provide more meaningful and contextual support to users. This can be a recommendation to buy a product based on the last product bought or the next medication based on the current treatment level and current symptoms being experienced. These recommendations not only consider the last event that occurred but can also take other user attributes into account to provide more direct support.

- **Provide self-service experiences**: Along with contextual support as needed, it is also possible to use the recommendations to provide more satisfactory self-service experiences. Users should be able to change the characteristics to be considered for recommendations, thus providing a system that adjusts how it responds to events for the user.

- **Incorporating feedback**: Using all the preceding strategies, it is possible to incorporate both positive and negative feedback so that the system can adapt to individual users' requirements as needed.

Personalized recommendations offer numerous advantages, including suggesting the next products based on current views, providing incentives based on user behavior, enhancing brand reputation, optimizing treatment regimens for patients, marketing new drugs more efficiently, improving supply chain processes, and determining optimal delivery routes. These tailored suggestions enable businesses to deliver more relevant and impactful experiences to their customers.

These are some of the ways the recommendations can be used. Some other interesting use cases of recommendation systems could be to boost sales (https://neo4j.com/developer-blog/graphs-acceleration-frameworks-recommendations/), manage the supply chain (https://neo4j.com/developer-blog/supply-chain-neo4j-gds-bloom/), and carry out patient journey mapping (https://www.graphable.ai/blog/patient-journey-mapping/).

Let's take a look at the traditional rule-based approach for recommendation systems and why this approach is not sufficient for building intelligent and personalized recommendation systems.

Limitations of traditional approaches

Traditionally, recommendation systems used **rule-based systems**. A rule-based system is one where the decision is made by executing a set of rules based on the data input provided. The logic can be simple, or it can be very complex based on the need. For example, any credit card transaction that is more than $1,000 in certain regions will be denied automatically. A slightly more complex rule can be to deny a transaction when a small transaction is successfully carried out and then a bigger transaction is attempted.

Rule-based systems usually apply two kinds of rules:

- **Static rules**: Here, rules are configured manually. Once these rules are in place, they work very efficiently and the system can execute them faithfully. They are good when you require fast responses with the least number of resources consumed. They can be as simple as case statements returning a value based on input.

- **Dynamic rules**: These are sophisticated rule engines. In these scenarios, the next decision made can be dependent on in which state the current decision tree lies and the next data input.

Some of the benefits of using rule-based systems are as follows:

- **Consistency**: They are consistent in their behavior and guarantee that for a given input or set of inputs, the output is the same.

- **Scaling**: These systems can scale very well to handle data and complexity with ease.

- **Efficient**: These are very efficient in terms of resources consumed and the cost of the system.

- **Maintenance and management**: These are easier to build and maintain. This in turn makes it easy to manage these systems.

Typically, use cases of these systems are fraud prevention and cybersecurity. While these systems are simple and easy to build, there are limitations to them. Some are listed here:

- **Complexity**: They can grow to be pretty complex as the business needs increase, if not handled correctly. With the added complexity, most of the benefits will slowly start to vanish.

- **Rigidness**: The system is too rigid to adapt to new types of data and scenarios. Even when we identify new scenarios, coding and configuring them might take too long for them to be effective.

- **Business needs adaptability**: It might take too much effort to adapt these systems to the growing business needs and requirements.

As we can see, as business needs evolve, we are stuck with limited options when relying on rule-based systems. It becomes more important to build an intelligent application that can adapt to the new data points as well as data complexity to provide better context to give good recommendations. These systems should be more adaptable to changing environments, data, as well as new requirements in a quick fashion.

This is where Neo4j as a graph database and the surrounding technology stack help us to build intelligent recommendation systems. Let's find out how.

Introducing Neo4j's LangChain4j and Spring AI frameworks

To build intelligent applications, we can utilize multiple frameworks available around Neo4j. For the specific use case of intelligent recommendation systems, we will take a look at the Java frameworks Spring AI and LangChain4j.

LangChain4j

LangChain4j (`https://github.com/langchain4j/`) is a Java framework inspired by the popular Python LangChain framework to build LLM applications in Java. Its goal is to simplify integrating LLM APIs into Java applications. Toward that, it builds an API that is a blend of LangChain, Haystack, LlamaIndex, and other concepts and adds its own flavor to build complex applications. This is how it achieves these objectives.

The following list helps us understand how it achieves these objectives:

- **Unified APIs**: All the LLM providers, such as Open AI and Google Gemini, have their own proprietary APIs to build applications. Vector stores such as Neo4j, Pinecone, and Milvus also provide their own APIs to store and retrieve the embeddings. LangChain4j provides a unified API to hide the complexity of all these APIs to make development easier.

- **Comprehensive toolbox**: The LangChain community has identified various patterns, abstractions, and techniques to build numerous LLM applications and examples in ready-to-use packages to jumpstart development. Its toolbox includes examples of low-level prompt templates, chat memory management, AI services, and RAG. Most of these examples are ready for easy integration into other applications.

LangChain4j provides the following features that help us in building intelligent applications:

- **More than 15 LLM providers**: LangChain4j provides a simple API to integrate the LLM providers into an application and use them easily. You can read more about the language model integrations at `https://docs.langchain4j.dev/category/language-models`.

- **More than 20 vector stores**: The vector store API allows storing the embeddings generated and querying them. Here is the vector store API for you to look at: `https://docs.langchain4j.dev/tutorials/embedding-stores`.

- **AI services**: LangChain4j has low-level APIs, such as those that directly interact with LLM providers and vector stores. But that might be too low level for some scenarios. To make things simple, it also provides more high-level API flows to integrate LLMs, vector stores, embedding models, and RAG as a pipeline. These are called AI services (`https://docs.langchain4j.dev/tutorials/ai-services`). We will use AI Services in the upcoming chapters.

- **RAG**: LangChain4j provides support for the RAG indexing, as well as RAG retrieval, stage. It has a simple **Easy RAG** feature that makes it easy to get started with RAG features. You can read more about the RAG capabilities provided by LangChain4j at `https://docs.langchain4j.dev/tutorials/rag`.

LangChain4j has good integration with the Spring Framework. But the Apache Spring framework has also built a separate AI integration framework similar to LangChain4j, called Spring AI. We will take a look at this framework next.

Spring AI

Spring AI is inspired by LangChain4j and LlamaIndex. While LangChain4j supports simple Java applications as well as Spring applications, Spring AI is optimized to work with Spring Framework. This means those who are well versed in the Spring Framework can develop LLM applications faster and easier.

Since the Spring Framework provides multiple modules to connect to various databases and coding patterns that are well defined and used by a lot of developers, this new feature makes it very easy for developers to adopt and build AI applications quickly. Some of the Spring AI capabilities that can help us in building intelligent applications are as follows:

- **LLM prompt templates**: LLM prompt templates provide a simple API to integrate LLMs easily.

- **Embedding models**: Spring AI can integrate various embedding model engines using configuration to generate vector embeddings.

- **Vector stores**: Spring AI also provides simple APIs to store and query vector stores. It provides easy, configuration-based integration to connect to various vector stores, such as Neo4j, Pinecone, and Milvus.

- **RAG**: You can also chain LLM prompt templates, embedding models, and vector stores to build effective RAG applications with Spring AI.

Both the LangChain4j and Spring AI frameworks provide core APIs to integrate with LLM chat models, prompt templates, embedding models, and vector stores. Along with providing the low-level APIs to talk with those systems, they also make it easy to build more sophisticated applications using higher-level APIs, such as RAG framework APIs.

Why Java-based frameworks?

There are a lot of frameworks in Python that can work with Neo4j. But there are a lot of applications that use Java frameworks. These frameworks provide a means to connect to various data sources, leveraging various packages available to build complex applications.

These frameworks support various vector stores, such as Neo4j, and multiple LLM providers, such as Amazon Bedrock, Azure OpenAI, Google Gemini, Hugging Face, and OpenAI. They offer high-level AI capabilities, from simple tasks such as formatting inputs and parsing outputs for LLMs to more complex features such as chat memory, tools, and RAG.

By combining these capabilities with Neo4j, these frameworks make it easier to build more complex applications, such as generating embeddings for graph features (paths, etc.) using LLMs, which can form the basis for enhancing the graph using similarity and community detection algorithms to group nodes into segments. This segmentation can provide the basis for next-level recommendations and other aspects. You can read more about Neo4j's GenAI ecosystem at `https://neo4j.com/labs/genai-ecosystem/`.

Overview of an intelligent recommendation system in Neo4j GenAI ecosystem

Let us look at how recommendation systems that are built on LLM/RAG principles would function in the Neo4j GenAI ecosystem (*Figure 7.1*).

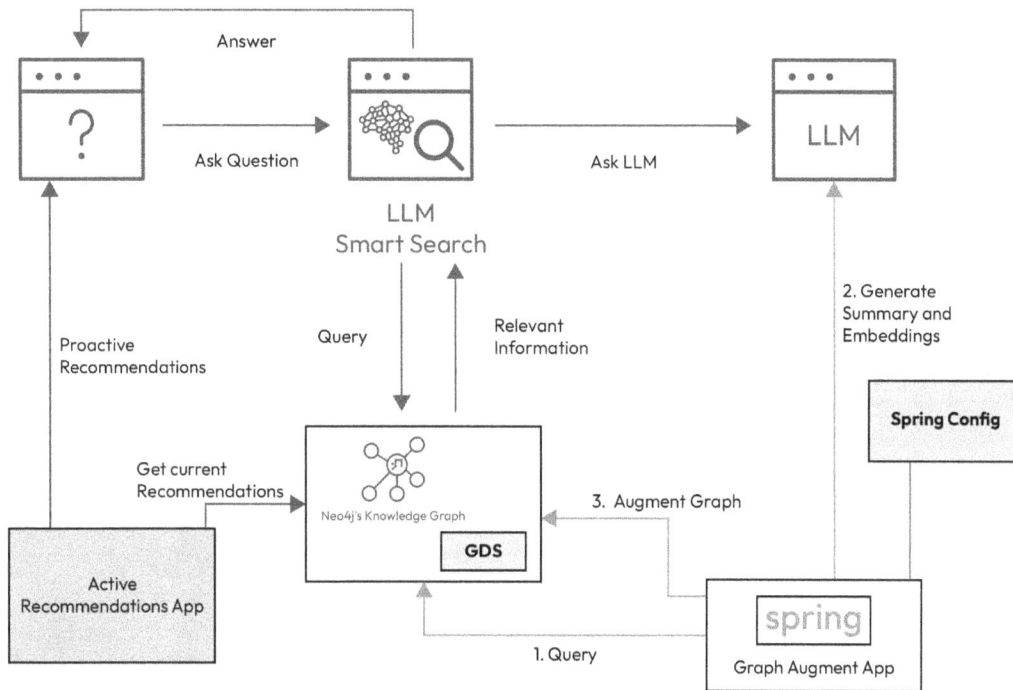

Figure 7.1 — Neo4j RAG recommendation architecture

We can leverage the features of these frameworks to build RAG applications backed by knowledge graphs. In this architecture, we are leveraging the Spring AI app to augment the graph to be able to provide more personal recommendations.

Also, for RAG, this architecture can leverage the vector indices as well as graph traversal to augment the response, to get the best of both worlds to get more accurate responses. This concept is called **Graph RAG**. Knowledge graphs can bring more accurate responses, rich context, and explainability for AI model interactions. Neo4j can integrate into LangChain4j and Spring AI to act as a vector store as well as a graph database to augment the LLM responses.

Summary

In this chapter, we looked at the capabilities of Neo4j that help us build intelligent applications, why the personalization that these applications can provide is useful, and how they are different from the existing rule-based applications. We looked at what Spring AI and LangChain4j are and their capabilities to build intelligent applications.

In the next chapter, *Chapter 8*, we will build a graph data model to support intelligent and personalized recommendations with the H&M dataset and see how this data can be loaded into a graph data model with the aim of providing recommendations. *Chapter 9* of this book will enable you to integrate this intelligent recommendation system with the Spring AI and LangChain4j frameworks.

8

Constructing a Recommendation Graph with H&M Personalization Dataset

While Neo4j is great for building knowledge graphs, it would be prudent to look at how we model the data. A good data persistence model can make data retrieval optimal and handle large loads better. In this chapter, we will take a step back to look at what constitutes a **knowledge graph** and how a different look at data modeling with a Neo4j data persistence approach can help build more powerful knowledge graphs. You might need to revisit the approaches defined in *Chapter 3*, which will enable you to build a knowledge graph with Personalized Fashion Recommendations (H&M personalization) data.

We will cover these topics in this chapter as we tackle data modeling evolution:

- Modeling a recommendation graph with the H&M Personalization dataset
- Optimizing for recommendations: Best practices in graph modeling

Technical requirements

You will need to be familiar with SQL and Cypher. We will be using SQLite and Neo4j to understand the various aspects of data modeling. We will use the following tools in this chapter:

- Neo4j Desktop (`https://neo4j.com/docs/desktop-manual/current/`) or Neo4j Aura (`https://neo4j.com/docs/aura/`)

- The H&M dataset to create the recommendation system: This dataset is available at `https://www.kaggle.com/c/h-and-m-personalized-fashion-recommendations/overview` (Carlos García Ling, ElizabethHMGroup, FridaRim, inversion, Jaime Ferrando, Maggie, neuraloverflow, and xlsrln. H&M Personalized Fashion Recommendations. 2022. Kaggle)

   Remember from *Chapter 3* that a good graph data model makes the *retrieval* part of RAG flow more effective. It makes retrieving relevant data faster and easier. You may revisit *Chapter 3* for a quick recap of graph data modeling. In this chapter, we model the data with time as a dimension. The chain of transactions with the time as a dimension makes data retrieval very efficient and performant.

Modeling the recommendation graph with the H&M personalization dataset

In this section, we will create a graph data model with the real-life large-scale H&M Personalization dataset. This graph data model will enable us to power up the recommendation engine that we will create in upcoming chapters.

In 2022, H&M posted customer transaction data along with other metadata related to customers, products, and so on, as part of a competition to build a recommendation engine. This dataset contains data from previous transactions, as well as from customer and product metadata. The available metadata spans simple data, such as garment type and customer age, to text data from product descriptions, to image data from garment images.

We will discuss the dataset's characteristics and load the data into a knowledge graph as we go, step by step.

We will take a look at the data available in this dataset:

- `images/`: This contains the images for a given `article_id`. Not all articles in the dataset may have images associated with them. We will not be using this data to build the graph. Storing the images in a graph would not only be inefficient, but it is not necessary for the graph flow we are building.

- `articles.csv`: This file contains the metadata for each article available for purchase. Each row represents one unique article with metadata such as the product family, color, style, section the article belongs to, and department.

- `customers.csv`: This file contains the metadata for each customer in the dataset, including customer ID, age, fashion news frequency, active flag, H&M club member status, and postal code.

- `transactions_train.csv`: This file contains the transactions made by customers. If a customer made multiple purchases of the same item, that data might come as multiple rows – one row for each item purchased, with the transaction date, article ID, customer ID, price, and sales channel.

We will take a look at the **graph data model** of this data in the next section and load the data for that model. When we build the knowledge graph for the H&M personalization dataset recommendations, we will have a list of transactions made by customers, and representing these as a chain of transactions with time as a dimension might work very well for us. By adding our understanding of the data into the graph data model can make our recommendations more valuable. For instance, the transactions are a sequence of events; hence modeling them as a sequence makes more sense. Unlike traditional databases, Neo4j makes it possible to store these transactions as a graph that is connected sequentially using relationships.

We can say, we are persisting our knowledge of data into the graph, thus creating a knowledge graph.

Building your recommendation graph

To build the recommendation model graph, we will take a look at the data within each of the files in the dataset and how they contribute to the graph. We will apply the process we discussed previously, in *Chapter 3,* to build the graph. Before loading the data, we need to use Neo4j Desktop and perform these steps:

1. Create a local database. You can follow the instructions at `https://neo4j.com/docs/desktop-manual/current/operations/create-dbms/` to perform this operation.

2. Copy the CSV files from the H&M recommendation dataset to the `import` directory of this database. If you are not sure how to do this, please visit `https://community.neo4j.com/t/where-is-neo4j-home/6488/5` for reference.

Now let us load the data into the graph database.

Loading the customer data

The customer data contains these elements: customer ID, age, fashion news frequency, active flag, H&M club member status, and postal code.

The customer ID is the unique ID of the customer. To make sure we have unique nodes representing the customer, we need to have a UNIQUE constraint. Also, we will make the postal code a node, as we might want to segregate customers by postal code easily.

Before loading this data, we need to create these unique constraints, by connecting to the Neo4j database we created:

```
CREATE CONSTRAINT customer_id_idx FOR (n:Customer) REQUIRE n.id IS UNIQUE
;
CREATE CONSTRAINT postal_code_idx FOR (n:PostalCode) REQUIRE n.code IS
UNIQUE ;
```

Once unique constraints are created, we can use this Cypher to load the data into the database:

Note

For the LOAD CSV queries, we need to prefix them with auto to be able to run them in Neo4j Browser.

```
LOAD CSV WITH HEADERS FROM "file:///customers.csv" as row
WITH row
CALL {
    WITH row
    MERGE (c:Customer {id:row.customer_id})
    SET c.age = row.age
    FOREACH( ignoreME in CASE WHEN row.fashion_news_frequency =
'Regularly' THEN [1] ELSE [] END |
        SET c:FN_REGULAR
    )
    FOREACH( ignoreME in CASE WHEN row.club_member_status = 'ACTIVE'  THEN
[1] ELSE [] END |
        SET c:CLUB_ACTIVE
    )
    FOREACH( ignoreME in CASE WHEN row.club_member_status = 'PRE-
CREATE'  THEN [1] ELSE [] END |
```

```
        SET c:CLUB_PRE_CREATE
    )
    FOREACH( ignoreME in CASE WHEN row.Active <> 'ACTIVE'  THEN [1] ELSE
[] END |
        SET c:INACTIVE
    )
    MERGE(p:PostalCode {code:row.postal_code})
    MERGE(c)-[:LIVES_IN]->(p)
} IN TRANSACTIONS OF 1000 ROWS
```

This script loads the customer data into the database, using 1,000 rows as one batch to commit. In this script, we can notice a couple of things:

- We have only one property, named age, on the Customer node, apart from the unique ID, customer_id
- We map the other properties of the customer data as labels on the Customer node

This approach follows the *consumption-based approach* to data modeling we discussed previously. Say we want to understand how the customers who are regular fashion news subscribers behave – this gives us an easy way to retrieve this information. Neo4j optimizes this type of retrieval using a label-based approach. We could make this customer behavior (fashion news subscription) a property and create an index to retrieve this data, but that would require more storage, as well as having an index lookup cost. Say we want to use the customers who are active club members and are regular fashion news consumers – this label-based approach gives us an edge to retrieve this information more effectively when compared to storing it as a property. Also, when we display this information as a graph, users can easily see the information in the labels, rather than looking for a property. It feels more natural to consume the data in this manner and queries also look more natural.

Next, we will load the article data.

Loading the article data

The article data contains other categories that describe the article, apart from the unique article ID and description. We will make other attributes that describe articles nodes themselves.

For this purpose, we need to create these unique constraints:

```
CREATE CONSTRAINT product_code_idx FOR (n:Product) REQUIRE n.code IS
UNIQUE ;
CREATE CONSTRAINT article_id_idx FOR (n:Article) REQUIRE n.id IS UNIQUE ;
CREATE CONSTRAINT product_type_id_idx FOR (n:ProductType) REQUIRE n.id IS
UNIQUE ;
CREATE CONSTRAINT colour_group_idx FOR (n:ColorGroup) REQUIRE n.id IS
UNIQUE ;
CREATE CONSTRAINT product_group_name_idx FOR (n:ProductGroup) REQUIRE
n.name IS UNIQUE ;
CREATE CONSTRAINT graphical_appearance_id_idx FOR (n:GraphicalAppearance)
REQUIRE n.id IS UNIQUE ;
CREATE CONSTRAINT perceived_colour_id_idx FOR (n:PerceivedColor) REQUIRE
n.id IS UNIQUE ;
CREATE CONSTRAINT department_id_idx FOR (n:Department) REQUIRE n.id IS
UNIQUE ;
CREATE CONSTRAINT section_id_idx FOR (n:Section) REQUIRE n.id IS UNIQUE ;
CREATE CONSTRAINT garment_group_id_idx FOR (n:GarmentGroup) REQUIRE n.id
IS UNIQUE ;
CREATE CONSTRAINT article_index_id_idx FOR (n:Index) REQUIRE n.id IS
UNIQUE ;
CREATE CONSTRAINT article_index_group_id_idx FOR (n:IndexGroup) REQUIRE
n.id IS UNIQUE ;
```

We can see that we have converted most of the attributes of the articles into nodes. This sort of normalizes the data represented in the graph. This Cypher will load the data into the graph:

```
LOAD CSV WITH HEADERS FROM "file:///articles.csv" as row
WITH row
CALL {
    WITH row
```

For each row, create an article, product, and product group and associate them:

```
MERGE(a:Article {id:row.article_id})
SET a.desc = row.detail_desc
MERGE(p:Product {code:row.product_code})
SET p.name = row.prod_name
MERGE(a)-[:OF_PRODUCT]->(p)
MERGE(pt:ProductType {id:row.product_type_no})
```

```
SET pt.name = row.product_type_name
MERGE(p)-[:HAS_TYPE]->(pt)
WITH row, a, p
MERGE(pg:ProductGroup {name:row.product_group_name})
MERGE(p)-[:HAS_GROUP]->(pg)
```

Now add the graphical appearance and colors associated with the article:

```
WITH row, a
MERGE(g:GraphicalAppearance {id:row.graphical_appearance_no})
SET g.name = row.graphical_appearance_name
MERGE (a)-[:HAS_GRAPHICAL_APPEARANCE]->(g)
WITH row, a
MERGE (c:ColorGroup {id: row.colour_group_code})
SET c.name = row.colour_group_name
MERGE (a)-[:HAS_COLOR]->(c)
WITH row, a
MERGE (pc:PerceivedColor {id: row.perceived_colour_value_id})
SET pc.name = row.perceived_colour_value_name
MERGE (a)-[:HAS_PERCEIVED_COLOR]->(pc)
MERGE (pcm:PerceivedColor {id: row.perceived_colour_master_id})
SET pcm.name = row.perceived_colour_master_name
MERGE (pc)-[:HAS_MASTER]->(pcm)
```

Now let us connect the department associated with it:

```
WITH row, a
MERGE (d:Department {id:row.department_no})
SET d.name = row.department_name
MERGE (a)-[:HAS_DEPARTMENT]->(d)
WITH row, a
MERGE (i:Index {id: row.index_code})
SET i.name = row.index_name
MERGE (a)-[:HAS_INDEX]->(i)
MERGE (ig:IndexGroup {id: row.index_group_no})
SET ig.name = row.index_group_name
MERGE (i)-[:HAS_GROUP]->(ig)
```

Finally, let us connect the section the article belongs to and the garment group:

```
    WITH row, a
    MERGE (s:Section {id: row.section_no})
    SET s.name = row.section_name
    MERGE (a)-[:HAS_SECTION]->(s)
    WITH row, a
    MERGE (gg:GarmentGroup {id: row.garment_group_no})
    SET gg.name = row.garment_group_name
    MERGE (a)-[:HAS_GARMENT_GROUP]->(gg)
} IN TRANSACTIONS OF 1000 ROWS
```

From the Cypher query, we can see that, in the graph, we are persisting the normalized data, without duplicating values for various aspects that describe the article.

We will load the transactions next.

Loading the transaction data

The `transaction_train.csv` data is in the order transactions have occurred. This makes it possible to load the data and preserve the sequence in the graph in an easy manner. We have this data in each row for transactions: transaction date, article ID, customer ID, price, and sales channel.

> **Note**
>
> We don't have a unique ID for each of the transactions.

We can use this Cypher to load the data:

```
LOAD CSV WITH HEADERS FROM "file:///transactions_train.csv" as row WITH
row
CALL {
    WITH row
    MATCH (c:Customer {id:row.customer_id})
    MATCH (a:Article {id:row.article_id})
    WITH a, c, row
    CREATE (t:Transaction {date: row.t_dat, price: row.price,
salesChannel: row.sales_channel_id})
    CREATE (t)-[:HAS_ARTICLE]->(a)
```

```
    WITH c, t
    CALL {
        WITH c, t
        WITH c, t
        WHERE exists((c)-[:START_TRANSACTION]->()) OR exists((c)-
[:LATEST]->())
        MATCH (c)-[r:LATEST]->(lt)
        DELETE r
        CREATE (lt)-[:NEXT]->(t)
        CREATE (c)-[:LATEST]->(t)
        UNION
        WITH c, t
        WITH c,t
        WHERE NOT ( exists((c)-[:START_TRANSACTION]->()) OR exists((c)-
[:LATEST]->()) )
        CREATE (c)-[:START_TRANSACTION]->(t)
        CREATE (c)-[:LATEST]->(t)
    }
} IN TRANSACTIONS OF 1000 ROWS
```

From this Cypher, we can see that we take the first transaction we find for a given customer and connect it to the customer using a *START_TRANSACTION* relationship. We use a *LATEST* relationship to track the last transaction the customer made. As we keep getting more transactions for the customer, we keep moving the *LATEST* relationship to the newest transaction. We connect the earlier transaction that was connected using a *LATEST* relationship and the new transaction with a *NEXT* relationship. So, in this graph, we are representing the transactions made by customers as a transaction train, true to the name of the dataset file transaction_train.csv.

Final graph

After loading all the data, our graph model will look as shown in *Figure 8.1*.

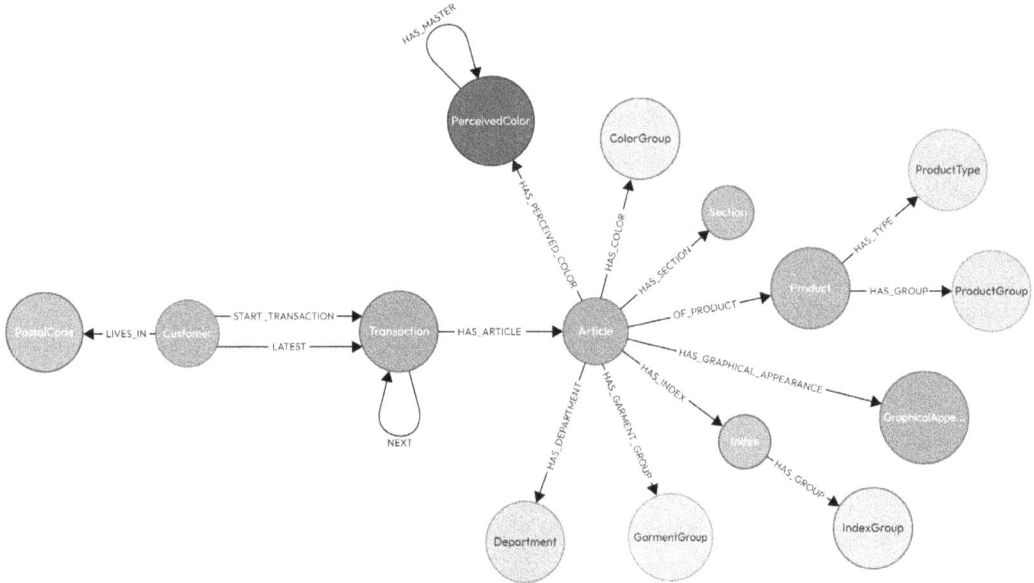

Figure 8.1 — Graph data model after loading the H&M data

We can see from this graph that the article attributes are fanned out into various individual nodes. The **Customer** node is connected to the postal code and first and last transactions. **Transaction** is associated with **Article**. The **Transaction** nodes are also connected to any next transactions available for a given customer.

Now that we have loaded the data, let us explore how we can further enhance the graph from this data, to add our own understanding of the data and ideas into the graph.

Optimizing for recommendations: best practices in graph modeling

We have a graph now, with data loaded the way we want to consume it and representing the context of the data. Still, the graph represents only the original context provided. Say we want to consume the data by season and year – we still need to build queries to retrieve it. Since Neo4j is schema optional, maybe we can do some post-processing and add extra relationships to consume the data in that way.

In this Cypher script, we are creating seasonal relationships:

1. For each customer, iterate through the transactions and assign a season value based on month and year:

```
MATCH (c:Customer)
WITH c
CALL {
    WITH c
    MATCH (c)-[:START_TRANSACTION]->(s)
    MATCH (c)-[:LATEST]->(e)
    WITH c,s,e
    MATCH p=(s)-[:NEXT*]->(e)
    WITH c, nodes(p) as nodes
    UNWIND nodes as node
```

2. For example, if the month is 1 and the year is 2020, we assign WINTER_2019 as the season name for that transaction as the context:

```
WITH c, node, node.date as d
WITH c, node, toInteger(substring(d, 0,4)) as year, substring(d,
5,2) as month
WITH c, node,
    CASE WHEN month="12" THEN year
        WHEN month="01" OR month="02" THEN year-1
        ELSE
            year
    END as year,
```

3. Collect transactions for each season value:

```
        CASE WHEN month="12" OR month="01" OR month="02" THEN
"WINTER"
            WHEN month="03" OR month="04" OR month="05" THEN
"SPRING"
            WHEN month="06" OR month="07" OR month="08" THEN
"SUMMER"
```

```
            WHEN month="09" OR month="10" OR month="11" THEN "FALL"
        END as season
    WITH c, node, season+'_'+year as relName
```

4. Get the first record of the collection for each season value:

    ```
    WITH c, relName, head(collect(node)) as start
    WHERE relName is not null
    ```

5. Create a relationship between the customer and that transaction with the season value
    as the relationship name. We are using the apoc method to create the relationship as the
    relationship name is dynamic:

    ```
    CALL apoc.create.relationship(c, relName, {}, start) YIELD rel
        WITH 1 as out
        return DISTINCT out
    } IN TRANSACTIONS OF 1000 ROWS
    WITH 1 as r
    RETURN DISTINCT r
    ```

Do note that this is a very basic approach. This shows we can create extra context in the graph
based on our understanding of the data. These approaches make Neo4j very suitable for building
knowledge graphs. When we make it easy to access data in this way, it can open up more ideas
on how we can look at the same data differently to extract more *intelligence* in a simple manner
that's traceable and understandable at the same time.

If you do not want to load the data manually, you can download the database snapshot from the
following URL: https://packt-neo4j-powered-applications.s3.us-east-1.amazonaws.com/
Building+Neo4j-Powered+Applications+with+LLMs+Database+Dump+files.zip

We have now added more context to the data. Let's look at the graph data model next.

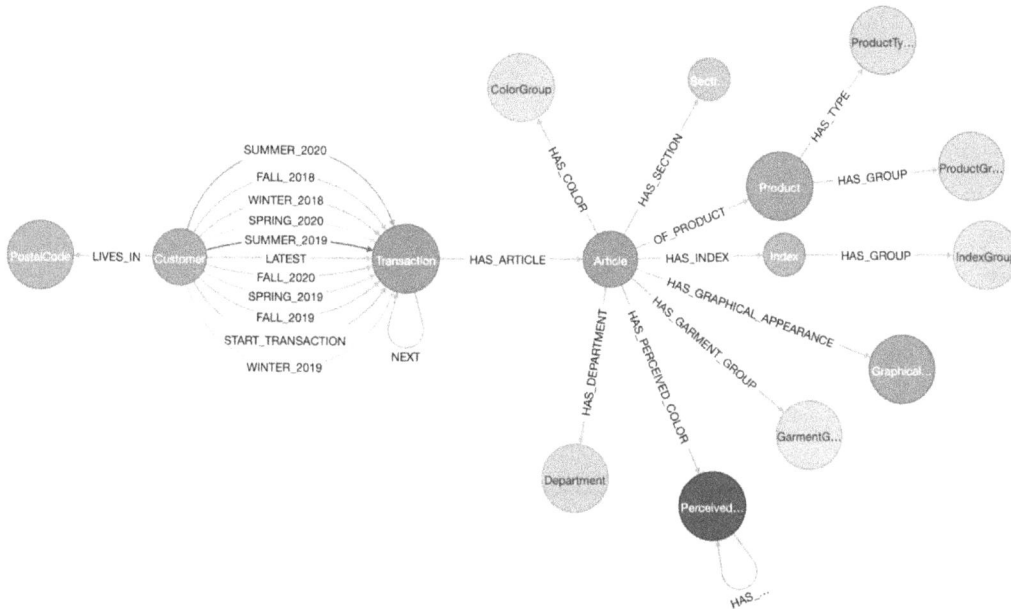

Figure 8.2 — H&M graph data model after enhancing with seasonal relationships

Let us use our understanding of the data to write a query to get articles bought by a random customer in the summer of 2019:

```
MATCH (c:Customer)-[:SUMMER_2019]->(start), (c)-[:FALL_2019]->()<-[:NEXT]-
(end)
WITH c, start, end SKIP 100 LIMIT 1
MATCH p=(start)-[:NEXT*]->(end)
WITH nodes(p) as nodes, relationships(p) as rels
UNWIND nodes as node
MATCH p=(node)-[:HAS_ARTICLE]->(a)
RETURN a.desc as article
```

With this query, we find customers who bought items both in the summer and fall of 2019, pick one customer from that list, and retrieve the article descriptions.

The output of the query will look like this:

```
1  MATCH (c:Customer)-[:SUMMER_2019]→(start), (c)-[:FALL_2019]→()←[:NEXT]-(end)
2  WITH c, start, end SKIP 100 LIMIT 1
3  MATCH p=(start)-[:NEXT*]→(end)
4  WITH nodes(p) as nodes, relationships(p) as rels
5  UNWIND nodes as node
6  MATCH p=(node)-[:HAS_ARTICLE]→(a)
7  RETURN a.desc as article
```

	article
1	"Ankle-length trousers in woven fabric with a high, elasticated waist, pleats at the front, a zip fly and buttons, side pockets, fake back pockets and straight, wide legs."
2	"V-neck T-shirt in soft cotton jersey."
3	"Round-necked T-shirt in soft jersey."
4	"Scarf in a soft weave with fringes on the short sides. Size 50x180 cm."

Started streaming 4 records after 436 ms and completed after 532 ms.

Figure 8.3 — Cypher query to retrieve SUMMER_2019 purchases for a customer

By looking at the query, it is easy to understand what the query is doing. We use SUMMER_2019 as the starting point and a transaction before FALL_2019 relationship as the endpoint, traverse from the start point to the endpoint, and retrieve the articles of those transactions.

We can see that we are completely relying on the graph traversals instead of property-based filters, which makes executing this query very efficient. Neo4j is built to execute these kinds of queries very efficiently.

Summary

In this chapter, we looked at how to look at a graph data model and how building a model based on how we consume it makes it easier to retrieve the data efficiently. We looked at the H&M recommendations dataset and loaded it using those principles, and also augmented it using the properties and our understanding of that data. This added more context to the graph and also made it simple to query the data – queries are more readable and explainable to others in a simpler way.

In the next chapter, we will build on this data, using an LLM to enhance it further, and will see how LLMs can provide us with more capable knowledge graphs.

9

Integrating LangChain4j and Spring AI with Neo4j

Now that we have loaded the data into a graph, in this chapter, we will look at how we can use LangChain4j or Spring AI to augment the graph to enhance its capabilities and build a knowledge graph. We will look into integrating the graph with LLMs to generate a summary of customer purchases and create an embedding of that summary to represent the customer purchase history. These embeddings are crucial for enabling machine learning and graph algorithms to understand and process graph data. These embeddings can help us build a knowledge graph to provide more personal recommendations for customers by understanding purchase behaviors. We will also look at how to create embeddings of the detailed description of each article present in the dataset.

In this chapter, we are going to cover the following main topics:

- Setting up LangChain4j and Spring AI
- Building your recommendation engine with LangChain4j
- Building your recommendation engine with Spring AI
- Fine-tuning your recommendation system

Technical requirements

We will be using a Java IDE environment to work with the LangChain4j and Spring AI projects. You need to have these installed and know how to work with them. You will need the following to get started:

- Maven will be used to build a project and manage dependencies. If you are going to use the IntelliJ IDE (or IntelliJ IDEA), then Maven will be installed along with it, and you need not install it separately. If you are new to Maven, you can read more about it at `https://maven.apache.org/`.

- Java 17.

- IntelliJ – These examples are built and tested with the IntelliJ IDE. You can use your preferred IDE, however. We will be using the IntelliJ IDEA tool to build and run our projects. You can download the tool from `https://www.jetbrains.com/idea/`. You can download the Community Edition to run the examples in this chapter. You can read more about using this IDE to build Spring applications at `https://www.jetbrains.com/idea/spring/`.

- Spring Boot – If you are new to Spring Boot, you can go to `https://spring.io/projects/spring-boot` to learn more about it.

- Neo4j Desktop with the following plugins installed. We will be starting from the graph database we built in the last chapter. You can download Neo4j Desktop from `https://neo4j.com/download/`. If you are new to Neo4j Desktop, you can learn more about it at `https://neo4j.com/docs/desktop-manual/current/`. The code is tested with the 5.21.2 version of the database. The following are the plugins required:

    - APOC plugin – 5.21.2
    - Graph Data Science library – 2.9.0

The following figure shows how to install these plugins for a DBMS.

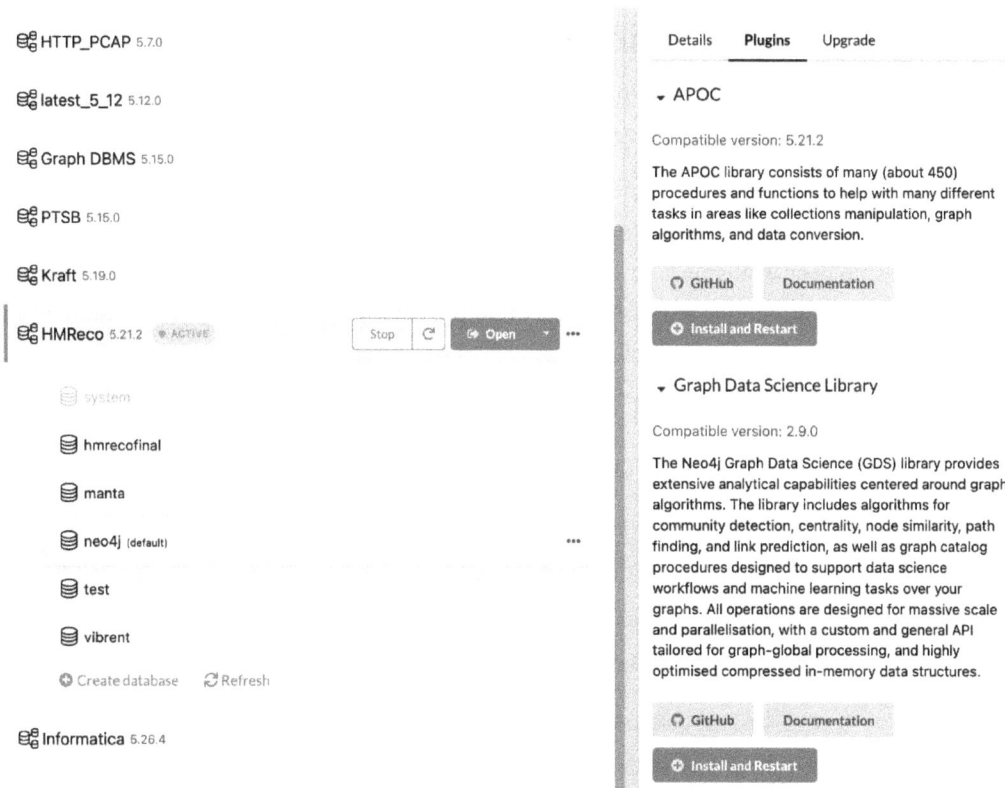

Figure 9.1 — Install plugins on Neo4j Desktop

When you select the DBMS on Neo4j Desktop, on the right side, it shows its details. Click on the **Plugins** tab and select the plugins you require. On the details pane, click on the **Install and Restart** button.

> **Note**
>
> You can find all the code you need at `https://github.com/PacktPublishing/Building-Neo4j-Powered-Applications-with-LLMs/tree/main/ch9`. These are complete projects and ready to run in an IDE. We will only show snippets of the code in this chapter to showcase the usage. So, it might be a good idea to download the code to follow the steps in this chapter.

We will start with setting up the LangChain4j and Spring AI projects.

Setting up LangChain4j and Spring AI

We will take a look at setting up the Spring AI and LangChain4j projects using the **spring initializr** website (`https://start.spring.io/`).

We will look at each of these technologies independently. LangChain4j and Spring AI are both options to perform the same tasks. We need only one of these frameworks to build GenAI projects. LangChain4j has been available for a bit longer than Spring AI. Both of them work pretty similarly in terms of the API and integrations. We will build the same application with both frameworks and see how similar they are. We will also identify the differences.

The following are the steps we need to follow to create the starter projects:

1. Setting up the LangChain4j project:

    a. Go to the website, `https://start.spring.io/`.

    b. Select **Maven** under the **Project** section.

    c. Select **Java** under the **Language** section.

    d. In the **Project Metadata** section, fill in the following values:

    - **Group**: `com.packt.genai.hnm.springai`
    - **Artifact**: `springai _graphaugment`
    - **Name**: `springai _graphaugment`
    - **Description**: `Graph Augmenting with Spring AI`
    - **Package Name**: `com.packt.genai.hnm.springai.graphaugment`
    - **Packaging**: `Jar`
    - **Java**: 17

    e. In the **Dependencies** section, click on the **Add Dependencies** button and select the **Spring Web** dependency.

    - There are no other dependencies that are currently listed by the initializer to add to the project. We will add LangChain4j dependencies manually to the project.

    f. Download and save the ZIP file that is generated.

2. Setting up the Spring AI project:

   a. Go to the website, `https://start.spring.io/`.

   b. Select **Maven** under the **Project** section.

   c. Select **Java** under the **Language** section.

   d. In the **Project Metadata** section, fill in the following values:

      - **Group**: `com.packt.genai.hnm.langchain`
      - **Artifact**: `langchain_graphaugment`
      - **Name**: `langchain_graphaugment`
      - **Description**: `Graph Augmenting with Langchain4J`
      - **Package Name**: `com.packt.genai.hnm.langchain.graphaugment`
      - **Packaging**: `Jar`
      - **Java**: 17

   e. In the **Dependencies** section, click on the **Add Dependencies** button to select the following dependencies:

      - **Spring Web**
      - **OpenAI**
      - **Neo4j Vector Database**

   f. Download and save the ZIP file that is generated.

This will only give us a skeleton project with which we will build the application. The skeleton project gives us a basic structure upon which we can add more logic.

Let us look at what we want out of our application before we go ahead and build it. We loaded the H&M transaction data into the graph database in the previous chapter. Currently, it holds the customers, articles, and transactions along with some helper relationships that mark the first transaction in a given season and year. As we want to build a personal recommendation system, we want to enhance the graph to understand customer behavior and provide recommendations. For this purpose, we will be taking the following approach:

1. Select a season for which to understand the purchase behavior. For example, say we want to find the customers who made purchases in summer 2019 and fall 2019 and use the transactions between those seasons to understand customer behavior. Note that there might be some customers who did not make any transactions in the fall of 2019, even

though they might have made transactions in the summer of 2019. We are ignoring those customers for this exercise, to make things a bit simpler.

2. Retrieve the articles purchased during these transactions. The articles should match the condition (purchases made in the summer and fall of 2019) in the order they are purchased. We will then use an LLM to summarize these purchases. This summarization preserves the order of the articles purchased.

3. Use the LLM to generate embedding for this summary text. We will be leveraging an OpenAI LLM for this part.

4. Store these embeddings. We will be storing them on the season relationship for which these embeddings are generated. For example, if we are generating a summary for the summer of 2019, we will store the resulting embeddings on the SUMMER_2019 relationship. An OpenAI LLM is used to generate the embeddings.

In the next section, we will take a look at building an application that performs the functions we described previously using LangChain4j.

Building your recommendation engine with LangChain4j

In this section, we will look at building a graph augmentation application that leverages LangChain4j. In this project, we will be using the GraphRAG approach to generate embeddings for a transaction chain that meets our requirements. We will be using the Neo4j graph retriever to retrieve the transaction chain that meets our requirements, as well as an LLM to generate a summary of those transactions to describe the customer purchase behavior and generate an embedding. The embedding generated will be a vector representation that describes the text summary in a manner that can be leveraged by machine learning or Graph Data Science algorithms. It can also be leveraged for vector search purposes. This article explains embeddings in the context of LLMs well: `https://ml-digest.com/architecture-training-of-the-embedding-layer-of-llms/`. We will start with the ZIP file downloaded in the last section. We need to unzip the file we have downloaded. Once it is unzipped, we will load the project into the IntelliJ platform using these steps:

1. Launch the IntelliJ IDE.

2. Click on **File** | **New** | **Project from Existing Sources....**

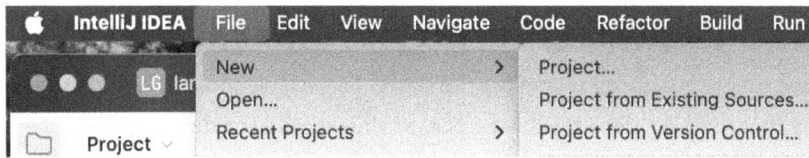

Figure 9.2 — Create a new project

3. Select the pom.xml file from the directory we unzipped.

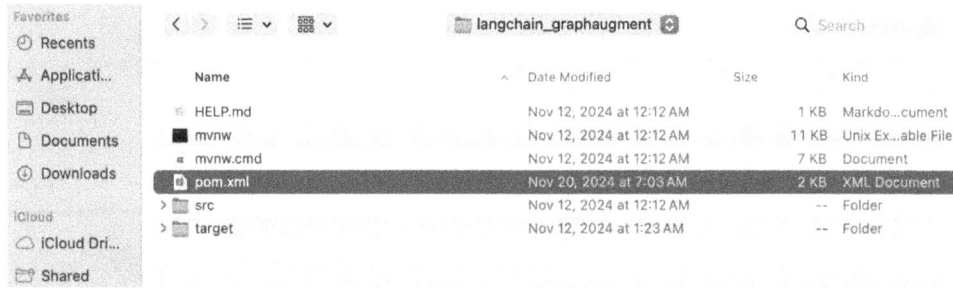

Figure 9.3 — Select pom.xml

4. Click on **Trust Project** to load the project.

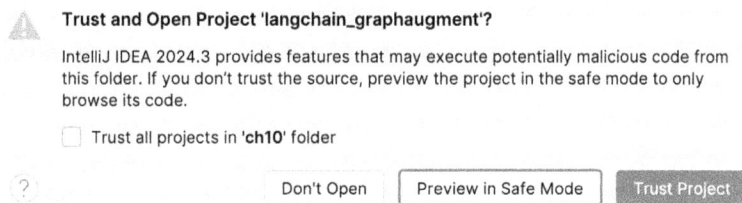

Figure 9.4 — Trust Project

5. Select **New Window** when prompted.

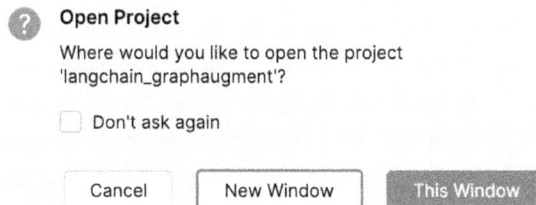

Figure 9.5 — Select New Window

6. Once the project is loaded, you can continue to the next section.

In the next section, we will update the project dependencies.

LangChain4j: updating the project dependencies

When we used the Spring starter to prepare the starter project, we could only add the dependencies identified by that tool. We need to edit the pom.xml file to add the dependencies.

The following are the dependencies we need to add to the project:

- LangChain4j Spring Boot starter – This dependency provides the Spring Boot integration of LangChain4j:

```xml
<!-- Langchain Springboot integration -->
<dependency>
    <groupId>dev.langchain4j</groupId>
    <artifactId>langchain4j-spring-boot-starter</artifactId>
    <version>0.36.0</version>
</dependency>
```

- LangChain4j OpenAI integration – This dependency provides the OpenAI integration:

```xml
<!-- Open AI integration -->
<dependency>
    <groupId>dev.langchain4j</groupId>
    <artifactId>langchain4j-open-ai-spring-boot-starter</artifactId>
    <version>0.36.0</version>
</dependency>
```

- LangChain4j Neo4j integration – This dependency provides the Neo4j integration:

```xml
<!-- Neo4j Vector Store integration -->
<dependency>
    <groupId>dev.langchain4j</groupId>
    <artifactId>langchain4j-neo4j</artifactId>
    <version>0.35.0</version>
</dependency>
```

- LangChain4j LLM embeddings integration – This dependency provides the LLM embeddings API:

```xml
<dependency>
    <groupId>dev.langchain4j</groupId>
    <artifactId>langchain4j-embeddings-all-minilm-l6-v2</artifactId>
```

```
        <version>0.35.0</version>
    </dependency>
```

The latest integration options and details can be found at `https://docs.langchain4j.dev/category/integrations`.

Now that we have added the project dependencies, we need to update the configuration properties that are required for the application. In the next section, we will be looking at updating the application properties.

> **Note**
>
> When you have made changes to the `pom.xml` file, you might have to reload the project for the IDE to update all the dependencies correctly. You can learn more about how to work with Maven projects with IntelliJ IDEA at `https://www.jetbrains.com/help/idea/delegate-build-and-run-actions-to-maven.html#maven_reimport`.

LangChain4j: updating the application properties

In this section, we need to update the application properties for the dependencies we added in the last section to be able to leverage the APIs. We need to add this configuration to the `application.properties` file in the project. Since we will be using the OpenAI LLM for the chat model and embeddings, we need to acquire an API key for this purpose. We need to visit the following website to acquire an API key for this purpose: `https://platform.openai.com/docs/overview`.

These are the configuration properties we need to add:

- OpenAI chat model integration – We need to add this configuration to `application.properties`:

  ```
  # Open AI LLM Integration for Generating Summary using Chat Model.
  langchain4j.open-ai.chat-model.api-key=<OPEN_AI_KEY>
  langchain4j.open-ai.chat-model.model-name=gpt-4o-mini
  langchain4j.open-ai.chat-model.log-requests=true
  langchain4j.open-ai.chat-model.log-responses=true
  ```

- OpenAI embeddings integration – We need to add this configuration to `application.properties`:

```
# Open AI LLM Integration for Generating Embeddings
langchain4j.open-ai.embedding-model.api-key=<OPEN_AI_KEY>
langchain4j.open-ai.embedding-model.model-name=text-embedding-3-
large
```

- Neo4j integration – We will add basic Neo4j integration this time, not the Neo4j vector database-related integration:

```
# Neo4j Integration
neo4j.uri=bolt://localhost:7687
neo4j.user=neo4j
neo4j.password=test1234
neo4j.database=hmreco

config.batchSize=5
```

Now that we have looked at the configuration properties, let us start building the application. We will start with Neo4j database integration, and then add chat model integration to summarize the transactions and generate embeddings for the summary. Finally, we will take a look at building a REST endpoint to invoke those requests as needed.

LangChain4j: Neo4j integration

We will take a look at Neo4j integration first. We will look at this first as we need a means to integrate with the database to perform these tasks:

1. Set up connectivity to be able to perform read and write transactions.
2. Read the articles for the transactions that occurred for the specified season.
3. Persist (save) the embeddings once they are generated.

Before we can build this logic, we need to create a **configuration bean** for Neo4j connectivity. We can define that bean like this to read from `application.properties`:

```
@ConfigurationProperties(prefix = "neo4j")
public class Neo4jConfiguration {

    private String uri;
    private String user ;
```

```
    private String password ;
    private String database ;
  /** Getter/Setters **/
}
```

The ConfigurationProperties annotation on top of the class definition will read application. properties and initialize the properties in the bean. The prefix option tells us to read only the properties that start with that prefix. For example, if we want the uri field to be populated, then we need to add the neo4j.uri property to the configuration. We have not included all the getter and setter code that is required to read the properties from this bean here.

Now, we will define a service to provide integration with the Neo4j database to read the articles and customer transactions data and update the embeddings as needed:

1. Define the service class using @Service annotation. We also need to inject Neo4JConfiguration here:

    ```
    @Service
    @Configuration
    @EnableConfigurationProperties(Neo4jConfiguration.class)
    public class Neo4jService {
        @Autowired
        private Neo4jConfiguration configuration ;

        private Driver driver ;
    ```

2. Add the setup method to initialize the connection to the Neo4j database:

    ```
    public synchronized void setup() {
        if( driver == null ) {
            driver = GraphDatabase.driver(
                    configuration.getUri(),
                    AuthTokens.basic(
                            configuration.getUser(),
                            configuration.getPassword()));
            driver.verifyConnectivity();
        }
    }
    ```

3. Add the method to get the customer transactions data for given start- and end-of-season values. Based on the start- and end-of-season values provided, it retrieves the `elementId` value of the start-of-season value and the article description in the sequence they are purchased. We need this `elementId` value to save the embeddings later. We can see that we are trying to get more related data from the article attributes instead of just the description. This way, we can include more attributes, such as color, as part of the summary, so that we can represent them as embeddings more accurately:

```
public List<EncodeRequest> getDataFromDB(String startSeason, String
endSeason) {
    setup();

    String cypherTemplate = """
        --- Cypher query to get the transactions
    """;

    String cypher = String.format(cypherTemplate, startSeason,
endSeason);

    SessionConfig config = SessionConfig.builder()
        .withDatabase(configuration.getDatabase())
        .build();

    try (Session session = driver.session(config)) {
        List<EncodeRequest> data = session.executeRead(tx -> {
            List<EncodeRequest> out = new ArrayList<>();
            var records = tx.run(cypher);

            while (records.hasNext()) {
                var record = records.next();
                String id = record.get("elementId").asString();
                String articles = record.get("articles").asString();
                out.add(new EncodeRequest(articles, id));
            }

            return out;
        });
        return data;
```

```
    } catch (Exception e) {
        e.printStackTrace();
    }

    return null;
}
```

4. Add the method to get the articles from the database:

```java
public List<EncodeRequest> getArticlesFromDB() {
    setup();

    String cypherTemplate = """
        -- Cypher query to get the articles.
    """;

    SessionConfig config = SessionConfig.builder()
        .withDatabase(configuration.getDatabase())
        .build();

    try (Session session = driver.session(config)) {
        List<EncodeRequest> data = session.executeRead(tx -> {
            List<EncodeRequest> out = new ArrayList<>();
            var records = tx.run(cypherTemplate);

            while (records.hasNext()) {
                var record = records.next();
                String id = record.get("elementId").asString();
                String article = record.get("article").asString();
                out.add(new EncodeRequest(article, id));
            }

            return out;
        });
        return data;
    } catch (Exception e) {
        e.printStackTrace();
    }
```

```
        return null;
    }
```

5. Add a method to save the embeddings for the selected season of a customer. We are keeping the summary in the graph to understand what the embedding represents. Once we understand this aspect, we don't need to store the summary in the database:

```java
public void saveEmbeddings(List<Map<String, Object>> embeddings) {
    setup();

    String cypher = """
        UNWIND $data as row
        WITH row
        MATCH ()-[r]->()
        WHERE elementId(r) = row.id
        SET r.summary = row.summary
        WITH row, r
        CALL db.create.setRelationshipVectorProperty(r, 'embedding',
row.embedding)
        """;

    SessionConfig config = SessionConfig.builder()
        .withDatabase(configuration.getDatabase())
        .build();

    try (Session session = driver.session(config)) {
        session.executeWriteWithoutResult(tx -> {
            tx.run(cypher, Map.of("data", embeddings));
        });
    } catch (Exception e) {
        e.printStackTrace();
    }
}
```

6. Add a method to save the embeddings for the `Article` text on an `Article` node:

```java
public void saveArticleEmbeddings(List<Map<String, Object>>
embeddings) {
    setup();
```

```
String cypher = """
    UNWIND $data as row
    WITH row
    MATCH (a:Article)
    WHERE elementId(a) = row.id
    CALL db.create.setNodeVectorProperty(a, 'embedding', row.
embedding)
    """;

SessionConfig config = SessionConfig.builder()
    .withDatabase(configuration.getDatabase())
    .build();

try (Session session = driver.session(config)) {
    session.executeWriteWithoutResult(tx -> {
        tx.run(cypher, Map.of("data", embeddings));
    });
} catch (Exception e) {
    e.printStackTrace();
}
}
}
```

From the code, we can see that this service depends on Neo4jConfiguration and provides these methods.

The code flow here is simple and provides utility methods to interact with a Neo4j database. The methods to get and save data have Cypher queries embedded into the code here.

Next, we will take a look at an OpenAI chat model integration that can generate a summary for the list of articles.

LangChain4j: OpenAI chat integration

To integrate the chat, we need to define AiService. This is the API exposed by Langchain4J to build Java applications.

Let's see how we can do this:

1. When we define `AiService`, the LangChain4j Spring Framework provides the implementation under the covers to make it very easy to invoke the chat service. Let's look at how this can be defined:

```
@AiService
public interface ChatAssistant {


    @SystemMessage("""
```

2. We set a role for the LLM chat engine. This sets the context for the engine on what guidelines to use to handle the data:

```
                ---Role---


                You are an helpful assistant with expertise in fashion
    for a clothing company.
```

3. We set a goal for the LLM engine here on how it should process the data. This describes what the input data is and how it is structured:

```
                ---Goal---


                Your goal is to generate a summary of the products
    purchased by the customers and descriptions of each of the
    products.\s
                Your summary should contain two sections -\s
                Section 1 - Overall summary outlining the fashion
    preferences of the customer based on the purchases. Limit the
    summary to 3 sentences
                Section 2 - highlight 3-5 individual purchases.


                You should use the data provided in the section below as
    the primary context for generating the response.\s
                If you don't know the answer or if the input data tables
    do not contain sufficient information to provide an answer, just say
    so.\s
                Do not make anything up.
```

```
                    Data Description:
                    - Each Customer has an ID. Customer ID is a numeric
        value.
                    - Each Customer has purchased more than one clothing
        articles (products). Products have descriptions.
                    - The order of the purchases is very important. You
        should take into account the order when generating the summary.
```

4. The response directive for the LLM gives directions on how the response should be structured:

```
                    Response:
                    ---

                    # Overall Fashion Summary:


                    \\n\\n


                    # Individual Purchase Details:


                    --
```

5. The Data section has the {text} variable defined, which is substituted with the input
   the method receives:

```
                    Data:
                    {text}
            """)
        String chat(String text);
    }
```

Here, we are defining an interface with an @AiService annotation. In this service, we need to define a chat method. We will be using a simple AI chat service with a System Message option here.
To read about the common operations and advanced operations that AIServices offers, please
read the documentation at https://docs.langchain4j.dev/tutorials/ai-services/. Here,
we are asking the LLM to act like a fashion expert and give us a summary of customer fashion
preferences and highlight the top purchases, keeping the order of purchases in mind. The input
parameter from the text is used as input data to the chat assistant.

Now we will take a look at how we can invoke this chat request:

```
@Service
public class OpenAIChatService

    private ChatAssistant assistant ;

    public OpenAIChatService(ChatAssistant assistant) {
        this.assistant = assistant;
    }

    public String getSummaryText(String input) {
        String out = assistant.chat(input) ;
        return out ;
    }
}
```

We can see from this code snippet that usage is pretty simple. The chat assistant is bound to this service via Spring initialization, and the getSummaryText method invokes the chat request. It is as simple as that to integrate the chat services into the application.

We will take a look at embedding model integration next.

LangChain4j: OpenAI embedding model integration

Embedding model integration is pretty simple since we have already enabled AiService for the chat service. The embedding model usage looks as shown in the following code:

```
@Service
public class OpenAIEmbeddingModelService {
    EmbeddingModel embeddingModel ;

    public OpenAIEmbeddingModelService(EmbeddingModel embeddingModel) {
        this.embeddingModel = embeddingModel;
    }

    Embedding generateEmbedding(String text) {
        Response<Embedding> response = embeddingModel.embed(text) ;
        return  response.content() ;
```

```
    }

  }
```

We can see from the code that it is as simple as adding `EmbeddingModel` to the class and initializing it using a constructor. When the Spring Boot application starts, the appropriate embedding model implementation based on properties is instantiated and assigned to this variable. This service provides a method to generate the embedding for a given text.

Now that we have looked at all the services defined, let us look at how we can use all of these to build the application to augment a customer transactions graph.

LangChain4j: final application

For the final application, we will build a REST endpoint to issue the request to perform the augmentation. Since the process itself can take time, it is split into two parts:

1. Issue a request to start the augmentation process. This returns a request ID.

2. We can use the request ID returned in step 1 to check the progress of the request.

Let us look at the REST controller first to issue requests:

1. We need to create a REST controller to handle the HTTP requests:

    ```
    @Configuration
    @EnableConfigurationProperties(RunConfiguration.class)
    @RestController
    public class LangchainGraphAugmentController {
    ```

2. Inject the individual services defined using the `Autowired` directive:

    ```
    @Autowired
    private OpenAIEmbeddingModelService embeddingModelService ;

    @Autowired
    private Neo4jService neo4jService ;

    @Autowired
    private OpenAIChatService chatService ;

    @Autowired
    ```

```
private RunConfiguration configuration ;
```

3. Define the global variable to hold the current processing requests:

```
private HashMap<String, IRequest> currentRequests = new
HashMap<>() ;
```

4. Add the method to start the customer transactions augmenting process. This method takes the start- and end-of-season values and creates a `ProcessRequest` object. It starts a process thread that requests and returns a UUID for this request. We keep the UUID and `ProcessRequest` mapping so that we can provide the status when requested:

```
@GetMapping("/augment/{startSeason}/{endSeason}")
public String processAugment(
        @PathVariable (value="startSeason") String startSeason,
        @PathVariable (value="endSeason") String endSeason
) {
    String uuid = UUID.randomUUID().toString() ;
    ProcessRequest request = new ProcessRequest(
            chatService,
            embeddingModelService,
            neo4jService,
            configuration,
            startSeason,
            endSeason
    ) ;
    currentRequests.put(uuid, request) ;
    Thread t = new Thread(request) ;
    t.start();
    return uuid ;
}
```

5. Add the method to start the article text augmentation process:

```
@GetMapping("/augmentArticles")
public String processAugmentArticles() {
```

```
String uuid = UUID.randomUUID().toString() ;
ProcessArticles request = new ProcessArticles(
        embeddingModelService,
        neo4jService,
        configuration
) ;
currentRequests.put(uuid, request) ;
Thread t = new Thread(request) ;
t.start();
return uuid ;
}
```

6. Add a method to get the status of the specified request ID:

```
@GetMapping("/augment/status/{requestId}")
public String getStatus(
        @PathVariable (value="requestId") String requestId) {
    IRequest request = currentRequests.get(requestId) ;

    if( request != null ) {
        if( request.isComplete() ) {
            currentRequests.remove(requestId) ;
        }
        return request.getCurStatus() ;
    } else {
        return "Request Not Found." ;
    }
}
}
```

Note

The graph augmenting process can take a lot of time. In particular, the summary generation part using the LLM chat API can be time-consuming and it can take quite a lot of time to augment all the customers that match the requirements, say, the summer of 2019 purchases. For that reason, the database dump that has the complete augmentation only covers around 10,000 customers.

Now, let us look at the process request implementation. This is where we tie in all the various APIs to perform the required process:

1. We need to define a class `ProcessRequest` that implements the `Runnable` interface. We will start a thread as these requests are long-running ones. The chat service, embedding model service, Neo4j service, and other parameters are passed as input when we create this request. This class keeps track of the current processing status:

```
public class ProcessRequest implements Runnable, IRequest {
    private OpenAIChatService chatService ;
    private OpenAIEmbeddingModelService embeddingModelService ;
    private Neo4jService neo4jService ;
    private RunConfiguration configuration ;

    private String startSeson ;
    private String endSeason ;

    private String curStatus = "0 %" ;

    private boolean isComplete = false ;

    public ProcessRequest(
            OpenAIChatService chatService,
            OpenAIEmbeddingModelService embeddingModelService,
            Neo4jService neo4jService,
            RunConfiguration configuration,
            String startSeson,
            String endSeason) {
        this.chatService = chatService;
        this.embeddingModelService = embeddingModelService;
        this.neo4jService = neo4jService;
        this.configuration = configuration ;
        this.startSeson = startSeson ;
        this.endSeason = endSeason ;
    }

    public String getCurStatus() {
```

```
            return curStatus ;
    }


    public boolean isComplete() {
        return isComplete;
    }
```

The run method implements the actual process:

```
@Override
public void run() {
    try {
```

2. Retrieve the customer transactions data from the Neo4j database. The output is a list, where each record contains the relationship ID for the start season as the context and the description of the articles in the order in which they were purchased:

```
            System.out.println("Retrieving Data from Graph");
            List<EncodeRequest> dbData = neo4jService.
getDataFromDB(startSeson, endSeason);
            System.out.println("Retrieved Data from Graph");
            int i = 0;
            int processingSize = dbData.size();
            List<Map<String, Object>> embeddings = new
ArrayList<>();

            for( EncodeRequest request: dbData ) {
```

Once you reach the required batch size of results collected, save the data to the Neo4j database:

```
            if (i > 0 && i % configuration.getBatchSize() == 0)
{
                System.out.println("Saving Embeddings to Graph :
" + i);

                neo4jService.saveEmbeddings(embeddings);
                embeddings.clear();
                curStatus = ( ( i * 100.0 ) / processingSize ) +
" %";
            }
```

```
i++;

Map<String, Object> embedMap = new HashMap<>();
```

3. Retrieve the customer purchase summary from the LLM chat service by passing the list of transactions retrieved from the graph:

```
String id = request.getId();
System.out.println("Retrieving Summary");
String summary = chatService.getSummaryText(request.
getText());
System.out.println("Retrieving embedding");
```

4. For the summary we get from the LLM chat service, create an embedding by leveraging the embedding service:

```
Embedding embedding = embeddingModelService.
generateEmbedding(summary);
```

5. Save the summary and embedding along with the relationship context ID into a record and then save it into a batch:

```
embedMap.put("id", id);
embedMap.put("embedding", embedding.vector());
embedMap.put("summary", summary);
embeddings.add(embedMap);
}
```

6. If any data is left in the batch, save that data to the Neo4j database:

```
if( embeddings.size() > 0 ) {
    System.out.println("Saving Embeddings to Graph");
    neo4jService.saveEmbeddings(embeddings);
    embeddings.clear();
}
curStatus = "100 %";
}catch (Exception e) {
    e.printStackTrace();
}
isComplete = true;
```

```
        }
    }
```

With this approach, we can augment the graph to perform the next steps to understand customer purchase behavior to be able to provide them with better recommendations.

The following code can process the article augmentation. The code is pretty much similar to the `ProcessRequest` class. We will look at only the differences here:

```
public class ProcessArticles implements Runnable, IRequest {
```

The `run` method reads the data from Neo4j and splits it into batches before invoking the batch embedding request:

```
@Override
public void run() {

        List<EncodeRequest> dbData = neo4jService.getArticlesFromDB();

        for( EncodeRequest request: dbData ) {
            if (i > 0 && i % batchSize == 0) {
```

Once the batch of article texts is collected, we will pass that batch to the embedding service to get the embeddings. We will save the embeddings generated to the Neo4j database:

```
                                List<Embedding> embedList =
  embeddingModelService.generateEmbeddingBatch(inputData);
                                                        neo4jService.
  saveArticleEmbeddings(embeddings);
                                            }
                        i++;
            }
```

Generate the embeddings for any of the remaining article texts and save them to the Neo4j database:

```
        if( inputData.size() > 0 ) {
                                List<Embedding> embedList =
  embeddingModelService.generateEmbeddingBatch(inputData);
                    neo4jService.saveArticleEmbeddings(embeddings);
```

```
                              }
            curStatus = "100 %";
        }catch (Exception e) {
            e.printStackTrace();
        }
    }
}
```

The flow of the operation is similar to the one in the ProcessRequest class. While we used a single request mode for season purchase embeddings, for article embeddings, we are using the *batch mode*. With the single request mode (using the API), we could generate only one summary at a time. However, with the batch mode, it is much faster to generate embeddings.

You can download the latest project from https://github.com/PacktPublishing/Building-Neo4j-Powered-Applications-with-LLMs/tree/main/ch9/langchain_graphaugment instead of building it from scratch if you would like to play with it.

To run the project, you can right-click on the LangchainGraphaugmentApplication.java file and select the **Run** menu option.

> **Note**
>
> If you are interested in customizing the run options and other aspects, then you can use the **Run**/**Debug** configurations provided by the IDE. To learn more about these aspects, please visit https://www.jetbrains.com/help/idea/run-debug-configuration-java-application.html.

In the next section, we will take a look at how we can build the same recommendation engine using Spring AI.

Building your recommendation engine with Spring AI

In this section, we will look at building the graph augmentation application leveraging Spring AI. This project approach is similar to what we built using LangChain4j. We will be leveraging the GraphRAG approach to generate embeddings for a transaction chain that meets our requirements. We will start with the ZIP file downloaded in the last section. We need to unzip the file we have downloaded. Once it is unzipped, we will load the project into the IntelliJ platform using these steps. This is similar to what we did in the previous section. Please follow the steps listed at the start of the *Building your recommendation engine with LangChain4j* section to import the project.

In contrast to LangChain4j, there are no significant steps to update Spring AI project dependencies. Let's see why.

Spring AI: updating the project dependencies

Unlike the LangChain4j project, we don't need to update any dependencies. We were able to add all the required dependencies from the Spring starter project. We will take a look next at updating the application properties.

Spring AI: updating the application properties

In this section, we need to update the application properties to be able to leverage the APIs. We need to add this configuration to the `application.properties` file in the project. Since we will be using an OpenAI LLM for the chat model and embeddings, we need to acquire an API key for this purpose, which we can do by visiting `https://platform.openai.com/docs/overview`.

These are the configuration properties we need to add:

- OpenAI chat model integration – We need to add this configuration to `application.properties`. We only need to add the OpenAI API key:

  ```
  # Open AI LLM Integration for Generating Summary using Chat Model.
  spring.ai.openai.api-key=<OPEN_AI_KEY>
  ```

- OpenAI embeddings integration – We need to add this configuration to `application.properties`. We don't need to add the OpenAI API key again, as it uses the same configuration as the LLM chat configuration:

  ```
  # Open AI LLM Integration for Generating Embeddings
  spring.ai.openai.embedding.options.model=text-embedding-3-large
  ```

- Neo4j integration – We will add basic Neo4j integration, not the Neo4j vector database-related integration:

  ```
  # Neo4j Integration
  neo4j.uri=bolt://localhost:7687
  neo4j.user=neo4j
  neo4j.password=test1234
  neo4j.database=hmreco

  config.batchSize=5
  ```

Now that we have looked at the configuration properties, let us start building the application. We will start with Neo4j database integration first, then add chat model integration for summarizing the transactions and generating embeddings for the summary. Finally, we will take a look at building a REST endpoint to invoke those requests as needed.

Spring AI: Neo4j integration

We are looking at Neo4j integration first as we need a means to integrate with the database to perform the following tasks:

1. Set up connectivity to be able to perform read and write transactions.

2. See the articles for the transactions that occurred for the specified period.

3. Persist the embeddings once they are generated.

The implementation here is exactly the same as the LangChain4j project discussed in the *Langchain4J – Neo4j integration* part of the previous section. We will take a look at an OpenAI chat model integration that can generate a summary for the list of articles.

Spring AI: OpenAI chat integration

To integrate the chat, it is a bit different from LangChain4j. We need to define `Service` and initialize `ChatClient`. We need to leverage this client and use chat APIs to make the request. It is not abstracted as it is with LangChain4j. Let us take a look at this service:

```
@Service
public class OpenAIChatService {
    private final ChatClient chatClient;
```

Let's now look at the steps to integrate OpenAI chat:

1. We have to provide the prompts for the LLM slightly differently in the Spring AI framework. In the LangChain4j framework, we had a single system message that defined the role the LLM is playing, the goal for the response, and data as a parameter in a single message. Here, we have to split the role and goal into a system prompt template, while the `data` parameter is passed into the user message. The outcome is the same in both cases:

```
        private final String SYSTEM_PROMPT_TEMPLATE = """
```

2. We are setting a role for the LLM chat engine. This sets the context for the engine on what guidelines to use to handle the data:

```
---Role---


        You are an helpful assistant with expertise in fashion
for a clothing company.
```

3. We are setting a goal for the LLM engine here on how it should process the data. This describes what the input data is and how it is structured:

```
---Goal---


        Your goal is to generate a summary of the products
purchased by the customers and descriptions of each of the
products.\s
        Your summary should contain two sections -\s
        Section 1 - Overall summary outlining the fashion
preferences of the customer based on the purchases. Limit the
summary to 3 sentences
        Section 2 - highlight 3-5 individual purchases.


        You should use the data provided in the section below as
the primary context for generating the response.\s
        If you don't know the answer or if the input data tables
do not contain sufficient information to provide an answer, just say
so.\s
        Do not make anything up.


        Data Description:
        - Each Customer has an ID. Customer ID is a numeric
value.
        - Each Customer has purchased more than one clothing
articles (products). Products have descriptions.
        - The order of the purchases is very important. You
should take into account the order when generating the summary.
```

4. The response directive for the LLM gives directions on how the response should be struc-
    tured:

```
Response:
---
# Overall Fashion Summary:

\\n\\n

# Individual Purchase Details:
--
""" ;
```

5. The data is passed as a user message here. It has the {text} variable defined, which is the
    property that is substituted with the input the method receives:

```
private final String userMessage = """

    Data:
    {text}
    """ ;
```

6. We need to initialize the chat client using ChatClient.Builder, which is injected by the
    Spring Framework into the constructor:

```
public OpenAIChatService(ChatClient.Builder chatClientBuilder) {
    this.chatClient = chatClientBuilder.build();
}

public String getSummaryText(String input)
```

7. We can see that the usage is different from the LangChain4j framework. Here, we need to create a prompt with a system template, pass the user message with data replacement, and invoke the chatResponse method:

```
        ChatResponse response = chatClient
                .prompt()
                .system(SYSTEM_PROMPT_TEMPLATE)
                .user(p -> p.text(userMessage).param("data", input))
                .call()
                .chatResponse() ;

        return response.getResult().getOutput().getContent() ;
    }


}
```

We will take a look at embedding model integration next.

Spring AI: OpenAI embedding model integration

Embedding model integration is pretty simple. We can use Autowired to initialize the embedding model instance. The embedding model usage looks as shown in the following code:

```
@Service
public class OpenAIEmbeddingModelService {
    private EmbeddingModel embeddingModel ;

    @Autowired
    public OpenAIEmbeddingModelService(EmbeddingModel embeddingModel) {
        this.embeddingModel = embeddingModel;
    }

    float[] generateEmbedding(String text) {
        float[] response = embeddingModel.embed(text) ;
        return  response ;
    }

    List<float[]> generateEmbeddingBatch(List<String> textList) {
```

```
        List<float[]> responses = embeddingModel.embed(textList) ;
        return responses ;
    }
}
```

From the code, we can see it is as simple as adding `EmbeddingModel` to the class and initializing it using a constructor. When the Spring Boot application starts, the appropriate embedding model implementation based on properties is instantiated and assigned to this variable. This service provides a method to generate the embedding for a given text.

Now that we have looked at all the services defined, let us look at how we can use all of these to build a graph augment application.

Spring AI: final application

The application flow is pretty much the same as the LangChain4j application we discussed in the *LangChain4j – final application* section. The code is similar, so we will not be adding that code here. The only difference would be the Java package names. For posterity, let us take a look at the application flow.

The REST endpoint is built to issue the request to perform the augmentation. Since the process itself can take time, this process is split into two parts:

1. Issue a request to start the augmentation process. This returns a request ID.
2. Use the request ID returned in step 1 to check the progress of the request.

The first step starts a thread and initiates processing the whole data. The request process follows these steps:

1. Retrieve the relationship ID for the start season as the context, and the description of the articles in the order in which they were purchased. We return a list of records as a response.
2. For each record we retrieved from Neo4j, we perform the following steps:

    1. Execute the chat request to generate the summary.
    2. For the summary returned from the chat request, generate an embedding using an LLM embedding API.
    3. Save the relationship ID, summary, and embedding to a map to build a batch.
    4. Once the batch size reaches the size specified in the configuration, write the summary and embedding to the relationship identified by the relationship ID.

With this approach, we can augment the graph to perform the next steps to understand customer purchase behavior to be able to provide customers with better recommendations.

You can download the latest project from `https://github.com/PacktPublishing/Building-Neo4j-Powered-Applications-with-LLMs/tree/main/ch9/springai_graphaugment` instead of building it from scratch if you would like to play with it.

To run the project, you can right-click on the `SpringaiGraphAugmentApplication.java` file and select the **Run** menu option.

> **Note**
>
> If you are interested in customizing the run options and other aspects, then you can use the **Run/Debug** configurations provided by the IDE. To learn more about these aspects, please visit `https://www.jetbrains.com/help/idea/run-debug-configuration-java-application.html`.

Let's now see how we can use this application we built to augment the graph and take a look at how we can provide recommendations from this.

Fine-tuning your recommendation system

Now that the project is ready, we can either run the application in the IDE or build a runnable JAR file. Here, we will run it from the IDE directly. We will be using a LangChain4j application for testing here. A Spring AI application would follow the same principles. We will be starting from the database we created in the previous chapter. If you do not want to start from scratch, you can download the database dump from `https://packt-neo4j-powered-applications.s3.us-east-1.amazonaws.com/Building+Neo4j-Powered+Applications+with+LLMs+Databas e+Dump+files.zip` and create a database from it.

You can double-click on the `LangchainGraphaugmentApplication.java` file to load it into the IDE. Once it is loaded, you can right-click on the class name to run the application. *Figure 9.6* shows how we can do this.

```
> import ...

@SpringBootApplication
public class LangchainGraphaugmen
```

💡 Show Context Actions	⌥↵
📋 Paste	⌘V
Copy / Paste Special	>
Column Selection Mode	⇧⌘8
Find Usages	⌥F7
Go To	>
Folding	>
Analyze	>
Rename...	⇧F6
Refactor	>
Generate...	⌘N
▷ Run 'LangchainGraph....main()'	^⇧R
⚙ Debug 'LangchainGraph....main()'	^⇧D
More Run/Debug	>

```
    public static void main(Strin
        SpringApplication.run(Lan
    }

}
```

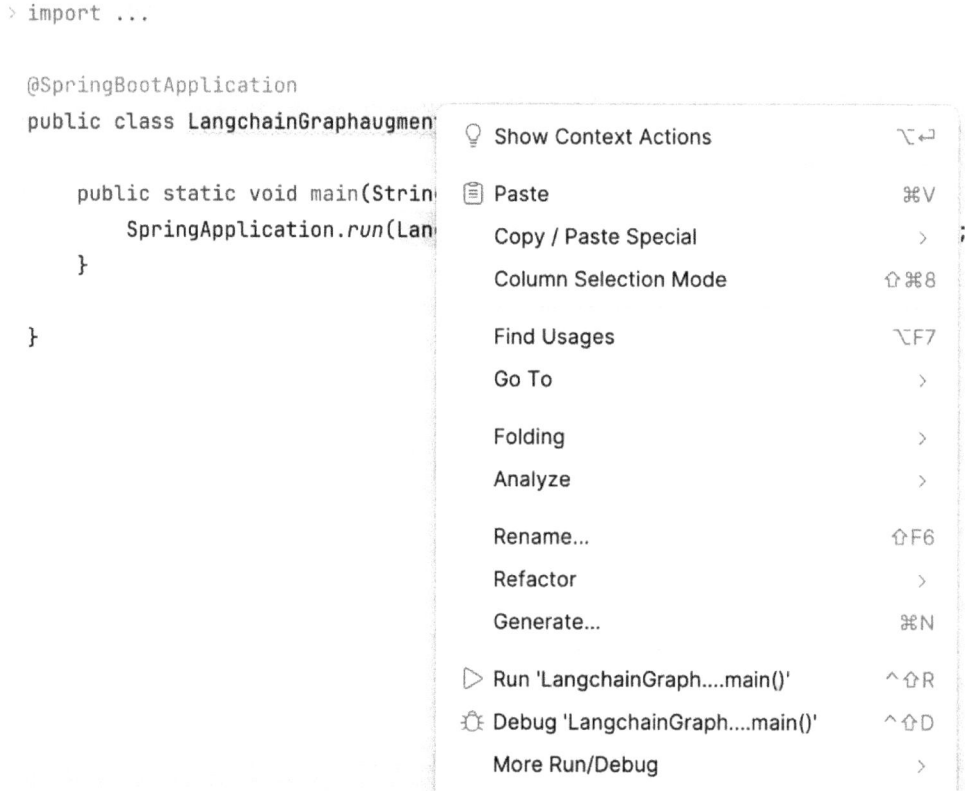

Figure 9.6 — Run the application from the IDE

Once you've right-clicked on the class name, click on the **Run** menu item to start the application. Once the application is ready, you should see this in the IDE console:

```
2024-12-12T14:52:30.075+05:30  INFO 5296 --- [langchain_graphaugment]
[           main] w.s.c.ServletWebServerApplicationContext : Root
WebApplicationContext: initialization completed in 1271 ms
2024-12-12T14:52:31.347+05:30  INFO 5296 --- [langchain_graphaugment]
[           main] o.neo4j.driver.internal.DriverFactory    : Direct driver
instance 1567253519 created for server address localhost:7687
2024-12-12T14:52:31.388+05:30  INFO 5296 --- [langchain_graphaugment]
[           main] o.s.b.w.embedded.tomcat.TomcatWebServer  : Tomcat
started on port 8080 (http) with context path '/'
2024-12-12T14:52:31.398+05:30  INFO 5296 --- [langchain_graphaugment]
[           main] g.h.l.g.LangchainGraphaugmentApplication : Started
LangchainGraphaugmentApplication in 3.146 seconds (process running for
3.746)
```

Once the application is up and running, we can open a browser and enter the URL `http://localhost:8080/augment/SUMMER_2019/FALL_2019` to start the augmentation process for the `SUMMER_2019` purchases of customers. When we issue this request, we get a UUID such as `aff867bd-08fb-42fb-8a27-3917e0ce83d1` as a response. While the process is running, we can inquire about the current completion percentage by entering the URL `http://localhost:8080/augment/status/aff867bd-08fb-42fb-8a27-3917e0ce83d1` in the browser.

> **Note**
>
> Note that the UUID value of `aff867bd-08fb-42fb-8a27-3917e0ce83d1` mentioned previously is a dynamic one. It is not guaranteed that you will get the same UUID as shown in the preceding text. This UUID is specific to the run in this example. You would need to take a look at the UUID returned by the request for your run and use it to check the status.

Generating a summary and embedding will take time. Once this process is complete, we should create embeddings on articles next. The process is similar to the previous step. We need to enter the URL `http://localhost:8080/augmentArticles` in the browser. It will also provide us with a UUID as a response. We need to keep checking the completion percentage until it is complete.

If you do not want to wait for this whole process to complete, you can download the database from `https://packt-neo4j-powered-applications.s3.us-east-1.amazonaws.com/Building+Neo4j-Powered+Applications+with+LLMs+Database+Dump+files.zip`.

Now, that we have performed the augmentation, let us take a look at how good these embeddings are and how they can help us provide recommendations. For this purpose, we can further enhance the graph by creating vector indexes for the embeddings we created.

You can execute this Cypher query to create a vector index for embeddings on articles:

```
CREATE VECTOR INDEX `article-embeddings` IF NOT EXISTS
FOR (a:Article)
ON a.embedding
OPTIONS { indexConfig: {
  `vector.dimensions`: 3072,
  `vector.similarity_function`: 'cosine'
}}
```

This creates a vector index on `Article` nodes named `article-embeddings`.

The following Cypher code can be used to create a vector index on the summer 2019 purchases embedding:

```
CREATE VECTOR INDEX `summer-2019-embeddings` IF NOT EXISTS
FOR ()-[r:SUMMER_2019]->() ON (r.embedding)
OPTIONS { indexConfig: {
 `vector.dimensions`: 3072,
 `vector.similarity_function`: 'cosine'
}}
```

This creates a vector index on the SUMMER_2019 relationship named summer-2019-embeddings.

Let us take a look at using the Article vector index first. This Cypher tries to find the top five matches for an article with an ID of 0748579001:

```
MATCH (a:Article {id:'0748579001'})
WITH a
CALL db.index.vector.queryNodes('article-embeddings', 5, a.embedding)
YIELD node, score
RETURN score, node.id as id, node.desc as desc
```

From the results (*Figure 9.7*), we can see that the first match is the best match and it is the Article node we looked for:

Score	Id	Desc
1.0	"0748579001"	"Ankle-length, A-line beach dress in an airy, patterned weave with a deep V-neck with gold-coloured studs, and long dolman sleeves with elastication and a decorative drawstring at the cuffs. Unlined."
0.882	"0748033001"	"Long beach dress in airy, crinkled chiffon with narrow, tie-top shoulder straps and an opening at the back of the neck. Unlined."
0.873	"0748582008"	"Short beach dress in an airy cotton weave with broderie anglaise. V-neck front and back with a crocheted lace trim, horizontal, tasselled straps at the back of the neck, dropped shoulders and short sleeves. Seam at the waist and a gently flared skirt. Unlined."
0.866	"0748025004"	"Kaftan in an airy weave with buttons down the front and high slits in the sides."
0.866	"0747737004"	"Sarong in an airy weave. Size 130x150 cm."

Figure 9.7 — Similar articles for a given article

Also, we can see that the articles that are less similar to each other have lower score values. From this result, let us take `Article` with an ID of `0748582008` and see what we can find:

```
MATCH (a:Article {id:'0748582008'})
WITH a
CALL db.index.vector.queryNodes('article-embeddings', 5, a.embedding)
YIELD node, score
RETURN score, node.id as id, node.desc as desc
```

When we run the Cypher, we can see these results:

Score	Id	Desc
1.0	"0748582008"	"Short beach dress in an airy cotton weave with broderie anglaise. V-neck front and back with a crocheted lace trim, horizontal, tasselled straps at the back of the neck, dropped shoulders and short sleeves. Seam at the waist and a gently flared skirt. Unlined."
0.969	"0748582001"	"Short beach dress in an airy cotton weave with broderie anglaise. V-neck front and back with a crocheted lace trim, horizontal, tasselled straps at the back of the neck, dropped shoulders and short sleeves. Seam at the waist and a gently flared skirt. Unlined."
0.893	"0848082001"	"Short beach kaftan in an airy weave with lace trims. Short, wide sleeves, and a drawstring at the waist."
0.884	"0854784001"	"Short beach dress in an airy cotton weave containing glittery threads. Round neckline with a V-neck opening and narrow ties at the front, dropped shoulders and long balloon sleeves with narrow, buttoned cuffs. Gathered tiers at the hem for added width."
0.884	"0850893001"	"Calf-length lace kaftan with a crocheted trim around the opening, a drawstring and twisted ties at the waist, and long sleeves. Scalloped trim around the cuffs and hem."

Figure 9.8 — Similar articles for a given article

From the results, we can see that when the score is closer to `0.9`, the articles are pretty similar. We can use this information to provide similar articles as recommendations, based on the articles customers have already purchased.

Now, let us look at the customer summer purchase behaviors for a customer whose ID ends in 92f0. Let's call this customer, A:

```
MATCH (c:Customer)-[r:SUMMER_2019]->() WHERE
c.id='0002b7a7ab270a638fcb2eb5899c58696db24d9d954ddb43683dd6b0ffa292f0'
WITH r
CALL db.index.vector.queryRelationships('summer-2019-embeddings', 5,
r.embedding)
YIELD relationship, score
MATCH (oc)-[relationship]->()
WITH oc, score, relationship
WITH oc, score, split(relationship.summary, '\n') as s
WITH oc, score, CASE when s[2] <> '' THEN s[2] ELSE s[3] end as desc
WITH score, oc.id as id, desc
RETURN round(score,3) as score,
substring(id,0,4)+".."+substring(id,size(id)-4) as id, desc
```

When we run this Cypher, we can see these results:

Score	Id	Desc
1.0	"0002..92f0"	"The customer exhibits a strong preference for vibrant colors and comfortable, casual styles, particularly in swimwear and denim. Their purchases suggest a love for playful yet practical clothing, suitable for both beach outings and everyday wear. The mix of swimwear, shorts, and casual tops indicates a versatile wardrobe focused on both style and comfort."
0.968	"044d..d47e"	"The customer exhibits a strong preference for swimwear, particularly in vibrant colors like light orange and dark red, indicating a fun and playful style. Their choices also reflect an inclination towards high-waisted designs and supportive tops, suggesting a desire for both comfort and fashion. Additionally, the purchase of a versatile playsuit and tailored jacket indicates an appreciation for stylish yet practical everyday wear."
0.967	"07fe..a87f"	"The customer exhibits a strong preference for swimwear, particularly in vibrant colors like orange and black, indicating a love for beach and poolside activities. There is also a notable inclination towards basic wardrobe staples, such as tank tops and shorts, suggesting a desire for comfortable yet stylish casual wear. The blend of swimwear and basic clothing reflects a versatile fashion sense suitable for both leisure and everyday wear."

| 0.966 | "0247..74b3" | "The customer demonstrates a preference for vibrant colors and versatile clothing items suitable for various occasions, including casual wear and swimwear. The repeated purchases of swimwear suggest a keen interest in beach or poolside activities. Additionally, the inclusion of dresses and accessories indicates a desire for stylish yet comfortable outfits." |
| 0.965 | "0686..5220" | "The customer displays a strong preference for vibrant colors, particularly orange and white, as seen in their selection of swimwear and casual attire. Their purchases indicate a blend of comfort and style, with a focus on versatile pieces that can be worn for various occasions. The inclusion of both swimwear and everyday clothing suggests a lifestyle that appreciates both leisure and fashion." |

Figure 9.9 — Purchase summaries for other customers similar to the given customer

From the basic summary, we can see that the customer purchase behaviors are pretty similar. Let us pick another customer (say, customer B) from this list to see whether the same customers are returned when we run the same query. We will pick the customer ID ending in 74b3:

```
MATCH (c:Customer)-[r:SUMMER_2019]->() WHERE c.id='
0247b7b564909181b2e552fe3d5cec01056ebc1b3d61d38f1ff0658db69174b3'
WITH r
CALL db.index.vector.queryRelationships('summer-2019-embeddings', 5,
r.embedding)
YIELD relationship, score
MATCH (oc)-[relationship]->()
WITH oc, score, relationship
WITH oc, score, split(relationship.summary, '\n') as s
WITH oc, score, CASE when s[2] <> '' THEN s[2] ELSE s[3] end as desc
WITH score, oc.id as id, desc
RETURN round(score,3) as score,
substring(id,0,4)+".."+substring(id,size(id)-4) as id, desc
```

Let us look at the results when we run this query:

Score	Id	Desc
1.0	"0247..74b3"	"The customer demonstrates a preference for vibrant colors and versatile clothing items suitable for various occasions, including casual wear and swimwear. The repeated purchases of swimwear suggest a keen interest in beach or poolside activities. Additionally, the inclusion of dresses and accessories indicates a desire for stylish yet comfortable outfits."
0.968	"05de..29df"	"The customer's fashion preferences indicate a strong inclination towards swimwear and dresses, particularly in vibrant and playful colors such as pink, orange, and blue. The selection of both swimwear and dresses suggests a versatile style that embraces both casual beachwear and stylish everyday attire. Additionally, the repeated purchases of high-waisted bikini bottoms showcase a preference for flattering and functional swimwear options."
0.967	"0322..3e92"	"The customer exhibits a strong preference for swimwear, as evidenced by multiple purchases of bikini tops and bottoms, showcasing a desire for stylish beach attire. Additionally, the selection of dresses and blouses reflects an inclination towards fashionable yet comfortable everyday wear. The use of vibrant colors and unique design elements indicates a taste for contemporary and eye-catching pieces."
0.966	"0002..92f0"	"The customer exhibits a strong preference for vibrant colors and comfortable, casual styles, particularly in swimwear and denim. Their purchases suggest a love for playful yet practical clothing, suitable for both beach outings and everyday wear. The mix of swimwear, shorts, and casual tops indicates a versatile wardrobe focused on both style and comfort."
0.965	"0863..c454"	"The customer displays a strong preference for swimwear, particularly in vibrant colors like dark red and orange, indicating a fondness for beachwear and summer styles. Additionally, their choices in everyday clothing, such as airy dresses and denim skirts, suggest an inclination towards comfortable yet stylish casual wear. The repetition of specific items also reflects a desire for consistency and reliability in their fashion selections."

Figure 9.10 — Purchase summaries for other customers similar to the given customer

We can see that the top five matches for customer B are very different from those of customer A, even though customer B's purchase summary was in the top five similar customer purchases of customer A.

We can use this approach to recommend articles to purchase based on customer purchase behavior. We are capturing the order of the purchases, but how the summary of these purchases is captured by an embedding defines who will be considered a similar customer. Let us see what this query would look like:

```
MATCH (c:Customer)-[r:SUMMER_2019]->() WHERE
c.id='0247b7b564909181b2e552fe3d5cec01056ebc1b3d61d38f1ff0658db69174b3'
WITH c, r
```

We want to find other customers similar to this customer based on purchases. We will use the vector index to get the top five similar customers:

```
CALL db.index.vector.queryRelationships('summer-2019-embeddings', 5,
r.embedding)
YIELD relationship, score
MATCH (oc)-[relationship]->()
WITH c, collect(oc) as others
CALL {
```

Collect the articles purchased by the customer:

```
    WITH c
    MATCH (c)-[:SUMMER_2019]->(start)
    MATCH (c)-[:FALL_2019]->(end)
    WITH start, end
    MATCH p=(start)-[:NEXT*]->(end)
    WITH p
    WITH nodes(p) as txns
    UNWIND txns as tx
    MATCH (tx)-[:HAS_ARTICLE]->(a)
    RETURN collect(a) as customerPurchases
}
WITH others, customerPurchases
CALL {
```

Collect the articles purchased by the other customers who are similar to the first customer:

```
    WITH others
    UNWIND others as a
    MATCH (a:Customer)-[:SUMMER_2019]->(start)
    MATCH (a)-[:FALL_2019]->(end)
    WITH start, end
    MATCH p=(start)-[:NEXT*]->(end)
    WITH nodes(p) as txns
    UNWIND txns as tx
    MATCH (tx)-[:HAS_ARTICLE]->(a)
    WITH DISTINCT a
    RETURN collect(a) as otherPurchases
}
WITH customerPurchases, otherPurchases
```

Remove the articles purchased by the original customer from the articles purchased by similar customers:

```
WITH apoc.coll.subtract(otherPurchases, customerPurchases) as others
UNWIND others as other
RETURN other.id as id, other.desc as desc
LIMIT 10
```

This Cypher first collects the purchases made by the customer, finds other customers who have similar purchase behavior, retrieves the purchases made by those customers, and recommends 10 articles to the original customer that they haven't previously purchased. The output of this query looks like this:

Id	Desc
"0471714036"	"Knee-length shorts in a cotton weave with a button fly, side pockets and a welt back pocket with a button."
"0699923078"	"T-shirt in soft, printed cotton jersey."
"0786663001"	"Short, off-the-shoulder dress in an airy, plumeti weave with elastication and a small frill trim at the top. Long sleeves with elastication at the cuffs, an elasticated seam at the waist and a flounce at the hem. Jersey lining."
"0728473001"	"Triangle bikini top with laser-cut scalloped edges and lightly padded cups with removable inserts. Narrow, adjustable shoulder straps that can be fastened in different ways and an adjustable metal hook fastening at the back."

"0689040001"	"Fully lined bikini bottoms with a mid waist, wide sides, a wide tie at one side and medium coverage at the back."
"0736046001"	"Metal hoop earrings in different sizes, three with charms in various designs. Diameter 1-2 cm."
"0713200006"	"Fully lined, waist-high bikini bottoms with wide sides and medium coverage at the back."
"0674606026"	"Short, A-line skirt with a high waist and buttons down the front."
"0562245064"	"5-pocket jeans in washed, superstretch denim with a regular waist, zip fly and button, and skinny legs."
"0557247005"	"Oversized top in sturdy sweatshirt fabric with dropped shoulders and ribbing around the neckline, cuffs and hem. Soft brushed inside."

Figure 9.11 — Recommendations for a customer based on purchases made by similar customers

By following the steps explained to fine-tune your graph, we can now provide recommendations based on customer purchase behavior by finding similar customers and their purchases or similar articles based on what customers bought. This approach is simple and works well. But we are determining who similar customers are, and so on. We might want to use **Graph Data Science** algorithms or machine learning to group customers better so that we can provide better recommendations. We will take a look at that aspect in the next chapter.

Summary

In this chapter, we looked at how to build intelligent applications by leveraging LangChain4j and Spring AI. We used these applications to augment the H&M transactions graph we loaded in the previous chapter, by leveraging LLM chat and embedding capabilities. Once the graph was augmented, we further enhanced the graph by leveraging vector indexes and saw how these indexes help us find similar articles or customers based on their purchases.

In the next chapter, we will step into **Graph Data Science** algorithms to see how we can further enhance these recommendations.

10

Creating an Intelligent Recommendation System

Now that we have loaded the data into a graph, and looked at how we can augment the graph using Langchain4j and Spring AI, along with generating recommendations, we will look at how we can go further to improve the recommendations by leveraging **Graph Data Science (GDS) algorithms** and machine learning. We will review the GDS algorithms provided by Neo4j to go beyond the recommendation system we created in the previous chapter. We will also learn how to use the GDS algorithms to build collaborative filtering as well as content-based approaches to provide recommendations. We will also take a look at the results after we run the algorithms to review how our approach is working and whether we are on the right path to build a better recommendation system. We will try to understand why these algorithms are better than the approach we implemented in the previous chapter.

In this chapter, we are going to cover the following main topics:

- Improving recommendations with GDS algorithms
- Understanding the power of communities
- Combining collaborative filtering and content-based approaches

Technical requirements

We will be using a Java IDE environment to work with the Langchain4j and Spring AI projects. You will need to have these installed and know how to work with them.

Setting up the environment

We will be starting from the graph database we built in the last chapter. The code is tested with the Neo4j 5.21.2 version of the database.

To set up the environment, you will need

- Neo4j Desktop with the following plugins installed. :

  - APOC plugin – 5.21.2
  - Graph Data Science library – 2.9.0

Figure 10.1 shows how to install these plugins for a DBMS.

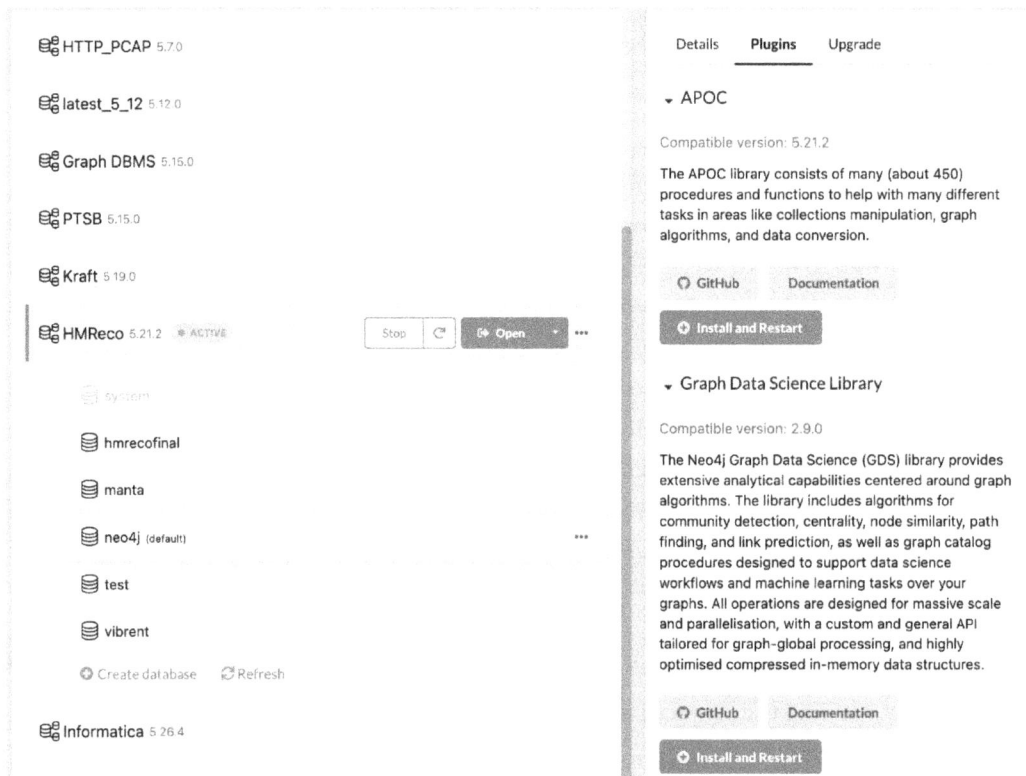

Figure 10.1 — Install plugins in Neo4j Desktop

When you select the DBMS in Neo4j Desktop, on the right side, it shows its details. Click on the **Plugins** tab and select the plugins. Once that is expanded, click on the **Install and Restart** button.

Next, we will look at the database dump required for this chapter.

Getting the database ready

Before you begin, you will need to create the communities. It will take some time for the similarity and community detection algorithms to complete. Thus, it is recommended to download the database dump from `https://packt-neo4j-powered-applications.s3.us-east-1.amazonaws.com/hmreco_post_augment_with_summary_communities.dump` and use it to create a database in Neo4j Desktop. You can use these instructions to load this dump into Neo4j Desktop: `https://neo4j.com/docs/desktop-manual/current/operations/create-from-dump/`.

This database dump has all the `SUMMER_2019_SIMILAR` relationships created and the communities are identified.

Let's start with using the GDS algorithms to enhance our knowledge graph for improved recommendations.

Improving recommendations with GDS algorithms

In this section, we will look at how we can enhance the graph further to gain more insights into the graph to build a better recommendation system. We will start with the graph database we created in the last chapter. For reference, you can download it from `https://packt-neo4j-powered-applications.s3.us-east-1.amazonaws.com/Building+Neo4j-Powered+Applications+with+LLMs+Database+Dump+files.zip`.

The Neo4j GDS algorithms (`https://neo4j.com/docs/graph-data-science/current/`) will help us enhance the graph. This process includes the following steps:

1. Calculate the similarity between customers based on the embeddings we have created and create a similar relationship between these customers. For this purpose, we will leverage the **K-Nearest Neighbors (KNN)** algorithm (`https://neo4j.com/docs/graph-data-science/current/algorithms/knn/`).

2. Run the community detection algorithm to group the customers based on similar relationships. For this purpose, we will leverage the **Louvain community detection** algorithm (`https://neo4j.com/docs/graph-data-science/current/algorithms/louvain/`).

First, we will utilize the KNN algorithm to enhance the graph.

Computing similarity with the KNN algorithm

The **K-Nearest Neighbors (KNN)** algorithm collects node pairs, computes a distance value between a node and its neighbors, and creates a relationship between the node and its **top K** neighbors. The distance is calculated based on node properties. We need to provide a homogeneous graph for this algorithm. When all the nodes and relationships are the same, it is called a **homogeneous graph**. The node pairs we provide to the KNN algorithm do not need any node labels or relationship types. The KNN algorithm just needs node pairs that are connected and an optional property that can be used as the context of the relationship between them. You can read more about this at https://neo4j.com/docs/graph-data-science/current/algorithms/knn.

To use this algorithm, we need to follow this process:

1. Project graph of interest to apply the algorithm.

2. Invoke the algorithm with the appropriate configuration. There are three modes of this algorithm:

    -   **Stream**: This applies the algorithm to the in-memory graph and streams the results. You can use the stream mode to inspect the results and see if they are what we want.

    -   **Mutate**: This applies the algorithm to the in-memory graph and writes the data back to the in-memory graph. The actual database does not change. The mutate method is used when we want to update the in-memory graph and want to process it later for different purposes.

    -   **Write**: This applies the algorithm to the in-memory graph and writes the relationships back to the actual database. This mode is used when we are sure of the process and want to write the results back to the graph immediately.

We will start with graph projection. Since we have written the embeddings on the SUMMER_2019 relationships, we will use those for processing.

This Cypher projects the graph in memory to be able to invoke this algorithm:

```
MATCH (c:Customer)-[sr:SUMMER_2019]->()
WHERE sr.embedding is not null
RETURN gds.graph.project(
  'myGraph',
  c,
  null,
  {
    sourceNodeProperties: sr { .embedding },
    targetNodeProperties: {}
  }
)
```

Normally, we will use the properties on the node to build a projection. Here, we have written the embedding value on a relationship, as this embedding is created to represent the summer 2019 season purchases. If we had written that embedding on the Customer node, then if we wanted to understand the customer purchase behavior for various scenarios, we would need to use some clever naming to write those to only the Customer node. By writing that embedding on the relationship, we are preserving the context of the embedding in the graph.

We can see from the preceding Cypher that we are retrieving the embedding from the relationship and adding it as a source node property in the projection. Now, let us invoke the algorithm to write back similar relationships to the graph.

This Cypher invokes the algorithm to write back the results:

```
CALL gds.knn.write('myGraph', {
    writeRelationshipType: 'SUMMER_2019_SIMILAR',
    writeProperty: 'score',
    topK: 5,
    nodeProperties: ['embedding'],
    similarityCutoff: 0.9
})
YIELD nodesCompared, relationshipsWritten
```

From the Cypher, we can see we are invoking the write mode of the algorithm. The algorithm will calculate the similarity between Customers by using **cosine similarity** on the embeddings, with a cut-off score of 0.9, pick the top 5 neighbors in the order of similarity score, and write a relationship named SUMMER_2019_SIMILAR between those customers.

> **Note**
>
> Cosine similarity calculates the angle between two vectors. So, if the vectors are farther apart, then the similarity value will be close to 0. If they are closer to each other, then the similarity value will be close to 1. If you want to read more about it, you can read at https://en.wikipedia.org/wiki/Cosine_similarity.

Similar scores can be between 0 and 1. If the score is closer to 0 between 2 entities, then they are not similar to each other. If it is close to 1, then they are more similar. We are using 0.9 as the similarity cutoff as we are generating embeddings based on the summary text generated – customers might have a higher similarity score. We don't want a similar relationship between customers because there are some keywords that are similar. We will validate this assumption in later steps. We are limiting ourselves to the top five (k =5) similar customer behaviors, to get closer recommendations.

> **Note**
>
> Please note that the KNN algorithm is a non-deterministic algorithm by default. This means that different runs might give different results. You can learn more about this at https://neo4j.com/docs/graph-data-science/2.14/algorithms/knn/. If you want deterministic results, then you must ensure that the concurrency parameter is set to one and the randomSeed parameter is explicitly set.

Once the algorithm is invoked, we need to remove the graph projection. Otherwise, it will keep using the memory in the database server:

```
CALL gds.graph.drop('myGraph')
```

This Cypher will drop the graph and clear the memory used by the graph projection.

We will take a look at community detection next, based on the SUMMER_2019_SIMILAR relationship.

For this, we will be leveraging the Louvain community detection algorithm, which is the most popular community detection algorithm.

Detecting communities with the Louvain algorithm

The **Louvain algorithm** relies on the similarity scores between entities and groups them into communities. It takes large, networked data and groups it into smaller, tighter-knit communities by looking at the neighbors and their relationships. This hierarchical clustering algorithm recursively merges communities into a single node and executes the modularity clustering on the condensed graphs. It maximizes a modularity score for each community, evaluating how much more densely connected the nodes within a community are compared to how connected they would be in a random network. We want to group our customers in more tight-knit groups in a more automated way to provide broader recommendations. You can read more about this at https://neo4j.com/docs/graph-data-science/current/algorithms/louvain/.

The approach is very similar to how we invoked the KNN algorithm. To use this algorithm, we need to follow this process.

1. Project graph of interest to apply the algorithm.

2. Invoke the algorithm with the appropriate configuration. There are three modes of this algorithm.

    - **Stream:** This applies the algorithm to the in-memory graph and streams the results. You can use the stream mode to inspect the results and see if they are what we want.

    - **Mutate:** This applies the algorithm to the in-memory graph and writes the data back to the in-memory graph. The actual database has not changed. The mutate method is used when we want to update the in-memory graph and want to process it later for different purposes.

    - **Write:** This applies the algorithm to the in-memory graph and writes the relationships back to the actual database. This mode is used when we are sure of the process and want to write the results back to the graph immediately.

Let's start with **graph projection**. We will use the SUMMER_2019_SIMILAR relationship and the score value saved on that relationship to perform community detection:

```
MATCH (source:Customer)-[r:SUMMER_2019_SIMILAR]->(target)
RETURN gds.graph.project(
  'communityGraph',
  source,
  target,
  {
    relationshipProperties: r { .score }
  },
  { undirectedRelationshipTypes: ['*'] }
)
```

The preceding Cypher creates an in-memory projection named communityGraph. It takes the source node, target node, and the score on the SUMMER_2019_SIMILAR relationship to build the projection.

Once the projection is built, we can use this Cypher to perform community detection:

```
CALL gds.louvain.write('communityGraph', { writeProperty: 'summer_2019_
community' })
YIELD communityCount, modularity, modularities
```

This Cypher performs the community detection and writes back the community ID as a property named `summer_2019_community` on the `Customer` node.

Once the community detection is complete, we need to drop the graph projection.

```
CALL gds.graph.drop('communityGraph')
```

This Cypher will drop the graph and clear the memory used by the graph projection.

We can use this Cypher to inspect how many communities are created:

```
MATCH (c:Customer) WHERE c.summer_2019_community IS NOT NULL
RETURN c.summer_2019_community, COUNT(c) as count
ORDER BY count DESC
```

This Cypher gives all communities, in the order of how many customers belong to that community. The response would look as shown in *Figure 10.2*.

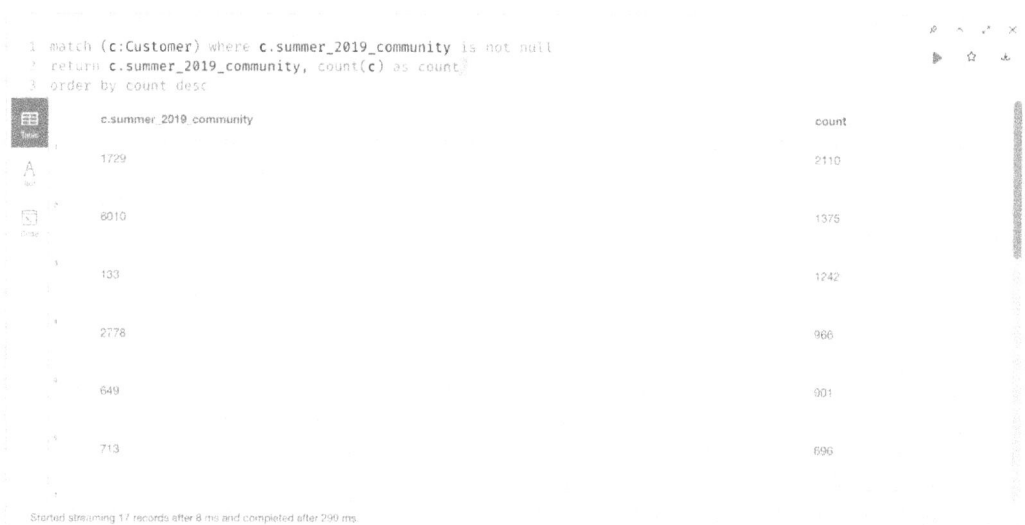

Figure 10.2 — Communities with customer counts

Note:

Please note that the Louvain community detection algorithm is a non-deterministic algorithm by default. This means that different runs might give different results. You can learn more about this at `https://neo4j.com/docs/graph-data-science/2.14/algorithms/louvain/`.

Now that we have built communities, let us take a look at the communities generated. In the next section, we will inspect a few of these communities to observe whether they group customers based on their purchase behavior.

Understanding the power of communities

Previously, in *Chapter 9*, we looked at finding similar customers using vector similarity and how to provide recommendations for a customer. Let's revisit *Figure 9.10* and *Figure 9.11*. *Figure 9.10* displays the purchase history of customers similar to a particular customer. *Figure 9.11* shows the recommendations for a customer based on the purchases of similar customers. The purchase history and customer recommendations are a result of the Cypher queries we worked on in the *Fine-tuning your recommendations* section to understand vector similarity usage.

In this section, we will take a deeper look at communities and see why they might be better than leveraging simple vector similarity to find similar customers.

> **Note**
>
> The following Cyphers are related to the database shared in the *Technical requirements* section.

From the Cypher we ran in the last section, *Detecting communities with the Louvain algorithm*, let us pick a community that has a good number of customers in it. We will take a look at the community with ID 133, which has around $1,242$ customers in it.

The following Cypher displays the customer purchase summary without the article details for the first five customers:

```
MATCH (c:Customer)-[r:SUMMER_2019]->()
WHERE c.summer_2019_community=133
WITH split(r.summary, '\n') AS s
WITH CASE WHEN s[2] <> '' THEN s[2] ELSE s[3] END AS d
return d LIMIT 5
```

When we run community detection, the community IDs generated can be different for each run. So, if you have run your own Cypher script to create the customer communities, you need to take a look at the communities and use those IDs to validate the data.

When we run the preceding Cypher script, the output looks like this:

```
The customer demonstrates a preference for stylish and modern pieces,
particularly favoring dresses and lingerie that offer both comfort and
elegance. The consistent choice of midi and short dresses paired with a
variety of non-wired bras suggests a desire for chic yet relaxed fashion
options. Additionally, the inclusion of tailored blouses and fashionable
outerwear indicates an appreciation for versatile styles suitable for
various occasions.

The customer exhibits a preference for comfortable yet stylish clothing,
favoring light and soft colors such as light pink and light blue. Their
purchases reflect a blend of casual and lingerie items, indicating á focus
on both everyday wear and intimate apparel. The selection features a mix
of high-waisted denim and lace detailing, suggesting an appreciation for
modern, flattering silhouettes.

The customer demonstrates a strong preference for versatile and stylish
pieces, favoring bold colors like pink and orange while incorporating
comfortable fabrics such as jersey and cotton. Their purchases include
a mix of casual wear, activewear, and lingerie, suggesting a balanced
lifestyle that values both comfort and aesthetics. The frequent selection
of shorts and dresses indicates a preference for easy-to-wear, fashionable
items suitable for various occasions.

The customer demonstrates a preference for comfortable and stylish
lingerie, favoring soft materials with unique design details such as lace
trims and laser-cut edges. Additionally, their choice of everyday wear
leans towards light and airy fabrics, showcasing a blend of casual and
chic styles suitable for various occasions. The color palette reflects
a soft and neutral aesthetic, with light pinks, beiges, and whites
dominating their selections.

The customer exhibits a preference for comfortable and functional
clothing, particularly in the realm of casual and lingerie wear. There is
a clear inclination towards basic styles in neutral colors such as black
and white, complemented by playful accents in perceived colors like orange
and pink. The focus on versatile pieces suggests a desire for practicality
combined with style.
```

From the summary descriptions, we can see the customers in this community prefer to buy casual and lingerie clothing together.

Let's take a look at the articles purchased by these customers:

```
MATCH (c:Customer)
WHERE c.summer_2019_community=133
WITH c LIMIT 10
MATCH (c)-[:SUMMER_2019]->(start)
MATCH (c)-[:FALL_2019]->(end)
WITH c, start, end
CALL {
    WITH start, end
    MATCH p=(start)-[:NEXT*]->(end)
    WITH nodes(p) as nodes
    UNWIND nodes as n
    MATCH (n)-[:HAS_ARTICLE]->(a)
    WITH a LIMIT 3
    RETURN collect(a.desc) as articles
}
WITH c, articles
RETURN articles
```

This Cypher gives this output:

```
["Calf-length dress in a crinkled weave with a V-neck, wrapover front
with ties at the waist and short sleeves with a slit and ties. Unlined.",
"Calf-length dress in a crinkled weave with a V-neck, wrapover front with
ties at the waist and short sleeves with a slit and ties. Unlined.",
"Soft, non-wired bras in cotton jersey with moulded, padded triangular
cups for a larger bust and fuller cleavage. Adjustable shoulder straps
that cross at the back and lace at the hem. No fasteners."]
["High-waisted jeans in washed superstretch denim with hard-worn details,
a zip fly and button, back pockets and skinny legs.", "Lace push-up
bra with underwired, moulded, padded cups for a larger bust and fuller
cleavage. Adjustable shoulder straps and a hook-and-eye fastening at the
back.", "Lace push-up bra with underwired, moulded, padded cups for a
larger bust and fuller cleavage. Adjustable shoulder straps and a hook-
and-eye fastening at the back."]
["Vest top in cotton jersey with a print motif.", "Soft, non-wired bras in
microfibre with padded cups that shape the bust and provide good support.
Adjustable shoulder straps and a hook-and-eye fastening at the back.",
"Chino shorts in washed cotton poplin with a zip fly, side pockets, welt
```

```
back pockets with a button and legs with creases."]
["Microfibre Brazilian briefs with laser-cut edges, a low waist, lined
gusset, wide sides and half-string back.", "Hipster briefs in microfibre
with lace trims, a low waist, lined gusset and cutaway coverage at the
back.", "Blouse in an airy weave with a V-neck, covered buttons down the
front, short dolman sleeves and a tie detail at the hem."]
["Round-necked T-shirt in soft cotton jersey.", "Round-necked T-shirt in
soft cotton jersey.", "Thong briefs in cotton jersey and lace with a low
waist, lined gusset, wide sides and string back."]
```

We are limiting ourselves to the first three articles so that we won't look at a lot of data here. We can see from the articles purchased that the summaries summarize the customer's purchase behavior well.

Let us look at how the customer age group to communities' correlation exists.

The following Cypher gives us the most frequently occurring age group in a community age group in a community:

```
MATCH (c:Customer) where c.summer_2019_community is not null
WITH  c.summer_2019_community as community, toInteger(c.age) as age,  c
WITH community,
    CASE WHEN age < 10 THEN "Young"
         WHEN 10 < age < 20 THEN "Teen"
         WHEN 20 < age < 30 THEN "Youth"
         WHEN 30 < age < 50 THEN "Adult"
         ELSE "Old"
    END as ageGroup,
    c
WITH community, ageGroup, count(*) as count
CALL {
    WITH community
    MATCH (c:Customer) where c.summer_2019_community=community
    RETURN count(*) as totalCommunity
}
WITH community, ageGroup,count, totalCommunity
WITH community, ageGroup, round(count*100.0/totalCommunity, 2) as ratio
WITH community, collect({ageGroup: ageGroup, ratio:ratio}) as data
CALL {
    WITH community, data
```

```
    UNWIND data as d
    WITH community, d
    ORDER BY d.ratio DESC
    RETURN community as c, d.ageGroup as a, d.ratio as r
    LIMIT 1
}
RETURN c as community, a as ageGroup, r as ratio
ORDER BY r DESC
```

The results will look as shown in *Figure 10.3*.

Community	Age Group	Ratio
1899	"Youth"	60.87
5823	"Adult"	56.68
770	"Youth"	47.9
1729	"Youth"	46.92
4602	"Youth"	45.71
133	"Youth"	44.61
921	"Youth"	44.17
3444	"Youth"	41.73
649	"Youth"	41.62
1881	"Youth"	41.26
1696	"Old"	41.06
2381	"Old"	40.94
6010	"Old"	37.67
713	"Youth"	37.64
760	"Youth"	36.09
1875	"Old"	35.09
2778	"Youth"	34.47

Figure 10.3 — Most frequently occurring age group and its ratio in every community

We can see most communities are dominated by the **Age Group, Youth**, who are aged between 20 and 30. Let us look at one of the communities where the **Youth** age group is not dominant. Let us look at community **5823**.

This Cypher gives us the first five customers' purchase summary of community 5823:

```
MATCH (c:Customer)-[r:SUMMER_2019]->()
WHERE c.summer_2019_community=5823
WITH c, split(r.summary, '\n') AS s
WITH c, CASE WHEN s[2] <> '' THEN s[2] ELSE s[3] END AS d
RETURN d LIMIT 5
```

When you perform a similarity search for a specific customer using their vector embedding, the results will primarily be other individual customers whose vector representations are close to the target customer's vector. You may observe a degree of heterogeneity. An important caveat is that when we solely rely on finding similar customers to a target customer, based on vector distance, we might miss out on potentially relevant recommendations.

Take a look at the following results:

The customer demonstrates a strong preference for **versatile and stylish pieces, with a notable inclination towards swimwear and casual skirts, reflecting an active and chic lifestyle.** The selection features a mix of practical and trendy items, highlighting an appreciation for both comfort and aesthetics. The color palette leans towards soft tones and earthy shades, suggesting a preference for understated elegance.

The customer exhibits a preference for stylish yet **comfortable footwear and swimwear, favoring pieces that blend functionality with trendy elements. The consistent use of white and orange in swimwear suggests a bold and lively aesthetic, while the choice of soft organic cotton for kids'** basics indicates an appreciation for quality and sustainability. Overall, there is a clear inclination towards versatile and fashionable pieces suitable for both leisure and casual settings.

The customer's fashion preferences indicate a strong inclination towards **relaxed and comfortable styles, particularly in children's denim wear. The consistent choice of blue tones across multiple purchases suggests a preference for classic and versatile colors.** Additionally, the inclusion of a dress with a structured yet casual design highlights an appreciation for both practicality and style in their wardrobe choices.

The customer exhibits a preference for **versatile and comfortable clothing, with a notable inclination towards knitwear and soft fabrics. Their choices reflect a balance of casual and practical styles suitable for everyday wear,** particularly in hues of black, dark orange, and grey, complemented by accents of pink. The selected items also indicate a focus on functionality, especially with the inclusion of nursing bras.

> The customer demonstrates a preference for **versatile and stylish pieces**
> **that blend comfort with contemporary design. They appreciate a mix of**
> **youthful and sophisticated styles, as seen in their selection of both**
> **kids' dresses and women's wear.** The choice of colors suggests a fondness
> for neutral tones with pops of color, reflecting both playful and elegant
> aesthetics.

These summaries show this community leans toward people who have kids. After observing the communities and a few customer summaries in those communities, we are able to understand the purchase behaviors better than just going by vector similarity.

Our next step is to combine collaborative filtering and content-based approaches to give better recommendations.

Combining collaborative filtering and content-based approaches

Collaborative filtering involves providing recommendations based on customer similarity based on their purchases, using which we have built customer communities, or using article similarity based on their characteristics. **Content-based filtering** allows providing recommendations based on article attributes or characteristics. We will take a look at how we can combine both of these approaches to provide better recommendations.

We will try these scenarios:

- **Scenario 1**: Filtering articles that belong to other communities
- **Scenario 2**: Filtering articles by characteristics and belonging to other communities

Let's discuss Scenario 1 first.

Scenario 1: Filtering articles that belong to other communities

In this scenario, we will first find all the articles purchased by all the customers in the same community. Next, we will find the articles purchased by customers who belong to other communities. The articles that belong to other communities will then be removed. This is followed by filtering out (removing) these articles (belonging to other communities).

For this scenario, we will pick the customer identified by `000ae8a03447710b4de81d85698dfc05`
`59258c93136650efc2429fcca80d699a` from community 1696.

1. Let us look at the purchase summary for this customer:

    ```
    MATCH (c:Customer)-[r:SUMMER_2019]->()
    WHERE
    .id='000ae8a03447710b4de81d85698dfc0559258c93136650efc2429fcca80d699
    '
    WITH c, split(r.summary, '\n') AS s
    WITH c, CASE WHEN s[2] <> '' THEN s[2] ELSE s[3] END AS d
    RETURN d
    ```

    This Cypher gives us this output:

    ```
    "The customer's fashion preferences indicate a strong inclination
    towards comfortable yet stylish pieces, often favoring soft fabrics
    and relaxed fits. The choices reflect a taste for versatile items
    that can be dressed up or down, particularly in a palette that
    leans towards darker shades with hints of pink. Overall, there is
    a notable emphasis on casual wear that combines simplicity with a
    touch of elegance."
    ```

2. Now let us get recommendations for this customer – the articles that they have not pur-
    chased earlier, using the following Cypher:

    ```
    MATCH (c:Customer {id:'000ae8a03447710b4de81d85698dfc-
    0559258c93136650efc2429fcca80d699a'})
    WITH c
    CALL {
    ```

3. Get the articles purchased by this customer:

    ```
            WITH c
            MATCH (c)-[:SUMMER_2019]->(start)
            MATCH (c)-[:FALL_2019]->(end)
            MATCH p=(start)-[:NEXT*]->(end)
            WITH nodes(p) as txns
            UNWIND txns as txn
            MATCH (txn)-[:HAS_ARTICLE]->(a)
            WITH DISTINCT a
            RETURN collect(a) as articles
    ```

```
}
WITH c, articles, c.summer_2019_community as community
CALL {
```

4. Get the articles purchased by customers in the same community as the original customer:

```
WITH community
MATCH (inc:Customer) WHERE inc.summer_2019_community = community
MATCH (inc)-[:SUMMER_2019]->(start)
MATCH (inc)-[:FALL_2019]->(end)
MATCH p=(start)-[:NEXT*]->(end)
WITH nodes(p) as txns
UNWIND txns as txn
MATCH (txn)-[:HAS_ARTICLE]->(a)
WITH DISTINCT a
RETURN collect(a) as inCommunityArticles
}
WITH c, articles,  community, inCommunityArticles
CALL {
```

5. Get the articles purchased by customers that are not in the same community as the original customer:

```
WITH community
MATCH (outc:Customer) WHERE outc.summer_2019_community is not
ull and outc.summer_2019_community <> community
MATCH (outc)-[:SUMMER_2019]->(start)
MATCH (outc)-[:FALL_2019]->(end)
MATCH p=(start)-[:NEXT*]->(end)
WITH nodes(p) as txns
UNWIND txns as txn
MATCH (txn)-[:HAS_ARTICLE]->(a)
WITH DISTINCT a
RETURN collect(a) as outCommunityArticles
}
WITH c, articles,  community, inCommunityArticles,
utCommunityArticles
```

6. Remove the articles purchased by customers outside the community the original customer belongs to:

```
WITH c, articles, apoc.coll.subtract(inCommunityArticles,
outCommunityArticles) as onlyInCommunity
```

7. Remove the articles purchased by the original customer from the `onlyInCommunityArticles`:

```
WITH c, apoc.coll.subtract(onlyInCommunity, articles) as
notPurchasedButInCommunity
```

8. Provide 10 recommended articles from the remaining list. We are limiting this to 10 articles for simplicity and demonstration purposes. We can look at all the articles and maybe group them by other aspects and provide different recommendations:

```
UNWIND notPurchasedButInCommunity as article
RETURN article.id as id, article.desc as desc
LIMIT 10
```

Here, we get the articles purchased by the customer first. Then, we retrieve all the articles of the community the customer belongs to. After that, we get all the articles customers belonging to other communities purchased. We get the subset of the articles purchased only by customers in the community. From this set, we remove the articles the customer purchased and provide the articles as recommendations.

The output of this query would look as shown in *Figure 10.4*.

Id	Desc
0708679001	Slim-fit, ankle-length jeans in washed, superstretch denim with a high waist, zip fly, fake front pockets and real back pockets.
0834749001	Oversized jumper in a soft rib knit containing some wool with a polo neck, low dropped shoulders, long, voluminous sleeves, and wide ribbing at the cuffs and hem. The polyester content of the jumper is recycled.
0513701002	V-neck T-shirts in organic cotton jersey.
0522374003	Jumper in a soft, fine knit with dropped shoulders, long sleeves and gently rounded hem.
0522374001	Jumper in a soft, fine knit with dropped shoulders, long sleeves and gently rounded hem.
0687041002	Long-sleeved, fitted top in soft, organic cotton jersey with a deep neckline, buttons at the top and a rounded hem.

0724567004	Pyjamas with a strappy top and shorts in soft satin with lace details. Top with a V-neck and narrow adjustable shoulder straps. Shorts with narrow elastication at the waist.
0785086001	Short satin nightslip with a V-neck, lace trims at the top and hem, and adjustable spaghetti shoulder straps.
0725353002	Bell-shaped, knee-length skirt in woven fabric with a high waist and a concealed zip and hook-and-eye fastening in one side. Lined.
0604655007	Pyjamas in printed cotton jersey. Short-sleeved top with a round neck. Bottoms with an elasticated waist and wide, gently tapered legs with ribbed hems.

Figure 10.4 — Recommendations by filtering out the articles purchased by a customer and by customers outside the community

These recommendations do seem to fit into the customer purchase summary.

Now let us look at scenario 2.

Scenario 2: Filtering articles by characteristics and belonging to other communities

In this scenario, we want to add article characteristics to the query. This means, for a customer, we will first find all the articles purchased by the community with certain characteristics. Then we will find the communities these articles belong to and remove the articles that belong to other communities.

For this purpose, we will choose community 5823 and the customer with ID 00281c683a8eb0942 e22d88275ad756309895813e0648d4b97c7bc8178502b33. Let us look at this customer's purchases.

1. This Cypher gives us this information:

    ```
    MATCH (c:Customer) where c.id='00281c683a8eb0942e22d88275ad-
    756309895813e0648d4b97c7bc8178502b33'
    WITH c
    CALL {
        WITH c
        MATCH (c)-[:SUMMER_2019]->(start)
        MATCH (c)-[:FALL_2019]->(end)
        MATCH p=(start)-[:NEXT*]->(end)
        WITH nodes(p) as txns
        UNWIND txns as txn
    ```

```
        MATCH (txn)-[:HAS_ARTICLE]->(a)-[:HAS_SECTION]->(s)
        WITH DISTINCT a,s
        RETURN collect({section:s.name, article:a.desc}) as articles
    }
    return articles
```

Based on the preceding Cypher we get this output:

```
{
  "article": "5-pocket jeans in washed stretch denim in a relaxed
fit with an adjustable elasticated waist, zip fly and press-stud and
tapered legs.",
  "section": "Kids Boy"}
,
{
  "article": "5-pocket jeans in washed stretch denim with hard-worn
details in a relaxed fit with an adjustable elasticated waist, zip
fly and press-stud, and tapered legs.",
  "section": "Kids Boy"
}
,
{
  "article": "Short dress in woven fabric with a collar, buttons
down the front and a yoke at the back. Narrow, detachable belt at
the waist and long sleeves with buttoned cuffs. Unlined.",
  "section": "Divided Collection"
}
,
{
  "article": "Dungarees in washed stretch denim with a three-part
chest pocket, adjustable straps with metal fasteners, and front and
back pockets. Fake fly, press-studs at the sides, jersey-lined legs
and a lining at the hems in a patterned weave.",
  "section": "Kids Boy"
}
```

Since this customer is buying clothing from the "Kids Boy" section, let us retrieve recommendations that belong to this section.

2. This Cypher gives us recommendations by adding this section's details to the earlier query. Let us get the Customer with ID: 00281c683a8eb0942e22d88275ad756309895813e0648d 4b97c7bc8178502b33 and the section named Kids Boy:

```
MATCH (c:Customer {id:'00281c683a8eb0942e22d88275ad-
756309895813e0648d4b97c7bc8178502b33'})
MATCH (s:Section) WHERE s.name='Kids Boy'
WITH c,s
CALL {
```

3. Get the articles purchased by this customer that belong to the section of importance:

```
WITH c,s
MATCH (c)-[:SUMMER_2019]->(start)
MATCH (c)-[:FALL_2019]->(end)
MATCH p=(start)-[:NEXT*]->(end)
WITH nodes(p) as txns
UNWIND txns as txn
MATCH (txn)-[:HAS_ARTICLE]->(a)-[:HAS_SECTION]->(s)
WITH DISTINCT a
RETURN collect(a) as articles
}
WITH c, articles,s, c.summer_2019_community as community
CALL {
```

4. Get the articles that belong to the section of importance purchased by customers in the same community as the original customer:

```
WITH community, s
MATCH (inc:Customer) WHERE inc.summer_2019_community = community
MATCH (inc)-[:SUMMER_2019]->(start)
MATCH (inc)-[:FALL_2019]->(end)
MATCH p=(start)-[:NEXT*]->(end)
WITH nodes(p) as txns, s
UNWIND txns as txn
MATCH (txn)-[:HAS_ARTICLE]->(a)-[:HAS_SECTION]->(s)
WITH DISTINCT a
RETURN collect(a) as inCommunityArticles
```

```
}
WITH c, articles,  community, inCommunityArticles, s
CALL {
```

5. Get the articles that belong to the section of importance purchased by customers in the communities outside the one the original customer belongs to:

```
    WITH community, s
    MATCH (outc:Customer) WHERE outc.summer_2019_community is not
ull and outc.summer_2019_community <> community
    MATCH (outc)-[:SUMMER_2019]->(start)
    MATCH (outc)-[:FALL_2019]->(end)
    MATCH p=(start)-[:NEXT*]->(end)
    WITH nodes(p) as txns, s
    UNWIND txns as txn
    MATCH (txn)-[:HAS_ARTICLE]->(a)-[:HAS_SECTION]->(s)
    WITH DISTINCT a
    RETURN collect(a) as outCommunityArticles
}
WITH c, articles,  community, inCommunityArticles,
utCommunityArticles
```

6. Remove the articles purchased by customers outside the community from the articles purchased by customers in the community of the original customer:

```
WITH c, articles, apoc.coll.subtract(inCommunityArticles,
outCommunityArticles) as onlyInCommunity
```

7. Remove the articles purchased by the original customer from the list of articles we got in the previous step:

```
WITH c, apoc.coll.subtract(onlyInCommunity, articles) as
notPurchasedButInCommunity
```

8. Provide 10 of these articles as recommendations:

```
UNWIND notPurchasedButInCommunity as article
RETURN article.id as id, article.desc as desc
LIMIT 10
```

When we run this query, we will see the output shown in *Figure 10.5*:

Id	Desc
0505507003	5-pocket slim-fit jeans in washed stretch denim with an adjustable elasticated waist and zip fly.
0704150011	Long-sleeved top in sweatshirt fabric with a motif on the front and ribbing around the neckline, cuffs and hem.
0701969005	Shorts in soft, patterned cotton twill with an elasticated drawstring waist, fake fly and side pockets.
0595548001	Shorts in soft, washed denim with an elasticated drawstring waist and a back pocket.
0704150006	Long-sleeved top in sweatshirt fabric with a motif on the front and ribbing around the neckline, cuffs and hem.
0626380001	Top in soft, patterned cotton jersey with long sleeves, an open chest pocket and slits at the hem. Slightly longer at the back.
0701972005	Shorts in woven fabric with an adjustable elasticated waist and decorative drawstring. Zip fly and button, diagonal side pockets and welt back pockets.
0771489001	T-shirts in airy cotton jersey with a chest pocket and short slits in the sides. Longer at the back.
0705911001	Vest top in cotton jersey with a print motif and a ribbed trim around the neckline and armholes.
0666327011	T-shirt in soft cotton jersey with a motif on the front.

Figure 10.5 — Recommendations that consider purchases and article attributes by filtering out the articles purchased by the customer and by customers outside the community

The demonstrations in this chapter showed how, by using these approaches, we can provide different types of recommendations based on similar purchases by other customers.

Summary

In this chapter, we looked at how to go beyond a basic recommendation application and leverage graph algorithms to enhance the graph and provide more appropriate recommendations. We explored how we can use the KNN similarity algorithm and community detection to gain hidden insights into the data.

In the upcoming chapters, we will take a look at how we can deploy these applications in the cloud and what best practices we can follow for deployment.

Part 4

Deploying Your GenAI Application in the Cloud

In this last part of the book, we focus on taking your GenAI application from development to production. We start by evaluating key factors in selecting the right cloud platform for deploying GenAI workloads, including scalability, cost, and service integrations. Then, we walk through the practical steps of deploying your application on Google Cloud, covering essential services and best practices to ensure a smooth and reliable launch. Whether you're a developer, architect, or AI practitioner, this section equips you with the knowledge to operationalize your GenAI solutions in real-world cloud environments.

This part of the book includes the following chapters:

- *Chapter 11, Choosing the Right Cloud Platform for GenAI Applications*
- *Chapter 12, Deploying Your Application on Google Cloud*
- *Chapter 13, Epilogue*

Stay tuned

To keep up with the latest developments in the fields of Generative AI and LLMs, subscribe to our weekly newsletter, AI_Distilled, at `https://packt.link/Q5UyU`.

11

Choosing the Right Cloud Platform for GenAI Applications

When you begin to deploy your GenAI application, one of the most critical decisions you will make is choosing the right cloud platform. The cloud landscape is vast and diverse, offering a range of options tailored to diverse needs, budgets, and technical requirements. However, selecting the best platform for your specific GenAI use case can be overwhelming without a clear framework to guide your decision. While this book focused on intelligent LLM applications, the learnings from this chapter will enable you to pick a cloud platform for any GenAI use case.

This chapter provides a comprehensive overview of the key factors to consider when evaluating cloud platforms. We will explore the unique features, strengths, and pricing models of leading providers, enabling you to make an informed decision based on your requirements—whether it is scalability, specialized AI services, or cost-effectiveness.

In this chapter, we are going to cover the following main topics:

- Understanding cloud computing options for GenAI
- Picking a cloud platform for GenAI applications: key considerations
- Making the right choice: a decision-making framework for selecting your cloud platform

Understanding cloud computing options for GenAI applications

The cloud has become the backbone of modern GenAI applications, providing the infrastructure and tools required to handle their demanding computational requirements. While traditional discussions about the cloud often focus on service models (IaaS, PaaS, and SaaS) and deployment types (public, private, and hybrid), this section shifts the focus to the unique role cloud providers play in supporting specialized AI services and why the cloud is indispensable for GenAI.

The cloud: an indispensable foundation of GenAI

GenAI applications are resource intensive, requiring vast amounts of computational power, storage, and scalability. The cloud offers several distinct advantages that make it essential for deploying GenAI solutions:

- **Scalability for growing workloads**: GenAI models can require thousands of GPUs or TPUs to train and deploy. Cloud platforms allow you to scale resources dynamically to meet these demands without upfront infrastructure investments.

- **Cost efficiency**: With pay-as-you-go pricing, you only pay for the resources you use, making the cloud a cost-effective choice compared to maintaining on-premises infrastructure.

- **Global accessibility**: Cloud platforms provide geographically distributed data centers, ensuring low-latency access to AI services and deployment flexibility across regions.

- **Reliability and security**: Cloud providers offer enterprise-grade security and high availability, ensuring that your GenAI applications are both safe and resilient.

- **Collaboration and integration**: GenAI workflows often involve cross-functional teams. The cloud provides collaborative environments and integrations with popular development tools, streamlining the process.

With the cloud, businesses can overcome the barriers of high infrastructure costs and complexity, focusing instead on building innovative, AI-driven solutions that deliver real-world impact.

Let's talk about some of the specialized AI services that leading cloud providers offer to support GenAI applications.

Specialized AI services by different cloud providers

Leading cloud providers offer more than just computing power; they provide an ecosystem of specialized AI and machine learning services tailored to the unique demands of GenAI. These services enable faster, more efficient development of AI applications by providing the following:

- **Pre-trained models and APIs**: Access to ready-to-use AI capabilities, such as text generation, speech recognition, and image analysis, eliminating the need to train models from scratch

- **Custom AI training services**: Tools for training and fine-tuning models on custom datasets, making it easier to build domain-specific AI applications

- **Managed AI workflows**: Automated tools for data preprocessing, model training, evaluation, and deployment, reducing the complexity of the development process

- **Integration with data services**: Seamless connectivity with storage and database solutions for managing the massive datasets required by GenAI

GenAI applications benefit from a rich ecosystem of pre-trained models, training services, managed AI workflows, and data integration tools provided by cloud platforms. The following figure outlines how major providers support these capabilities, helping developers accelerate AI development and deployment.

Capability	Google Cloud (Vertex AI)	Amazon Web Services (AWS SageMaker)	Microsoft Azure (Azure AI and ML)
Pre-trained models and APIs	Gemini models and Model Garden (open source and proprietary foundation models); AI APIs for NLP, speech, vision, and structured data tasks	AWS Bedrock (supports multiple foundation models, such as Anthropic Claude, Meta Llama, and AI21); AI APIs for text, image, video, and speech	Azure AI Model Catalog with diverse open source and proprietary models (e.g., OpenAI GPT-4 and Meta Llama); Cognitive Services APIs for NLP, vision, and speech
Custom AI training services	Vertex AI custom model training with AutoML and fine-tuning; supports PyTorch, TensorFlow, and JAX	SageMaker AI with pre-trained models as well as custom training Docker images	Azure ML with AutoML, fine-tuning capabilities, and built-in ML pipelines

Managed AI workflows	Vertex AI pipelines for MLOps automation (preprocessing, training, evaluation, and deployment)	SageMaker pipelines for full ML lifecycle automation; Amazon Step Functions for workflow orchestration	Azure ML pipelines for automated AI workflows and integration with data engineering tools
Integration with data services	BigQuery ML for in-database ML, Cloud Storage, and Dataflow for scalable AI data pipelines	AWS S3, Redshift ML, and Glue for ETL and AI-driven analytics	Azure Synapse, Data Lake, and Databricks for AI-powered data analytics and processing

Figure 11.1 — Comparison of AI capabilities of various cloud providers

Utilizing these capabilities, businesses can streamline AI model development, from using pre-trained models to custom fine-tuning and large-scale AI deployments.

In the next section, we will explore the critical considerations that can help you align your platform choice with your project's technical and business requirements.

Picking a cloud platform for GenAI applications: key considerations

Selecting the right cloud platform for your GenAI application involves more than just comparing features and pricing. Each platform has unique strengths and trade-offs, and understanding them is vital to ensure the platform aligns with your project's goals, budget, and operational needs.

Selecting a cloud platform for GenAI deployment involves weighing several technical and business factors. Here, we explore the most critical aspects to guide your decision-making process.

Scalability and performance

GenAI applications are inherently resource-intensive, requiring substantial computational power and the flexibility to handle diverse workloads. Whether you are training massive language models, running inference on large datasets, or serving real-time predictions, the scalability and performance of your chosen cloud platform are critical to your application's success.

The ability to scale resources dynamically ensures that your system can handle spikes in demand, such as during model training or high-traffic periods, without over-provisioning and incurring unnecessary costs. At the same time, high-performance infrastructure, including access to specialized hardware such as GPUs and TPUs, is essential for speeding up model training and optimizing inference times. Apart from this, low-latency data processing capabilities are crucial for real-time applications, such as chatbots or recommendation engines, where even slight delays can negatively impact user experience.

Therefore, by focusing on these factors, you can ensure that your GenAI application operates efficiently and reliably, even as your needs evolve over time.

Some of the important considerations for scalability and performance are as follows:

- **Elastic scaling**: Look for platforms that support autoscaling to adjust resources automatically based on workload intensity. This ensures you are not paying for unused resources during low activity periods while still meeting peak demands.

- **High-performance hardware**: Evaluate the availability of GPUs, TPUs, or FPGAs that can significantly accelerate training and inference tasks. Platforms such as Google Cloud, AWS, and Azure provide extensive support for such hardware.

- **Regional availability and latency**: For applications serving users globally, ensure the platform has a wide network of data centers to minimize latency and provide consistent performance across regions.

- **Batch and real-time processing**: Consider whether the platform can efficiently handle both batch processing tasks (e.g., bulk training jobs) and real-time requirements (e.g., generating chatbot responses).

The following figure highlights the key scalability and performance capabilities of the leading cloud providers, with an overview of their unique strengths in handling GenAI workloads.

Factor	Google Cloud (Vertex AI)	Amazon Web Services (AWS SageMaker)	Microsoft Azure (Azure AI and ML)
Elastic scaling	AutoML and AI Platform scale automatically based on workload and integrate with Kubernetes (GKE) for containerized scaling.	AutoScaling Groups and SageMaker automate scaling for training and inference workloads.	Virtual Machine Scale Sets and Azure Machine Learning Autoscale for AI/ML workloads.
High-performance hardware	TPUs, NVIDIA GPUs (A100, H100), custom AI chips (Axion)	AWS Inferentia, NVIDIA GPUs, Trainium for deep learning acceleration	NVIDIA GPUs, FPGAs, AMD-based virtual machines

Latency and regional availability	Data centers in 35+ regions; strong presence in North America, Europe, and Asia-Pacific	Widest global footprint (32+ regions); high-speed inter-region networking	Data centers in 60+ regions; strong hybrid cloud options
Batch processing	Supports batch inference via Vertex AI pipelines and AI platform jobs	Managed batch transform jobs for large-scale ML inference	Azure ML pipelines support batch predictions and large dataset processing.
Real-time processing	Low-latency predictions via Vertex AI Endpoints	SageMaker Real-Time Inference with auto-scaling	Azure ML Endpoints for low-latency model serving

Figure 11.2 — GenAI workload processing capabilities of various cloud platforms

To choose a cloud provider, you should factor in scalability and performance but also ensure you account for efficiency, cost-effectiveness, and responsiveness to user needs.

Cost and pricing models

Cost is often a decisive factor when selecting a cloud platform for GenAI applications, as the resource-intensive nature of AI workloads can quickly escalate expenses if they are not managed carefully. Cloud providers offer various pricing models and cost management tools, but understanding and selecting the right combination of services to fit your budget is critical.

From training large models on GPUs and TPUs to managing vast datasets and serving real-time inferences, GenAI applications incur costs across multiple dimensions. These include compute power, storage, data transfer, and additional charges for specialized AI services. Selecting the right pricing model and utilizing cost-saving strategies can also provide a competitive advantage, ensuring that you stay within budget while scaling your AI capabilities.

There are a variety of cost and pricing considerations that may impact your choice of cloud provider:

- **Pay-as-you-go pricing:** Cloud platforms typically charge on a usage basis, where you only pay for the resources you consume. This is ideal for dynamic workloads where resource requirements fluctuate, as it eliminates the need for upfront infrastructure investment. For example, **AWS On-Demand Instances** and **Google Cloud Compute Engine** offer pay-as-you-go pricing for compute and storage services. Consider an e-commerce company that uses GenAI to generate personalized recommendations; it may experience higher traffic during holidays and sales events. With pay-as-you-go pricing, they can scale up compute resources during peak periods (e.g., Black Friday) and scale down during low-traffic months, optimizing costs.

Provider	Pricing Details	Pricing Link
Google Cloud	Compute Engine and AI services billed per second/minute/hour. Supports autoscaling.	`https://cloud.google.com/pricing/`
AWS	EC2 On-Demand Instances charge per second/minute. Supports dynamic scaling.	`https://aws.amazon.com/pricing/`
Azure	Virtual Machines and AI services are billed based on per-second usage.	`https://azure.microsoft.com/en-in/pricing`

Figure 11.3 — Pay-as-you-go pricing options

- **Reserved instances and discounts**: Many platforms offer significant discounts (up to 75%) if you commit to a long-term usage plan (e.g., 1 or 3 years). Reserved instances are a good option if you have predictable workloads, such as hosting an inference model with consistent traffic. For instance, **Azure Reserved VM** instances provide predictable cost savings for steady-state usage. Consider a hospital AI system that processes radiology images for diagnostics, which has consistent demand year-round. Committing to a reserved instance for GPU/TPU workloads significantly reduces costs compared to on-demand pricing.

- **Spot instances for cost-sensitive workloads**: Spot instances offer unused compute capacity at significantly lower prices but can be interrupted if the platform needs the resources for higher-priority tasks. These are ideal for non-critical or batch processes, such as model training jobs that can tolerate interruptions. Consider **AWS Spot Instances** and **Google Preemptible VMs**, which provide up to 90% savings compared to on-demand pricing.

- **Data storage costs**: GenAI applications often rely on large datasets for training and inference. Understand the storage options available, including hot (frequently accessed), warm, and cold (archival) tiers. Evaluate the costs associated with storing and retrieving data, as they can vary significantly depending on usage patterns. For example, **Amazon S3** and **Google Cloud Storage** offer tiered pricing to optimize costs based on access frequency. In the case of a video streaming service, for example, that uses AI to recommend content, it needs frequent access to trending videos (hot storage) while archiving older videos in cold storage. Choosing the right storage tier ensures cost-effectiveness while maintaining performance.

- **Data transfer costs**: Moving data between regions, services, or platforms can incur significant expenses. Ensure you understand these charges, especially for distributed applications. For instance, **egress costs** (data transferred out of the cloud) can add up quickly for applications serving large volumes of data to end-users globally. Consider a financial services company analyzing transactions worldwide that needs real-time fraud detection powered by AI. Frequent cross-region data transfers between Europe and the US can be costly, and also, understanding egress costs helps optimize traffic routing and minimize expenses.

Provider	Pricing Details	Pricing Link
Google Cloud	Charges vary by region, with free in-region transfers	`https://cloud.google.com/storage-transfer/pricing`
AWS	Charges for inter-region and internet data transfers	`https://aws.amazon.com/ec2/pricing/on-demand/#Data_Transfer`
Azure	Egress charges apply beyond free limits	`https://azure.microsoft.com/en-us/pricing/details/bandwidth/`

Figure 11.4 — Data transfer costs

- **Cost management and monitoring tools**: Cloud platforms provide cost calculators and monitoring tools to help you estimate and manage expenses effectively:

  - **AWS Cost Explorer**: Tracks usage patterns and identifies cost-saving opportunities.
  - **Google Cloud Billing Reports**: Offers real-time insights into spending across projects.
  - **Azure Cost Management**: Allows for forecasting and budget allocation.
  - **Free tiers and trial credits**: Many platforms provide free-tier services or trial credits, enabling you to experiment with features without incurring immediate costs. For example, **Google Cloud Free Tier** and **AWS Free Tier** offer limited resources for new users to explore their services.

While understanding pricing models is essential, proactively optimizing costs is equally important to ensure sustainable cloud spending. Cloud resources can quickly become expensive if not managed effectively, especially for GenAI workloads that require substantial compute power, storage, and data processing.

Therefore, to manage and optimize costs, you should consider the following:

- **Right-sizing resources**: Continuously monitor your usage and scale resources appropriately to avoid paying for idle capacity. This can be achieved using cloud-native monitoring tools such as Google Cloud Recommender, AWS Compute Optimizer, and Azure Advisor, which analyze usage patterns and suggest optimizations. Implementing autoscaling policies (e.g., AWS Auto Scaling, Google Managed Instance Groups, and Azure Scale Sets) ensures resources adjust dynamically to workload demands. Choosing the right instance type based on performance needs prevents over-provisioning, while serverless computing (AWS Lambda, Google Cloud Functions, and Azure Functions) and containerized workloads (Kubernetes) further optimize costs by allocating resources only when needed.

- **Data lifecycle management**: Use appropriate storage tiers to optimize costs for infrequently accessed data.

- **Centralized billing**: Consolidate multiple accounts or projects under one billing system to simplify tracking and optimize bulk pricing.

By understanding the cost structures and leveraging pricing strategies, you can significantly reduce the expenses associated with deploying and running GenAI applications in the cloud. This will help you achieve a balance between performance and cost-effectiveness.

With an increasing reliance on cloud-based GenAI applications, we must ensure robust security and regulatory compliance mechanisms. In the next section, we will explore key security considerations, identity and access management strategies, and regulatory compliance requirements that ensure your GenAI deployment remains secure, resilient, and legally compliant.

Security and compliance

Security and compliance are critical considerations when deploying GenAI applications in the cloud. These applications often handle sensitive data, such as proprietary datasets, user information, or industry-specific records, making security an essential feature. Furthermore, compliance with legal and regulatory standards is a non-negotiable requirement for businesses operating in regulated industries, such as healthcare or finance, and diverse geo-political locations.

Understanding the security and compliance capabilities of a cloud platform allows you to protect your data, build trust with users, and avoid costly legal or reputational risks. While leading cloud providers—Google Cloud, AWS, and Azure—offer robust security features, it is the user's responsibility to configure many of them properly based on their use cases.

Some security features, such as basic encryption at rest and identity management, are enabled by default, while others, such as custom **role-based access control** (**RBAC**) and compliance configurations, require manual setup. To ensure proper configuration, cloud providers offer detailed documentation and best practices:

- Google Cloud security best practices: `https://cloud.google.com/security/best-practices?hl=en`

- AWS security best practices: `https://aws.amazon.com/security/`

- Azure security best practices: `https://learn.microsoft.com/en-us/security/`

In general, you need to focus on some of the key security considerations and configurations:

- **Data encryption**: Ensures that sensitive information remains protected both in transit and at rest. Cloud providers offer built-in encryption features, but additional configurations may be required, depending on your security and compliance needs:

  - **In transit**: Data moving between systems or services should use secure protocols such as TLS/SSL. This requires manual setup in some cases, such as forcing TLS/SSL connections for data movement between services.

  - **At rest**: Data stored in databases, filesystems, or object storage should be encrypted using robust algorithms such as AES-256, which is enabled by default for most cloud storage services. However, users can configure custom encryption keys for enhanced security.

This table details configuring encryption in Google Cloud, AWS, and Azure:

Cloud Provider	Encryption at Rest	Encryption in Transit	Documentation
Google Cloud	Default encryption using Google-managed keys; users can configure **Customer-Managed Encryption Keys** (**CMEKs**) with Cloud KMS	Uses TLS/SSL by default; additional encryption options for APIs and databases are available	`https://cloud.google.com/docs/security/overview/whitepaper`
AWS	AWS S3, RDS, and EBS encryption enabled by default; AWS KMS allows customer-managed key encryption	Enforced using AWS Certificate Manager and TLS settings	`https://docs.aws.amazon.com/whitepapers/latest/logical-separation/encrypting-data-at-rest-and--in-transit.html`

Azure	Encryption at rest enabled for Blob Storage, SQL, and Disks; **Customer-Managed Keys (CMKs)** available via Azure Key Vault	Uses TLS/SSL for in-transit encryption; additional network encryption settings are available	`https://learn.`
			`microsoft.com/en-`
			`us/azure/security/`
			`fundamentals/`
			`encryption-overview`

Figure 11.5 — Data security options

- **Identity and access management (IAM)**: IAM is essential for controlling who can access cloud resources and ensuring that only authorized users or services have the required permissions. Cloud providers offer built-in IAM frameworks that allow organizations to manage access securely:

  - **Role-Based Access Controls (RBAC)**: IAM enables fine-grained permissions by assigning roles (e.g., Admin, Developer, and Viewer) to users and services, ensuring that access is granted only as needed.

  - **Multi-Factor Authentication (MFA)**: Enhances security by requiring users to verify their identity through an additional authentication factor (e.g., SMS or authenticator apps) beyond passwords.

  - **Integration with enterprise identity providers**: **Single sign-on (SSO)** and federated authentication using **Azure Active Directory (AAD)**, AWS IAM Identity Center, and Google Cloud IAM.

  - For example: AAD and AWS IAM provide granular control over user roles and permissions, allowing organizations to enforce least privilege access and secure authentication methods for sensitive cloud workloads.

- **Network security**: Enables protection of cloud workloads from unauthorized access, data breaches, and cyber threats. Cloud providers offer a range of network security tools to create secure perimeters, restrict access, and monitor traffic:

  - **Virtual private clouds (VPCs)**: Allow users to create isolated network environments within the cloud infrastructure, ensuring controlled access to sensitive resources.

  - **Firewalls and private endpoints**: Cloud-native firewalls and private connectivity options (e.g., AWS PrivateLink, Azure Private Link, and Google Private Service Connect) secure internal traffic while limiting exposure to public networks.

- **Logging and monitoring**: Security tools such as Google Cloud VPC Service Controls, AWS VPC Flow Logs, and Azure Network Watcher detect and respond to suspicious activities in real time.

- For example, **Google Cloud VPC Service Controls** allow organizations to define secure perimeters around sensitive workloads, restricting data movement across cloud services while preventing unauthorized access.

- **Threat detection and incident response**: Crucial for identifying security threats in real time and mitigating risks before they escalate. Cloud providers offer AI-driven security tools to detect anomalies, prevent intrusions, and automate security responses.

  - **Anomaly detection and intrusion prevention**: Built-in security tools use machine learning to identify suspicious activity, unauthorized access, and potential threats before they impact workloads.

  - **Automated incident response**: Cloud providers offer automated remediation services that contain security threats, reducing the need for manual intervention.

  - **Security event logging**: Threat intelligence services collect, analyze, and respond to security events, integrating with **security information and event management (SIEM)** platforms for advanced monitoring.

  - For example, **AWS GuardDuty** and **Azure Security Center** use AI-driven threat detection to identify security risks, analyze anomalous activity, and trigger automated alerts to security teams, enabling a rapid response to potential breaches.

Ensuring compliance with industry regulations and data protection laws is critical when deploying GenAI applications in the cloud. While major cloud providers—Google Cloud, AWS, and Azure—offer built-in compliance frameworks, most regulatory settings require user configuration based on business needs, industry standards, and data residency requirements.

- Some compliance measures, such as default encryption and security logs, are pre-configured.

- Other settings, such as data residency controls, auditing tools, and regulatory adherence (such as HIPAA, the GDPR, and SOC 2), require manual setup during cloud resource configuration.

- Cloud providers often prompt users during setup to configure compliance settings, but businesses must ensure they align with specific legal and operational requirements.

Some of the key compliance and regulatory requirements are as follows:

- **Regulatory standards**: Cloud providers comply with multiple industry standards but require manual setup to ensure business-specific adherence.

  - **Health Insurance Portability and Accountability Act (HIPAA)**: For healthcare-related applications handling **protected health information (PHI)**

  - **The General Data Protection Regulation (GDPR)**: Governs how businesses handle the personal data of EU citizens and requires explicit user consent mechanisms

  - **Service Organization Control 2 (SOC 2)**: Ensures cloud services follow strict data security and privacy controls for handling customer data.

  - For example, **Azure Compliance Manager** provides pre-configured templates to help align workloads with regulatory standards.

- **Data residency and sovereignty**: Data sovereignty laws require businesses to store and process data within specific geographic regions to comply with local regulations. This is not pre-configured; cloud providers offer regional data storage options, but businesses must manually select data residency settings. For example, **Google Cloud Regional Services** and **AWS Regions** allow users to choose data storage locations to meet regulatory requirements.

- **Auditability**: Audit logging is partially enabled by default but requires manual configuration for custom compliance needs:

  - Ensure that the platform provides tools for auditing access and actions taken on sensitive data.

  - Maintain logs and records of all data interactions to demonstrate compliance during audits.

  - For example, **AWS CloudTrail** and **Azure Monitor Logs** enable comprehensive auditing capabilities.

- **Certifications and trust programs**: Cloud providers participate in external certifications and trust programs to validate their compliance with industry security and regulatory standards. These certifications help businesses meet legal and security requirements for data protection, privacy, and governance. All three major cloud providers—Google Cloud, AWS, and Azure—comply with global certifications, but organizations must ensure their cloud configurations align with compliance needs based on their specific use case.

Certification	Google Cloud	AWS	Azure
ISO 27001 (information security management)	✓ Compliant	✓ Compliant	✓ Compliant
Payment Card Industry Data Security Standard (PCI DSS)	✓ Compliant	✓ Compliant	✓ Compliant
FedRAMP (US Government Security Compliance)	✓ Compliant (FedRAMP High for select services)	✓ Compliant (FedRAMP High for GovCloud)	✓ Compliant (FedRAMP High for government services)
SOC 2 (secure handling of customer data)	✓ Compliant	✓ Compliant	✓ Compliant
HIPAA (healthcare data protection)	✓ Compliant (requires manual setup)	✓ Compliant (requires manual setup)	✓ Compliant (requires manual setup)
General Data Protection Regulation (GDPR) for EU data	✓ Compliant	✓ Compliant	✓ Compliant

Figure 11.6 — Compliance certifications available

Implementing security and compliance measures is only the first step—maintaining them effectively is just as crucial. With evolving cybersecurity threats and ever-changing regulatory landscapes, a proactive approach to security and compliance is necessary to protect your GenAI applications from vulnerabilities.

Let's now explore some of the best practices that help maintain a secure and legally compliant GenAI deployment.

Best practices for security and compliance in GenAI deployments

Ensuring robust security and compliance is essential for the successful deployment of GenAI applications, especially when dealing with sensitive data or operating in regulated industries. Adopting best practices helps mitigate risks, maintain regulatory alignment, and build trust with users, ensuring your application is both secure and reliable:

- **Regular security audits**: Periodically review and update your security configurations to address new threats.

- **Automated compliance checks**: Use cloud-native tools to continuously monitor and enforce compliance requirements.

- **Shared responsibility model**: Understand the division of responsibility between you and the cloud provider—while the provider secures the infrastructure, you are responsible for securing applications and data.

- **Data minimization**: Store only the data necessary for your application to reduce exposure to security risks.

While best practices provide a foundation, selecting the right cloud provider requires understanding which platforms best support security and compliance needs. The following figure outlines how Google Cloud, AWS, and Azure address these key areas:

Best Practice	Google Cloud	AWS	Azure
Security Audits	Security Command Center, Cloud Audit Logs	AWS Security Hub, AWS Inspector	Microsoft Defender for Cloud, Azure Security Center
Automated Compliance Checks	Assured Workloads, Policy Intelligence	AWS Config, Audit Manager, AWS Artifact	Azure Policy, Compliance Manager
Shared Responsibility Model	Documentation on shared security best practices	Clear AWS shared security model	Azure's shared security responsibility guide
Data Minimization	**Data Loss Prevention (DLP)** API, cloud storage life cycle policies	Amazon Macie (DLP for S3), IAM data access policies	Azure Purview (data governance), DLP
Compliance Frameworks	HIPAA, GDPR, FedRAMP, ISO 27001, PCI DSS (certified)	HIPAA, GDPR, FedRAMP, ISO 27001, PCI DSS (certified)	HIPAA, GDPR, FedRAMP, ISO 27001, PCI DSS (certified)

Figure 11.7 — Security compliance availability

For further evaluation, you can explore the official security and compliance documentation provided by each cloud provider:

- Google Cloud security and compliance: `https://cloud.google.com/compliance?hl=en`
- AWS security and compliance: `https://aws.amazon.com/compliance/`
- Azure security and compliance: `https://learn.microsoft.com/en-us/compliance/`

If you are looking for detailed comparisons of cloud provider security frameworks, the **Cloud Security Alliance (CSA)** maintains a publicly accessible database of security assessments at `https://cloudsecurityalliance.org/star`.

This resource lists cloud providers' security controls, compliance certifications, and third-party risk assessments, helping you evaluate which platform best meets your needs.

It is important to prioritize security and compliance, to help safeguard sensitive data, adhere to regulatory standards, and build a trustworthy GenAI application. This not only protects your organization from potential threats and legal issues but also fosters user confidence in the reliability and safety of your solution.

By carefully evaluating these factors, you can select a cloud platform that not only meets your technical and operational needs but also ensures long-term scalability, cost efficiency, and compliance for your GenAI project. While implementing best practices for security and compliance lays a solid foundation for your GenAI deployment, understanding the offerings of leading cloud providers is equally critical.

Key takeaways

Summarizing the analysis of leading cloud providers, these key takeaways highlight the unique strengths and ideal use cases for each platform. Here is a quick reference to help you align your GenAI deployment needs with the most suitable cloud solution.

- **Google Cloud** excels in AI analytics and end-to-end machine learning workflows, with strong data integration capabilities.
- **AWS** offers unparalleled scalability and cost-saving options, making it ideal for high-volume and flexible workloads.
- **Microsoft Azure** stands out for its hybrid cloud support and enterprise-grade AI services, catering to businesses with diverse infrastructure needs.

As you process and understand the unique strengths of each platform, you can align your choice with your project's requirements, ensuring the success of your GenAI deployment. This includes carefully analyzing the features and pricing of leading cloud providers and checking that they are in alignment with your goals and constraints.

In the next section, we will introduce a decision-making framework to help you select the cloud platform that best meets the needs of your GenAI application.

Making the right choice: a decision-making framework for selecting your cloud platform

Choosing the right cloud platform for your GenAI application is a multifaceted decision that depends on your project's unique requirements, priorities, and constraints. A structured framework simplifies this process by providing a clear methodology to evaluate platforms based on factors such as scalability, cost, specialized features, and compliance.

Let's look at a step-by-step decision-making process to help you balance technical and business considerations effectively. Whether you are focused on optimizing performance, controlling costs, or leveraging specialized AI tools, this framework ensures that your choice aligns with both short-term goals and long-term scalability.

- **Define your requirements and priorities**: Start by identifying the specific needs of your GenAI application. This step helps you focus on platforms that align with your priorities and ignore unnecessary features.

    - **Performance needs**: Assess your compute and storage requirements. Do you need access to GPUs, TPUs, or high-performance storage?

    - **Scalability requirements**: Consider whether your workload is steady or fluctuates significantly, as this will impact your need for dynamic scaling.

    - **AI-specific features**: Identify essential AI tools or services, such as pre-trained models, APIs, or custom model training capabilities.

    - **Budget constraints**: Set a clear budget and determine how much flexibility you have for unexpected costs.

    - **Compliance and security**: Ensure your chosen platform adheres to industry regulations (e.g., HIPAA and the GDPR) and provides robust security measures.

- **Shortlist potential providers**: Based on your defined requirements, narrow down your options to a few cloud providers that align with your needs. Use the following criteria to create your shortlist:

  - **AI services and tools**: Evaluate platforms such as Google Cloud (Vertex AI), AWS (SageMaker), and Azure (Cognitive Services) for their GenAI offerings.

  - **Cost models**: Compare pricing structures, including pay-as-you-go, reserved instances, and spot instances.

  - **Integration and ecosystem**: Consider compatibility with your existing tools, frameworks, and workflows (e.g., TensorFlow, PyTorch, or data services).

  - **Regional availability**: Ensure the provider has data centers in regions that are critical to your application's performance and compliance.

- **Evaluate trade-offs**: Compare the shortlisted providers by analyzing their trade-offs in key areas:

  - **Performance versus cost**: Does the provider offer the performance you need at a price point that is within your budget?

  - **Flexibility versus specialization**: Are you prioritizing flexibility across a range of tasks, or do you need highly specialized tools for GenAI?

  - **Support and reliability**: Assess the provider's support offerings and track record for reliability, especially for critical workloads.

- **Leverage decision-making tools**: Many cloud providers offer tools to assist with selection and planning:

  - **Cost calculators**: Use tools such as AWS Pricing Calculator, Google Cloud Pricing Estimator, or Azure Cost Management to predict expenses.

  - **Trials and free tiers**: Take advantage of free-tier offerings or trial credits to test services before committing.

  - **Performance benchmarks**: Review publicly available benchmarks or run your own tests on model training, inference, and data transfer tasks.

- **Future-proof your decision**: Think beyond your immediate needs to ensure scalability and adaptability for future growth:

    - **Long-term cost efficiency**: Evaluate options such as reserved instances or hybrid models to control long-term costs.

    - **Evolving AI needs**: Consider whether the platform can support emerging AI technologies or scaling requirements as your project grows.

    - **Vendor lock-in risks**: Assess the portability of your application and whether switching providers in the future would be feasible.

- **Make a data-driven decision**: Consolidate your findings into a comparison matrix, scoring each provider on key criteria such as cost, performance, scalability, compliance, and feature support. Assign weights to each criterion based on its importance to your project, then use the scores to identify the best-fit platform.

This decision-making framework ensures that your cloud platform choice is strategic, data-driven, and aligned with your GenAI project's unique requirements. By carefully defining your priorities, evaluating trade-offs, and planning for the future, you can select a platform that maximizes the success of your GenAI deployment.

Summary

In this chapter, we explored the essential considerations for deploying GenAI applications in the cloud, equipping you with the knowledge to make informed decisions. We began by emphasizing the importance of specialized AI services and the cloud's role in supporting the scalability and performance needs of GenAI. We then discussed the key factors for evaluating cloud platforms, such as cost, security, compliance, and feature offerings. A detailed analysis of leading cloud providers—Google Cloud, AWS, and Microsoft Azure—helped highlight their unique strengths, pricing models, and suitability for different use cases. Finally, we introduced a structured decision-making framework to help you choose the best platform tailored to your specific requirements.

In the next chapter, we will take a hands-on approach to deploying your GenAI application. Building on the foundational knowledge from this chapter, we will guide you through implementing a practical deployment workflow on Google Cloud.

12

Deploying Your Application on the Google Cloud

You have come a long way in designing and developing your GenAI application. Now, it is time to take that next crucial step—deployment. While a true production-grade deployment involves various complexities such as CI/CD pipelines, scalability considerations, observability, cost optimization, and security hardening, this chapter is designed to give you a foundational, hands-on introduction to cloud deployment using Google Cloud Run. **Cloud Run** by Google Cloud provides a powerful yet developer-friendly way to deploy containerized applications without managing infrastructure, making it ideal for rapid prototyping and small-scale production use cases.

The deployment steps and services may vary slightly across other cloud platforms, such as AWS or Microsoft Azure, but we will focus on Google Cloud for brevity. However, once you are comfortable with the core concepts here, you are encouraged to experiment with similar workflows on other providers to broaden your cloud deployment expertise.

We will walk through the process of deploying the Haystack chatbot you built in *Chapter 5* as a serverless application on Google Cloud. The process of deploying the intelligent recommendation system using Spring AI is mentioned later in the chapter with the links to the resources to follow the steps. By the end of this chapter, you will have a working chatbot live on the cloud and the confidence to build on this foundation for more advanced deployments.

In this chapter, we are going to cover the following main topics:

- Preparing your search chatbot using Haystack for deployment
- Containerizing the application with Docker
- Setting up a Google Cloud project and services
- Deploying to Google Cloud Run
- Testing and verifying the deployment

Technical requirements

To deploy your Haystack chatbot using Google Cloud Run, you need the following:

- An active Google Cloud account with billing enabled. If you are new to Google Cloud, you can start by creating an account at `https://console.cloud.google.com/` and take advantage of the free tier and credits offered for new users.
- Access to a Neo4j database:
  - If you are using a local Neo4j instance, you must expose it publicly using ngrok or a similar tool, so that the deployed chatbot can connect to it. Here is an example to expose Neo4j's bolt port:

    ```
    ngrok tcp 7687
    ```

  - Update your .env with the ngrok public URL:

    ```
    NEO4J_URI=bolt://0.tcp.ngrok.io:XXXXX
    ```

- If you are using AuraDB Free, the preceding step can be ignored.

Preparing your Haystack chatbot for deployment

We will be deploying our application on Google Cloud. The approach we will be talking about is similar from a deployment perspective on all the popular cloud environments. We will be looking at building a docker compose and running it in the cloud. Google Cloud was chosen because it is convenient rather than having any technical advantage as such. Once we deploy and run the application on Google Cloud, the official documentation links for other clouds to deploy the same docker compose will be provided. Just repeating those steps in the book will not make much of a difference.

Before jumping into containerization and deployment, it is important to ensure that your Haystack chatbot code is organized in a way that is compatible with serverless deployment. In this section, you will structure your code base appropriately and prepare the essential configuration files needed for deploying to Google Cloud Run.

We will be reusing the working search chatbot from *Chapter 5* by creating a copy of the main script (search_chatbot.py), renaming it app.py (as this is the default entry point many cloud services expect when serving a Python web application), and placing it in a simplified folder ready for containerization. Since the chatbot logic is already functional, we will skip local testing and move directly to packaging and deploying it to the cloud.

> **Note**
>
> These steps to help you containerize and deploy your Haystack chatbot to Google Cloud Run are also presented in the README.md file in the book's GitHub repo at https://github.com/PacktPublishing/Building-Neo4j-Powered-Applications-with-LLMs/tree/main/ch12.

Next, prepare a requirements.txt file that lists all the necessary Python dependencies your chatbot needs to run. This file allows the container to install the required packages during the build process. The content of this file will look something like this:

```
haystack-ai==2.5.0
openai==1.67.0
gradio==4.44.1
python-dotenv>=1.0.0
neo4j==5.25.0
neo4j-haystack==2.0.3
```

To manage sensitive credentials and environment-specific configurations securely, it is recommended to use a .env file. In the ch12 directory of the GitHub repo, you will find a file named example.env that serves as a template. This file includes placeholders for key variables such as your OpenAI API key and Neo4j database credentials. To use it, simply create a copy of this file, rename it .env, and populate it with your actual values. The application leverages the python-dotenv library to load these variables at runtime, keeping secrets out of your code base while still making them accessible to your application:

```
OPENAI_API_KEY=<insert-your-openai-api-key>
NEO4J_URI=<insert-your-neo4j-uri>
NEO4J_USERNAME=neo4j
NEO4J_PASSWORD=<insert-your-neo4j-password>
```

At this point, you have set up the core components needed for deployment—your application script, dependencies, and environment variables. To ensure everything is organized correctly for containerization and deployment, your project directory should now follow this structure:

```
haystack-cloud-app/
├── app.py                    # Renamed chatbot server file (originally
search_chatbot.py)
├── requirements.txt          # Python dependencies
├── Dockerfile                # Will be created in the next step
├── .env                      # For storing configuration variables
├── example.env               # Template file for environment variables
```

The example.env file acts as a reference for users to create their own .env file with valid credentials and configuration values. With all the core components now in place—including your application script, dependencies, and environment setup—you are ready to containerize your application for deployment.

Let us move on to the next step, which is to containerize your application with Docker.

Containerizing the application with Docker

Before deploying your Haystack chatbot to Google Cloud Run, the application must be packaged into a Docker container. **Containerization** allows you to bundle your code, dependencies, and environment into a single, portable unit that runs consistently across different systems—including the cloud.

In this section, you will create a Dockerfile, which defines the steps required to build a Docker image of your chatbot. This image will then be deployed to Cloud Run as a serverless web service.

Here is the Dockerfile used to containerize your Haystack chatbot:

```
FROM python:3.11

EXPOSE 8080
WORKDIR /app

COPY . ./

RUN pip install -r requirements.txt

CMD ["python", "app.py"]
```

Let us break down what each line does:

- `FROM python:3.11`: This sets the base image to Python 3.11, which includes everything needed to run Python applications.

- `EXPOSE 8080`: Cloud Run expects the application to listen on port 8080. This line documents the port that the container will expose at runtime.

- `WORKDIR /app`: This sets the working directory inside the container to /app. All subsequent commands will run from this directory.

- `COPY . ./`: This copies the entire contents of your local project directory into the container's /app directory.

- `RUN pip install -r requirements.txt`: This installs all Python dependencies listed in your `requirements.txt` file.

- `CMD ["python", "app.py"]`: This specifies the command to run when the container starts—in this case, it runs your chatbot application using `app.py`.

Once your Dockerfile is in place, you now have a fully containerized version of your Haystack chatbot, ready to be deployed to the cloud. The next step is to configure your Google Cloud environment so that you can push your container and run it using Cloud Run.

Let us move on to setting up your Google Cloud project and services.

Setting up a Google Cloud project and services

Google Cloud provides a robust, developer-friendly platform for deploying modern applications, including GenAI-powered solutions. With tools such as Cloud Run, Artifact Registry, and Cloud Build, Google Cloud enables you to go from code to scalable, serverless deployment with minimal operational overhead.

Although your Haystack chatbot uses OpenAI for language processing, Google Cloud plays a critical role in hosting the application, managing container builds, and securely storing your Docker images. In this section, you will configure your Google Cloud project, enable only the necessary services (such as Cloud Run, Cloud Build, and Artifact Registry), and prepare your environment for deployment.

By the end of this section, your project will be cloud-ready, with all the services and permissions in place to deploy your chatbot using Google Cloud's serverless infrastructure.

Let us get started by setting up your project and enabling the required APIs.

Creating a project

In the Google Cloud console (`https://console.cloud.google.com/`), on the project selector page, select or create a Google Cloud project (`https://cloud.google.com/resource-manager/docs/creating-managing-projects`).

Make sure that billing is enabled for your Cloud project. Learn how to check whether billing is enabled on a project at `https://cloud.google.com/billing/docs/how-to/verify-billing-enabled`.

Launching Google Cloud Shell

To simplify the setup and avoid installing any tools locally, we will use Google Cloud Shell, which comes pre-installed with Docker, the `gcloud` CLI, and Git. Here is how to get started:

1.   Go to the Google Cloud console (`https://console.cloud.google.com/`).
2.   Click the Cloud Shell icon in the top-right corner of the navigation bar (the terminal icon).

A terminal window will open at the bottom of your screen. This is a fully functional shell with access to your Google Cloud project and services.

> **Note**
>
> Cloud Shell provisions a temporary VM with 5 GB of persistent storage—more than enough for this walkthrough.

Setting your active project

Make sure you are working on the right Google Cloud project. You can either create a new one or use an existing one. Set it using the following:

```
gcloud config set project YOUR_PROJECT_ID
```

You can verify the active project with the following:

```
gcloud config list project
```

Enabling the required services

Now, enable the Google Cloud services required for deploying your container:

```
gcloud services enable cloudresourcemanager.googleapis.com \
                       servicenetworking.googleapis.com \
                       run.googleapis.com \
                       cloudbuild.googleapis.com \
                       cloudfunctions.googleapis.com
```

On successful execution of the command, you should see a message similar to the one shown here:

```
Operation "operations/..." finished successfully.
```

The alternative to the preceding gcloud command is through the console by searching for each product. If any API is missed, you can enable it during the implementation. Refer to the documentation for gcloud commands and usage: https://cloud.google.com/sdk/gcloud/reference/config/list.

Adding your project files to Cloud Shell

Before continuing with the deployment steps, make sure your Haystack chatbot files are available in your Google Cloud Shell environment.

You have two options to do this:

1. **Upload your existing files**: If you have been developing the project locally (e.g., as part of earlier chapters), you can upload your working directory to Cloud Shell using the **Upload** option in the Cloud Shell editor. Just click the **Open Editor** button (pencil icon), then use **File | Upload Files** or drag and drop your folder directly into the editor.

2. **Clone from GitHub (recommended for clean setup)**: Alternatively, you can clone the *Chapter 12* code directly from the official book repository using the following command:

    ```
    git clone https://github.com/PacktPublishing/Building-Neo4j-Powered-
    Applications-with-LLMs.git
    cd Building-Neo4j-Powered-Applications-with-LLMs/ch12
    ```

    Once you are inside the ch12 folder, you will find all the necessary files—app.py, requirements.txt, Dockerfile, and example.env.

If you decide to clone the repo, make sure to follow the step mentioned earlier to generate the
.env file. Now that your project files are in place and ready inside Cloud Shell, it is time to move
on to the final stage—deploying your Haystack chatbot to Google Cloud Run.

Deploying to Google Cloud Run

In this section, you will walk through the full deployment workflow—from setting environment
variables and configuring Artifact Registry to building your container and deploying it live using
Cloud Run. Let us break it down step by step:

1. Set up environment variables. Begin by exporting the key environment variables for your
    Google Cloud project and deployment region. Replace the placeholders with your actual
    values:

    ```
    # Set your Google Cloud project ID
    export GCP_PROJECT='your-project-id'  # Replace with your actual
    roject ID
    # Set your preferred deployment region
    export GCP_REGION='us-central1'        # You can choose a different
    supported region
    ```

2. Create an Artifact Registry instance and build the container. Configure your Artifact Reg-
    istry repository and build your container image using Cloud Build:

    ```
    # Set Artifact Registry repo name and Cloud Run service name
    export AR_REPO='your-repo-name'        # Choose a name like 'genai-
    chatbot'
    export SERVICE_NAME='movies-chatbot'  # Or any descriptive name
    ```

    a. Create the Docker repository:

    ```
    gcloud artifacts repositories create "$AR_REPO" \
      --location="$GCP_REGION" \
      --repository-format=Docker
    ```

    b. Authenticate Docker with Artifact Registry:

    ```
    gcloud auth configure-docker "$GCP_REGION-docker.pkg.dev"
    ```

c. Then, build and push your container image:

```
gcloud builds submit \
  --tag "$GCP_REGION-docker.pkg.dev/$GCP_PROJECT/$AR_
REPO/$SERVICE_NAME"
```

This command uses your Dockerfile to package the app and pushes the resulting container image to Artifact Registry.

3. Deploy to Cloud Run. Before deploying, make sure your .env file contains all the required environment variables, such as OPENAI_API_KEY, NEO4J_URI, and any project-specific configuration.

To pass these variables during deployment, convert your .env file into a format compatible with the --set-env-vars flag:

```
ENV_VARS=$(grep -v '^#' .env | sed 's/ *= */=/g' | xargs -I{} echo
-n "{},")
ENV_VARS=${ENV_VARS%,}
```

- Now, deploy your application to Cloud Run:

```
gcloud run deploy "$SERVICE_NAME" \
  --port=8080 \
  --image="$GCP_REGION-
docker.pkg.dev/$GCP_PROJECT/$AR_REPO/$SERVICE_NAME" \
  --allow-unauthenticated \
  --region=$GCP_REGION \
  --platform=managed \
  --project=$GCP_PROJECT \
  --set-env-vars="GCP_PROJECT=$GCP_PROJECT,GCP_REGION=$GCP_
REGION,$ENV_VARS"
```

Once complete, Google Cloud Run will return a URL where your chatbot is live and accessible via the web.

Congratulations—your Haystack chatbot is now successfully deployed and running as a serverless application on Google Cloud!

Let us move on to the final step: testing and verifying the deployment to ensure everything works as expected.

Testing and verifying the deployment on Google Cloud

Once your deployment is complete, Google Cloud Run will return a public service URL, typically in the following format:

```
https://movies-chatbot-[UNIQUE_ID].${GCP_REGION}.run.app
```

Open this URL in your browser. You should see your Gradio-powered chatbot interface live on the web—identical in functionality to your local version. You can now interact with the chatbot, submit queries, and receive movie recommendations just as before, but this time, it is running fully in the cloud.

If something does not work as expected, keep the following checklist ready for troubleshooting:

- **Dependency check**: Make sure your Dockerfile correctly installs all dependencies using `pip install -r requirements.txt`. Missing dependencies can result in build or runtime errors on Cloud Run.

- **Cloud Shell versus local environment**: If you are not using Google Cloud Shell, ensure your local environment is authenticated with Google Cloud using a service account that has appropriate permissions for Cloud Run, Artifact Registry, and (if applicable) Vertex AI.

- **Monitor logs and metrics**: You can monitor your service's logs, request history, and performance metrics directly from the Google Cloud console under **Cloud Run**. This is especially useful for debugging and performance tuning.

- **Cloud Run service management**: Navigate to **Cloud Run** in the Cloud console, where you will see a list of deployed services. Your chatbot (e.g., `movies-chatbot`) should appear here. Clicking on the service name will give you access to the following:

  - The public service URL
  - Deployment history
  - Container configuration
  - Environment variables
  - Logs and error reports

This visibility makes it easy to track and manage your application post-deployment.

With your chatbot now live, deployed on a scalable serverless platform, and publicly accessible, you have successfully completed the deployment journey. Your GenAI-powered movie recommendation chatbot is now ready to be used, shared, and further enhanced.

Deploying the chatbot to other clouds

As mentioned in the initial section, once you have docker compose prepared, you can follow the instructions provided to deploy the same application to other clouds:

- **Azure deployment**: Please follow the instructions provided at this link: `https://techcommunity.microsoft.com/blog/appsonazureblog/how-to-deploy-a-local-docker-container-to-azure-container-apps/3583888`.

- **AWS deployment**: Docker provides a clear guide on deploying docker compose files to AWS. Please follow this link for more details: `https://www.docker.com/blog/docker-compose-from-local-to-amazon-ecs/`.

When you follow the instructions in these links, you can see the similarity with the deployment approach when we chose to containerize the applications.

There is a lot of information available in each cloud's official documentation to deploy Spring Boot applications to the cloud. For example, if you are looking to run the application we created in *Chapters 9* and *10*, you can follow the steps in the documentation provided by various cloud vendors:

- **Google Cloud**: This article (`https://cloud.google.com/run/docs/quickstarts/build-and-deploy/deploy-java-service`) lists detailed steps to deploy on Google Cloud Run

- **Azure**: This article (`https://learn.microsoft.com/en-us/azure/spring-apps/basic-standard/how-to-maven-deploy-apps`) shows how to deploy the Spring Boot application on Azure

- **AWS**: For Azure here are some articles for your reference.

  - This article (`https://community.aws/content/2qk6oFuOPiA4G0N83ocU0REbtdN/step-by-step-guide-to-deploying-a-spring-boot-application-on-aws-ec2-with-best-practices`) shows us how to deploy the Spring Boot application on AWS EC2

  - This article (`https://www.geeksforgeeks.org/deploy-a-spring-boot-application-with-aws/`) shows how to deploy the Spring Boot application using AWS Elastic Beanstalk

These articles are good enough to guide you through deploying our GenAI application as, at its heart, it is a simple application that does not need scaling as such since it only performs the augmentation—that, too, as a batch process.

The production deployment of these applications is a more complex procedure that requires you to focus on various supporting elements, such as database, monitoring, and so on. Discussing the whole deployment is out of the scope of this book, but we will highlight the deployment architecture and key considerations to deploy your applications in production in the next section.

Preparing for deployment in production: key considerations

In this section, we will look at a typical architecture deployment for intelligent applications. There are a lot of other aspects we need to keep in mind when we are moving to production. For simplicity, we will refer to the augmentation application we built in *Chapters 9* and *10*.

Let us look at all the tasks we did from loading data to reviewing the results:

1.   We loaded the data into a graph.

2.   The graph was enhanced with seasonal relationships. We augmented the graph using the augmentation application—articles as well as customer behavior aspects.

3.   We also utilized KNN similarity and community detection algorithms to enhance the graph and reviewed how this approach gives us better results.

In a production deployment, all of these aspects may need to be automated and deployed as individual applications. Let us take a brief look at all of these aspects that we need to take care of.

When we are deploying intelligent applications to production, we need to make sure we take care of data ingestion, data consumption, the LLM or ML pipeline to augment the graph, and the graph database deployment architecture for scale.

Let's first take a look at the deployment architecture in *Figure 12.1*.

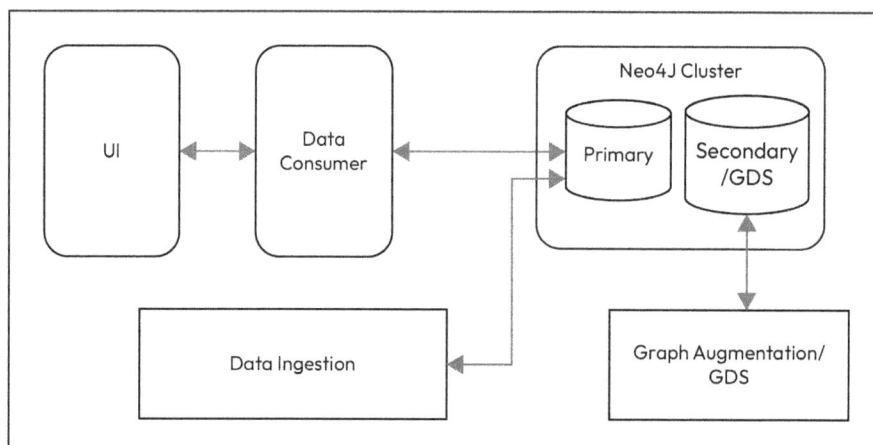

Figure 12.1 — Deployment architecture of Neo4j intelligent applications

We can see there are two different Neo4j databases shown here. In Neo4j for regular interaction, we will have Primary, which can perform both READ and WRITE capabilities. For analytical, **Graph Data Science (GDS)**, and other uses, we will use Secondary, which provides only the READ capability. We can have more than one Primary database to provide high availability and more than one Secondary database to provide horizontal scalability. We can see from the diagram that all the regular interactions, including data ingestion and data consumption, are handled by Primary and the analytical workload that augments the graph is handled by Secondary.

This type of deployment architecture also makes it easy to maintain and monitor the system. The Neo4j database comes with **Neo4j Ops Manager** (https://neo4j.com/docs/ops-manager/current/) for deploying and monitoring Neo4j servers. It provides dashboards to monitor the current health of the system as well as to set up alerts to be notified in case of errors.

For the other applications, we need to have similar monitoring, especially for data ingestion and augmentation applications. When they fail in the middle, we should be able to restart from where we have failed. The augmentation application is built to handle the data that way.

When we are building the ingestion pipeline, we need to keep in mind these aspects:

- What is our initial data size?
- What are our day-to-day changes (incremental data changes) and their size?
- How does incremental data come? Is it coming in near-real time, as a batch at regular intervals, a big batch at the end of the day, or interactive changes made by end users via the UI?

We will look at best practices for these scenarios.

Initial data load

If we are migrating from another data source or database, we might have to move the data into Neo4j for the first time. Depending on this data size, we must decide whether we can take a transactional approach to load the data or leverage the offline data import approach called neo4j-admin import.

In *Chapter 9*, we used a transactional approach to load the data. If the amount of data we are loading is under a few million records, say 100 million, we can load this data in a reasonable amount of time. When we load the data transactionally, the Neo4j database needs to update the indexes and keep transaction logs apart, committing the data to the database. This adds a good amount of overhead to the process. But this approach gives us more flexibility and reusable code to use with incremental data loading. If we are loading data into a cluster, we can use this approach to make sure the data is available across the cluster, as the Neo4j database server makes sure the changes are replicated across the cluster. We have used the **LOAD CSV** option to load the data. You can read more about this at `https://neo4j.com/docs/cypher-manual/current/clauses/load-csv/`.

This approach is fine for proofs of concept and ad hoc data load purposes, but for production systems, the data ingestion should be performed using a client by connecting to the database using the Neo4j protocol. While the **LOAD CSV** option is simple and attractive, it uses up the database heap to load the data and perform the data ingestion, which might not be desirable. A basic Python client application that can ingest data into a graph can be found at `https://github.com/neo4j-field/pyingest`. Note that this is a sample client, and you need to build one that suits your production needs.

If the data sizes are bigger, then using the **Neo4j Admin Import** process would be best. For this purpose, we need to prepare CSV files for nodes and relationships in a specific format and use the `neo4j-admin` tool to prepare the database. You can read more about the CSV file formats and examples at `https://neo4j.com/docs/operations-manual/current/tools/neo4j-admin/neo4j-admin-import/`.

Incremental data load

The approaches for incremental data loading depend on the framework we will use to load the data. If there is a lot of streaming data, then leveraging a framework such as Apache Kafka might be a good idea. Also, it is easy to build applications to interact with databases to ingest the data using language frameworks such as Java, JavaScript, .NET, or Python.

You can read about building client applications for Neo4j at `https://neo4j.com/docs/create-applications/`. One thing we need to keep in mind is to leverage the managed transactional functions so that the driver can retry the transactions as needed in a cluster when the cluster topology changes due to network failures or server failures. You can read more about this at `https://neo4j.com/docs/java-manual/current/transactions/`. This link points to Java usage, but the same feature is available for all supported language frameworks.

Graph augmentation

While we have built the article augmentation and customer augmentation as a Spring Boot application, there are other aspects that we have not investigated automating. After we generated embeddings for a specified season for the customer, we ran the ML aspects as individual commands such as KNN similarity and community detection. We might have to automate these aspects, too. Whenever new data is ingested into the graph, we might have to trigger the augmentation application to generate the embeddings to adapt to the new data we have loaded, and then trigger the GDS algorithms after that is completed. Note that the ML pipeline we looked at is simple chaining of KNN similarity and community detection; they can be much more complex based on the needs.

If you want to read more about ML pipelines with Neo4j, you can visit `https://neo4j.com/docs/graph-data-science/current/machine-learning/machine-learning/`.

We explored how to look at recommendations as Cypher queries as part of analysis and validation. Once we are satisfied with queries, we might have to build an application to provide recommendations as needed on demand.

We have built our application on the Spring Framework, which provides various capabilities and options to build a production-grade application that makes it easier to deploy and monitor applications. You can read more about how we can package the Spring applications for production deployment at `https://docs.spring.io/spring-boot/reference/packaging/index.html`. You can read more about the production-level features that help us monitor the application at `https://docs.spring.io/spring-boot/reference/actuator/index.html`.

These are the key principles and considerations for deployment; for production deployment, multiple aspects need to be considered, including a proper deployment architecture along with application development. Several processes need to be deployed for monitoring and performance evaluation to make sure the application scales with usage as data and traffic grows.

Summary

In this concluding chapter, you learned how to take your Haystack-powered GenAI chatbot from local development to a fully deployed, cloud-hosted application using Google Cloud Run. We walked through preparing your project structure, containerizing your application with Docker, configuring essential Google Cloud services, and deploying your chatbot in a scalable and serverless environment. You also learned how to verify the deployment, monitor performance, and troubleshoot common issues—equipping you with practical skills that extend far beyond just this project.

More importantly, this chapter brought everything full circle. From understanding knowledge graphs and vector search to integrating GenAI workflows using Haystack and Neo4j and, finally, deploying your application to the cloud—you now have a complete end-to-end blueprint for building intelligent, scalable, and production-ready GenAI applications.

We've now wrapped up our journey of building Neo4j-powered apps with LLMs. Up next, we'll take a quick look at the key takeaways of this journey.

13

Epilogue

We have looked at quite a few topics and explored how to build intelligent applications. Now, we will revisit what we learned in the earlier chapters and look at the next steps in our journey. We will review how Neo4j is best suited to build knowledge graphs and how it integrates with the GenAI ecosystem to build intelligent search and recommendation applications with ease. We will cover the following topics:

- The combined power of GenAI and Neo4j
- Beyond the book: exploring advanced techniques and resources for continued learning
- Closing remarks

The combined power of GenAI and Neo4j

In *Chapters 1–3*, we looked at how GenAI and the evolution of LLMs came into the picture and how they jumpstarted technology, enabling natural interactions and ease of use. We also looked at how these same capabilities, because of the way they work, can provide information that is believable but might actually be false, as well as information that might not exist, which is referred to as hallucinations. We looked at how RAG can help with reducing these hallucinations.

We looked into knowledge graphs and how we can model them effectively to participate in RAG flows, called GraphRAG approaches. GraphRAG can be more effective and accurate than traditional RAG by integrating evolving knowledge graphs, which can ground LLMs with ease of use.

GraphRAG for search applications

In *Chapters 4–6*, we embarked on a hands-on journey to build a powerful and intelligent search experience using a movie knowledge graph. Starting with structured data, we modeled and constructed the graph using Python and enriched it with vector embeddings generated through the Haystack framework. These embeddings, stored directly in the graph, helped us achieve a similarity search for our GraphRAG pipeline.

Using vector search with the power of knowledge graphs, we created a hybrid retrieval system capable of answering not just simple keyword queries but also complex questions that might require multi-hop traversal to retrieve results. Through the integration of LLMs and GraphRAG, we moved on to intelligent search, which is capable of both document retrieval and context-aware understanding.

These chapters demonstrated the real-world potential of combining structured knowledge from graphs with the expressive power of LLMs.

GraphRAG for recommendations

In *Chapters 7–10*, we looked at building a recommendations application by leveraging GraphRAG. We leveraged Langchain4J and Spring AI to understand how we can build GraphRAG applications using Java and the Spring framework. We followed numerous steps to build an intelligent recommendation application. The first one was building a knowledge graph by loading H&M customer transaction data. The next important step was to augment the graph by adding seasonal relationships, which helped consume the data in a more granular fashion. We then used these seasonal relationships as part of the GraphRAG flow to generate a summary of customer purchases for a given season, along with embeddings to enrich the graph with more context. These embeddings and graph data science algorithms captured relationships between similar customers, with the help of the KNN algorithm. Upon creating similarity relationships, community detection algorithms were utilized to group the customers into communities to provide better recommendations. We also looked at why this pipeline gives us better recommendations than relying on a simple vector search itself.

When we built this application, we used GraphRAG not to generate text for end user consumption but to enrich the knowledge graph, to provide better recommendations. This showed how LLMs can play a part not just as chatbots but also in enriching the data to understand it better and in a new light.

Choosing your cloud platform

Chapters 11–12 focused on various available cloud services. We drew a detailed comparison to help you select a cloud for your GenAI applications. In the last chapter, we demonstrated how to deploy your application to the Google Cloud.

Next up, we will talk about how we can go beyond what we have discussed in this book.

Beyond the book: exploring resources for continued learning

While we have discussed, with simple examples, the importance of graph data modeling and looked at two specific graph data model examples, it would be prudent to understand how Neo4j helps in building better graphs and how its architecture can assist with building knowledge graphs in a scalable manner. Neo4j provides the following resources to learn more about Neo4j, knowledge graphs, and GraphRAG implementations:

- **Neo4j Graph Academy**: You can find Neo4j Graph Academy at `https://graphacademy.neo4j.com/`. This contains a wealth of resources to understand Neo4j concepts and build knowledge graphs. For example, the course at `https://graphacademy.neo4j.com/courses/genai-workshop-graphrag/` provides an easy-to-follow workshop to understand GraphRAG principles.

- **Neo4j GraphRAG Python package**: Neo4j provides a simple-to-use GraphRAG Python package. You can read more about it at `https://neo4j.com/docs/neo4j-graphrag-python/current/index.html`.

- **Neo4J GenAI ecosystem**: You can read more about the GenAI ecosystem integrations at `https://neo4j.com/labs/genai-ecosystem/`. This link contains documentation about the integration with Haystack, LangChain, Spring AI, and other frameworks.

Let's head over to the closing remarks.

Closing remarks

We have looked at various aspects of emerging LLM frameworks and how we can build better solutions using these frameworks. While this technology is exciting and opening new doors for how we look at and solve problems, it is still in its nascent stages. It requires a lot of processing power and may not have the **service-level agreement (SLA)** response times we might be looking for. While we might get excited about solving all the problems using this approach, it's important to evaluate whether trying to solve a given problem really needs to leverage these technologies or whether we can solve them more reasonably and effectively. For example, many people are excited about LLM capabilities and trying to generate data models (be it graphs, SQL, or other) by describing a problem. This can be a double-edged sword. If we are not familiar with the data we are working with, we may not be able to validate the model generated. If we are very familiar with the data, we might have better context and nuances of the data that LLMs might be missing. So, we might not benefit as much when we try to solve the problems in this manner. So, keep in mind that this might be a surgical knife to solve the problems effectively, not an axe, so use it effectively.

While this book concludes here, your journey does not have to. Armed with the foundational knowledge, tools, and working examples, you are now ready to experiment, expand, and elevate your own GenAI solutions. Whether you are building smart assistants, contextual search engines, or personalized recommender systems, the future of intelligent applications is now in your hands.

Keep building. Keep exploring. And most importantly, keep connecting ideas, data, and people through the power of knowledge graphs and generative AI.

Stay tuned

To keep up with the latest developments in the fields of Generative AI and LLMs, subscribe to our weekly newsletter, AI_Distilled, at `https://packt.link/Q5UyU`.

Have questions about the book or want to contribute to discussions on Generative AI and LLMs?

Join our Discord server at `https://packt.link/4Bbd9` and our Reddit channel at `https://packt.link/wcYOQ` to connect, share, and collaborate with like-minded enthusiasts.

‹packt›

Other Books You May Enjoy

If you enjoyed this book, you may be interested in these other books by Packt:

EXPERT INSIGHTS

Generative AI with Python and PyTorch

SECOND EDITION

Navigating the AI frontier with LLMs, Stable
Diffusion, and next-gen AI applications

Joseph Babcock | Raghav Bali   ‹packt›

Generative AI with Python and PyTorch

Joseph Babcock, Raghav Bali

ISBN: 978-1-83588-444-7

- Grasp the core concepts and capabilities of LLMs
- Craft effective prompts using chain-of-thought, ReAct, and prompt query language to guide LLMs toward your desired outputs
- Understand how attention and transformers have changed NLP
- Optimize your diffusion models by combining them with VAEs
- Build text generation pipelines based on LSTMs and LLMs
- Leverage the power of open-source LLMs, such as Llama and Mistral, for diverse applications

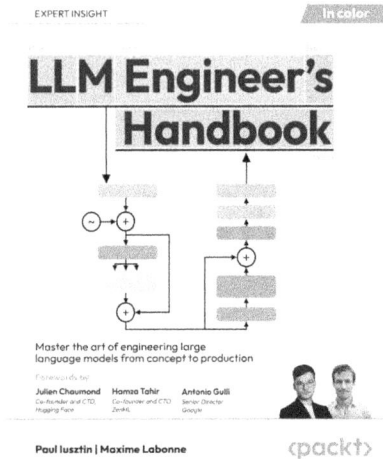

LLM Engineer's Handbook

Paul Iusztin, Maxime Labonne

ISBN: 9781836200079

- Implement robust data pipelines and manage LLM training cycles
- Create your own LLM and refine it with the help of hands-on examples
- Get started with LLMOps by diving into core MLOps principles such as orchestrators and prompt monitoring
- Perform supervised fine-tuning and LLM evaluation
- Deploy end-to-end LLM solutions using AWS and other tools
- Design scalable and modular LLM systems
- Learn about RAG applications by building a feature and inference pipeline

Packt is searching for authors like you

If you're interested in becoming an author for Packt, please visit authors.packtpub.com and apply today. We have worked with thousands of developers and tech professionals, just like you, to help them share their insight with the global tech community. You can make a general application, apply for a specific hot topic that we are recruiting an author for, or submit your own idea.

Share your thoughts

Now you've finished Building Neo4j-Powered Applications with LLMs, we'd love to hear your thoughts! Scan the QR code below to go straight to the Amazon review page for this book and share your feedback or leave a review on the site that you purchased it from.

https://packt.link/r/1836206232

Your review is important to us and the tech community and will help us make sure we're delivering excellent quality content.

Index

Download a free PDF copy of this book

Thanks for purchasing this book!

Do you like to read on the go but are unable to carry your print books everywhere?

Is your eBook purchase not compatible with the device of your choice?

Don't worry, now with every Packt book you get a DRM-free PDF version of that book at no cost.

Read anywhere, any place, on any device. Search, copy, and paste code from your favorite technical books directly into your application.

The perks don't stop there, you can get exclusive access to discounts, newsletters, and great free content in your inbox daily.

Follow these simple steps to get the benefits:

1. Scan the QR code or visit the link below:

https://packt.link/free-ebook/9781836206231

2. Submit your proof of purchase.
3. That's it! We'll send your free PDF and other benefits to your email directly.

www.ingramcontent.com/pod-product-compliance
Lightning Source LLC
Chambersburg PA
CBHW081053220326
41598CB00038B/7079

*9 78 1 83 6 2 0 6 2 3 1 *